Safeguarding Adults in Social Work

Safeguarding Adults in Social Work

Second Edition

**Edited by
ANDY MANTELL
and
TERRY SCRAGG**

Series Editors: Jonathan Parker and Greta Bradley

LearningMatters

First published in 2008 by Learning Matters Ltd
Reprinted in 2009 (twice)
Second edition 2011

British Library Cataloguing in Publication Data

A CIP record for this book is available from the British Library

ISBN 978 0 85725 401 6
Adobe ebook ISBN 978 0 85725 403 0
EPUB ebook ISBN 978 0 85725 402 3
Kindle ISBN 978 0 85725 404 7

Cover design by Code Design Associates ltd
Project Management by Deer Park Productions, Tavistock
Typeset by PDQ Typesetting, Newcastle-under-Lyme
Printed and bound in Great Britain by Bell & Bain Ltd, Glasgow

Learning Matters Ltd
20 Cathedral Yard
Exeter EX1 1HB
Tel: 01392 215560
info@learningmatters.co.uk
www.learningmatters.co.uk

MIX
Paper from
responsible sources
FSC
www.fsc.org   FSC® C007785

Contents

Editors and contributors   viii
Series Editors' Preface   ix
Acknowledgements   x
Introduction   1

Part 1: The policy framework

Chapter 1   **Policy to practice**   9
              David Gaylard

              What do we mean by abuse? • Key concepts in adult abuse
              Categories of adult abuse • How do you assess seriousness?
              Why do people abuse? • The evolution of adult protection
              Adult social care – the need for reform? • Developing a legal
              perspective • No Secrets Review 2009 • The vetting and barring
              scheme review • A new system of regulation • Putting policy
              into practice

Chapter 2   **Human rights and wrongs: The Human Rights
              Act 1998**   34
              Andy Mantell

              Background to the Human Rights Act 1998 • Guiding principles
              Your rights

Chapter 3   **Making choices: The Mental Capacity Act 2005**   48
              Andy Mantell and Alex Clark

              Capacity, choice and difference • The Mental Capacity Act 2005
              Mental capacity in practice • Engaging with people who use services

Chapter 4   **Adult protection: The Scottish legislative
              framework**   66
              Kate Fennell

              Background • Adults who lack capacity • The Adult Support and
              Protection (Scotland) Act 2007 • The Adult Support and Protection
              Act 2007 in practice

Part 2: Empowering practice

Chapter 5 Learning from safeguarding children   81
             Sam Baeza

The emotive response to abuse • Features and categories
of child abuse • The evolution of child protection
Safeguarding adults and children: Similarities and differences
The court process

Chapter 6 Domestic violence: Understanding the
             connections   94
             Gill Butler

Defining domestic violence • Who are the abusers?
Understanding and reponding to domestic violence • Women's
views about helpful responses • Tensions in the social work role
Links to safeguarding adults: Key points • Practice implications

Chapter 7 Working with difference   108
             Gill Constable

What do we mean by difference? • Making the connections – What
makes some adults more vulnerable than others? • The concept
of power • Anti-discriminatory and anti-oppressive practice
Empowering practice

Chapter 8 Developing user-focused communication skills 121
             Colin Goble

The importance of communication • Causes of impaired
communication

Part 3: Effective practice

Chapter 9 Organisational cultures and the management of
             change   141
             Terry Scragg

What are organisational cultures? • The influence of culture
on an organisation • Processes of change

Chapter 10 **Effective collaborative working**   154
          Teri Cranmer

What do we mean by collaborative working? • Collaboration in the
context of safeguarding • The drivers for collaborative working
Working collaboratively across statutory organisations
Developing your own collaborative practice

Chapter 11 **Working with risk**   168
          Chris Smethurst

What do we mean by 'risk'? • The social construction of risk:
Implications for practice • Working with risk: Principles of
good practice • Ensuring safe practice

Chapter 12 **Inquiries and Serious Case Reviews:**
          Listening and learning   180
          Jill Manthorpe and Stephen Martineau

The importance of Inquiries and Serious Case Reviews
Inquiry summary • Learning the lessons at organisational level

Conclusion   190
Appendix: Subject benchmark for social work   192
References   195
Index   207

Editors and contributors

Sam Baeza is Senior Lecturer in Social Work, Department of Social Work and Social Care, University of Chichester

Gill Butler is Deputy Dean, Department of Social Work and Social Care, University of Chichester

Alex Clark is Assistant Director, Business, Health and Social Studies, Moray College, University of the Highlands and Islands

Gill Constable is Senior Lecturer in Social Work, Department of Social Work and Social Care, University of Chichester

Teri Cranmer is Social Care Professional Lead, West Sussex Adults' and Children's Services

Kate Fennell is Adult Protection Officer, City of Edinburgh Council

David Gaylard is Senior Lecturer in Social Work, Department of Social Work and Social Care, University of Chichester

Colin Goble is Senior Lecturer, Childhood, Youth and Community Services, University of Winchester

Andy Mantell (editor) is Senior Lecturer in Social Work, Department of Social Work and Social Care, University of Chichester

Jill Manthorpe is Professor of Social Work and Director of the Social Care Workforce Research Unit, Kings College London

Stephen Martineau is Research Fellow, Social Care Workforce Research Unit, Kings College London

Terry Scragg (editor) is a Social Work Practice Assessor and Visiting Fellow, Department of Social Work and Social Care, University of Chichester

Chris Smethurst is Senior Lecturer in Social Work, Department of Social Work and Social Care, University of Chichester

Series Editors' Preface

The Western world including the UK, and England in particular, faces numerous challenges over forthcoming years. These include dealing with the impact of an increasingly ageing population, with its attendant social care needs, and working with the financial implications that such a changing demography brings. At the other end of the life span the need for high quality child care, welfare and safeguarding services have been highlighted as society develops and responds to a changing complexion.

Migration has developed as a global phenomenon and we now live and work with the implications of international issues in our everyday and local lives. Often these issues influence how we construct our social services and determine what services we need to offer. It is likely that as a social worker you will work with a diverse range of people throughout your career, many of whom have experienced significant, even traumatic, events that require a professional and caring response. As well as working with individuals, however, you may be required to respond to the needs of a particular community disadvantaged by world events or excluded within local communities because of assumptions made about them.

The importance of social work education came to the fore again following the inquiry into the death of baby Peter, the subsequent report from the Social Work Task Force set up in its aftermath and the Reform Board process. It is timely to reconsider elements of social work education – indeed, we should view this as a continual striving for excellence! – as this allows us to focus clearly on what knowledge is useful to engage with in learning to be a social worker.

The books in this series respond to the agendas driven by changes brought about by professional body changes, Government and disciplinary reviews. They aim to build on and offer introductory texts based on up-to-date knowledge and to help communicate this in an accessible way preparing the ground for future study as you develop your social work career. The books are written by people passionate about social work and social services and aim to instil that passion in others. The current text focuses on the fraught area of adult safeguarding. This is a difficult, emotionally challenging and, at times, controversial area but one which you will need to engage with and immerse yourself in if you are to develop as a social work practitioner within a rapidly changing, increasingly politicised world of welfare. The meanings of social work are evolving in line with social and political change and the safeguarding elements of social work throughout the lifespan are increasingly central to practice within the UK. This is set to continue at a time of public service retrenchment. This book provides information and learning specific for social work practice in this complex world. Although focusing on adult safeguarding, the knowledge introduced in this book is important for all student' social workers, and for whichever fields of practice you may seek to enter: adults belong to families and may have contact with children and vice versa. Learning about people across the lifespan, their needs for well-being and being safeguarded affirms your commitment to those people whom the profession serves.

Professor Jonathan Parker, Bournemouth University
Greta Bradley, University of York

Acknowledgements

We would like to thank Jane Bennett, Stuart Brazington, Mick Collins, Belinda Schwehr, Sandra Wallis and Paul Yeomans for their valuable feedback on earlier drafts. Kate Lodge, Luke Block and Jonathan Parker provided help and encouragement throughout the process of preparing this book for publication.

Introduction

Safeguarding adults is increasingly acknowledged as a critical issue for society, with continuing revelations of abusive and oppressive regimes and practices which challenge social care services and practitioners who work with adults deemed as at risk (previously referred to as vulnerable). Increased awareness and reporting have revealed that the scale of the problem is significantly higher than originally thought, partly because of a lack of understanding and acknowledgement as to what constitutes abuse. This situation mirrors the public and professionals' 'discovery' of child abuse in the past with increasing scrutiny being paid to abusive situations by the media, researchers and practitioners. It is now recognised that abuse can take place in a wide range of settings, which means it is essential that professionals are alert to the factors that may increase individual vulnerability, for example, a traumatic brain injury, but also environmental factors which can reduce risk and promote individuals' well-being. An understanding of the dimensions of abuse, the legal and policy context, and knowledge of best practice to prevent abuse, is what this book aims to achieve.

This second edition is intended to be of value to any practitioner working to promote the well-being of adults at risk but is aimed primarily at student social workers and explores a range of approaches to safeguarding adults that will be useful across the whole of your programme of study. It has been updated to enable you to gain an understanding of the evolving legal framework, policies and practice in relation to safeguarding adults that will also be invaluable in subsequent years when you move into practice as a qualified social worker, particularly if you are working with adult service users. Likewise, experienced and qualified social workers will also find the book provides an overview of the current legislative and policy positions in England, Wales and Scotland and a discussion of a range of perspectives that can inform and refresh your practice.

Book structure

This book is written by staff of the Social Work Department at the University of Chichester, Kings College, London, the University of Winchester and colleagues from Edinburgh and West Sussex Adults' Services. As you will see below, the book starts with a broad exploration of research, policy and practice in safeguarding adults, drawing on some of the key legislation and policy that have informed the development of the main concepts, and some of the processes that can be adopted in practice. In particular the book has been adapted to take account of the implications of the progression of the wider policy initiative on personalisation. Terminology is also developing, for example, the concept of the 'vulnerable' adult is being replaced by that of 'adults at risk', shifting the emphasis from the individual to social and environmental factors. This book reflects both how the term vulnerable adult has been utilised in the past and how listening to the voices of carers and people who use services has led to a change in this terminology. There has also been a shift from the use of terms like 'alleged perpetrator' to the less stigmatising language of 'person alleged responsible', more accurately reflecting the complexity of adult abuse. This policy framework is then used as the basis for the following chapters that are concerned with different aspects of safeguarding adults from a range of standpoints, including what can be learnt from practice with children and domestic violence. Finally there is an exploration of issues in the management of change and work in multidisciplinary settings, consideration of risk and its implications for practice that is person-centred and concluding with what can be learned from where things have gone wrong.

Part 1 The policy framework

Chapter 1 has been significantly expanded to examine the legislation and social policy in England and Wales with regard to safeguarding adults. It reviews the key elements of social policy that have influenced the evolving safeguarding adults practice. We will see that although there remains no single or consolidating piece of legislation in England and Wales, it is clear that there are numerous pieces of legislation supplemented by policy aimed at preventing abuse and increasing protection which practitioners can consider. It starts by defining key concepts before exploring how policy has been incorporated into current guidance and procedures and concludes with a consideration of the challenges which exist within practice.

Chapter 2 considers the relevance of the Human Rights Act 1998 (HRA 1998) to safeguarding adults. You will be introduced to the context and guiding principles behind the HRA 1998 and its central role in safeguarding vulnerable adults. The chapter then explores the articles and key principles of the Act in relation to safeguarding adults and practice situations, with activities and case examples that will increase your understanding of the Act. This discussion will highlight the tensions between competing rights and the significance of the concept of proportionality. It emphasises the importance of the Human Rights Act 1998 in guiding best practice to prevent adult abuse occurring.

Chapter 3 starts with an exploration of how certain individuals and social groups have been perceived within our society as less capable of making choices and decisions. It will be argued that these perceptions have contributed to the social construction of notions of 'vulnerability' and risk, which are key concerns within safeguarding adults policy and practice. The chapter will then explore the contents of the Mental Capacity Act 2005 (MCA 2005), followed by the implications of the Act in relation to anti-oppressive practice. It will be argued that professionals need to adopt a critical and reflective approach when deciding when to apply the MCA 2005, particularly exploring the social context in which the individual is placed and the nature of power relations in the professional–client relationship.

Chapter 4 presents a Scottish perspective, highlighting how the legislative basis for practice differs from that in England and Wales. This chapter describes the Adults with Incapacity (Scotland) Act 2000 and the Adult Support and Protection (Scotland) Act 2007 and the relationship between these pieces of legislation and social work practice in Scotland, which has significantly increased the ability of social workers to intervene to protect adults from abuse.

Part 2 Empowering practice

Chapter 5 examines the way that policy and practice in respect of safeguarding children have evolved and developed and what lessons this offers for safeguarding adults. The chapter describes how changes have been reactive in tending to follow well-publicised cases of child abuse and poses the question whether safeguarding adults practice will follow a similar course, or whether more proactive reform can be introduced. The chapter examines the similarities and differences between safeguarding children and adults, and whether the history of responses to child abuse and the well-established processes used in these situations have application in adult practices, while at the same time learning from the mistakes made in child protection.

Chapter 6 examines the overlap between domestic violence and other adults at risk of abuse, and summarises the nature and extent of domestic violence in England. The chapter introduces a framework for analysing and understanding domestic violence and the responses that you can adopt when working in the context of adult abuse. With the aid of research findings the chapter makes connections between what has been helpful to women subject to domestic violence and how this can inform the design and delivery of services that safeguard adults. The chapter argues that procedures should be developed in consultation with service users who have experienced abuse and which recognise their strengths and expertise in identifying solutions.

Chapter 7 explores the concept of difference, which is intended to help you understand values, beliefs and attitudes through the process of reflection, based on research. An understanding of difference is intended to enable you to consider how life chances and circumstances can increase and expose individuals to potential abuse. The concept of power and its relationship to vulnerability are also discussed and how the use of an audit tool can help to change practice. The chapter will examine what is meant by anti-discriminatory and anti-oppressive practice and the differences between the two concepts, drawing on legislation and research findings. Finally the chapter will focus on how you can support your ongoing development as a reflective social worker.

Chapter 8 examines the importance of user-focused communication skills in work with adults in social care contexts. The chapter argues that good communication skills are central to high-quality services and therefore essential in safeguarding adults at risk. Central to this chapter is the importance of service user involvement in all aspects of service design in response to the legacy of social care where service users were powerless, which in turn resulted in abusive and oppressive practices. This chapter will argue that the ability to communicate effectively heightens the opportunity for the service user's voice to be heard, with reference to people with severe learning difficulties.

Part 3 Effective practice

Chapter 9 introduces you to the concept of organisational culture and how it can have a pervasive influence on services through its power to shape responses to change. The chapter draws on recent inquiries into institutional abuse in services for people with learning difficulties which exposed the powerful role culture played in frustrating previous attempts to improve these services. The chapter argues for leadership and sensitive change-management processes. These approaches need to be driven by values and beliefs in the importance of engaging with service users to ensure that deeply entrenched cultures are challenged and the vital work of all staff in ensuring that open and responsive cultures are created and so reduce the risks of abusive practices.

Chapter 10 explores what is meant by collaborative working and its importance in safeguarding adults. The chapter introduces you to the theoretical and legislative frameworks that underpin collaborative working and how these impact on local practice, and some of the strengths and barriers to more effective joint working. The expectations contained in *No secrets* (Department of Health, 2000), which provides the guidance for collaboration between agencies and some of the factors that can inhibit partnership working, are explored. The chapter then offers you some well-established tools that can be used to develop more effective collaborative practice, with emphasis on reflection as an important means of improving working relationships.

Chapter 11 considers risk, which is seen as integral to an understanding of practice in safeguarding adults. The chapter examines what is meant by risk and argues that it has come to dominate service responses at a time when professionals struggle with the assessment and management of risk, leading to defensive practice. This situation has resulted in more mechanistic approaches to practice which can provide an illusion of security but can result in practices that are potentially oppressive. The importance of organisational support for workers in order to reduce the tendency to practise defensively can enable more creative decisions to be made that assess risk realistically and at the same time provide reassurance for workers.

Chapter 12 is a new contribution to this second edition. It considers the value of Serious Case Reviews in local authorities and their equivalent inquiries within Strategic Health Authorities. It explores what is involved in a serious case review and their current impact. It goes on to consider some of the findings from these case reviews and how they can impact on our current practices. It highlights how such reviews can help us to see beyond individual incidents to systemic failings.

Learning features

This book is interactive. You are encouraged to work through the book as an active participant, taking responsibility for your learning, in order to increase your knowledge, understanding and ability to apply this learning to your practice. You will be expected to reflect creatively on how your immediate learning needs can be met in working with adult service users and how your professional learning can be developed in your future career.

Case studies and research summaries throughout the book will help you to examine theories and models of practice with vulnerable adults. We have devised activities that require you to reflect on experiences, situations and events and help you to review and summarise learning undertaken. In this way your knowledge will become deeply embedded as part of your development. When you come to practise learning in an agency the work and reflection undertaken here will help you to improve and hone your skills and knowledge.

This book serves as an introduction to the subject of safeguarding adults, but we realise that there are many other sources of information that you may wish to access that provide more detailed information on specific aspects of work with adults at risk of abuse and safeguarding practice. We have suggested further reading at the end of each chapter for you to follow up.

PART 1
THE POLICY FRAMEWORK

Chapter 1

Policy to practice
David Gaylard

ACHIEVING A SOCIAL WORK DEGREE

This chapter will help you to meet the following National Occupational Standards.

Key Role 1: Prepare for, and work with, individuals, families, carers, groups and communities and other professionals.

- Address behaviour which presents risk to individuals, families, carers, groups and communities.

Key Role 3: Support individuals to represent their views and circumstances.

Key Role 4: Assess and manage risk to individuals, families, carers, groups and communities.

Key Role 5: Manage and be accountable, with supervision and support, for your own social work practice within your organisation.

- Work within multi-disciplinary and multi-organisational teams, networks and systems.

Key Role 6: Demonstrate professional competence in social work practice.

- Research, analyse, evaluate and use current knowledge of best social work practice.
- Review and update your own knowledge of legal, policy and procedural frameworks.
- Manage complex ethical issues, dilemmas and conflicts.
- Contribute to the promotion of best social work practice.

Introduction

This revised chapter examines legislation and social policy in England, Wales and Northern Ireland (see Chapter 4 for discussion of Scottish law) with regard to safeguarding adults at risk (formerly known as 'vulnerable adults'). It critically reviews key social policy that has influenced evolving safeguarding adult practice. It starts by defining key concepts before exploring how policy in practice has been incorporated into current procedural guidance and concludes with a consideration of the challenges which exist within empowering practice. Although currently there is no single consolidating piece of legislation in England, Wales and Northern Ireland, there are numerous pieces of legislation supplemented by policy aimed at detecting and preventing abuse.

What do we mean by abuse?

Where there are regional variations in definitions of abuse, *No secrets* (Department of Health, 2000) provides the following definitions:

Abuse may consist of a single act or repeated acts. It may be physical, verbal or psychological, it may be an act of neglect or failure to act, or it may occur when a vulnerable person is persuaded to enter into a financial or sexual transaction to which he or she has not consented, or cannot give consent.

Abuse can occur in any relationship and may result in significant harm to, or exploitation of, the person subjected to it.

Physical, sexual, financial, emotional, discriminatory or psychological violation or neglect of a person unable to protect him/herself to prevent abuse from happening or to remove him/herself from the abuse or potential abuse by others.

a violation of individuals' human and civil rights by another person or persons. (p9)

Key concepts in adult abuse

No secrets (2000) and other policies concerned with safeguarding adults have developed a number of terms and concepts that will aid your understanding of this complex field.

'Vulnerable adult' (now referred to as 'adult at risk') refers to:

any person aged 18 years and over who is or may be in need of community care services including services due to their role as carer by reason of mental or other disability, age, illness; and who is or may be unable to take care of him or herself, or unable to protect him or herself against significant harm or serious exploitation.

(Lord Chancellor's Department, 1997)

'Vulnerability' is a broader concept which may apply to a wide range of disabilities and situations including those adults at risk because of their caring or dependent role or family responsibilities. Vulnerability is a contentious concept and there are often conflicting views concerning an individual's capacity and social situation. Therefore, this terminology has consequently been replaced by 'adult at risk' in revised multiagency safeguarding adults policy and procedures. The UK prevalence survey (Comic Relief and Department of Health, 2007) highlights that it is often an individual's context that makes them more vulnerable to abuse. Therefore, you have to be careful not to locate the cause of the abuse with the victim rather than the perpetrator.

This book seeks to acknowledge the range of situations and relationships in which people suffer abuse, but particularly focuses on the empowerment of adults:

who are or may be eligible for community care services to retain independence, well-being and choice and have access to their human rights to live a life that is free from abuse and neglect.

(ADSS, 2005 p5).

This definition specifically includes individuals assessed as being able to purchase all or part of their own care services, plus those deemed eligible for local authority commissioned community care services (e.g. low, moderate, substantial or critical need index of the Fair Access to Care eligibility criteria). This may include a need to access mainstream services, e.g. the police, trading standards, legal advice, in relation to a safeguarding issue.

'Significant harm' is a key concept within safeguarding adults work which helps practitioners to determine how serious or extensive abuse must be to warrant intervention.

> *Harm should be taken to include not only ill-treatment (including sexual abuse and forms of ill treatment that are not physical); the impairment of, or an avoidable deterioration in, physical or mental health; and the impairment of physical, emotional, social or behavioural development or the impairment of health.*

> (Lord Chancellor's Department, 1997)

The *Law Commission Review of Adult Social Care Law Consultation* (2010) added 'unlawful conduct' which appropriates or adversely affects property , rights or interests (e.g. theft, fraud, embezzlement or extortion) to help determine how serious or extensive harm must be to justify intervention.

'Proportionality' remains a fundamental concept since the implementation of the Human Rights Act 1998. The Act places a duty upon public authorities to intervene to protect the rights of the citizen, but requires that intervention must not be excessive in comparison with the risk posed (see Chapter 2).

'Capacity to consent'. The Mental Capacity Act 2005 enshrines *a presumption of capacity*. Individuals are assumed to have capacity to make informed decisions, unless there is clear evidence to the contrary. This is often a critical issue when deciding whether a person has been abused or not and is discussed in detail in Chapter 3.

Categories of adult abuse

In highlighting the forms of abuse experienced by adults it is important to acknowledge their limitations. Such definitions cannot fully convey the impact upon the individual and their families. The Comic Relief and Department of Health UK prevalence survey (O'Keefe et al., 2007) conveys the complexity of abuse, with people sometimes being subject to multiple forms, overlapping or incremental abuse.

Physical abuse has been defined as *the non-accidental infliction of physical force that results in bodily injury, pain or impairment* (Stein, 1991, quoted in McCreadie, 1994). Practice examples include falls and injuries without satisfactory explanation or that are not conducive to present injuries. Other examples include pinching, scalding, slapping, pushing, hitting, kicking or hair pulling. Inadvertent physical abuse sometimes originates from poor practice, e.g. inappropriate application of outdated moving and handling techniques, involuntary isolation or confinement and the misuse of pre-scribed medication.

Sexual abuse is the involvement of adults in sexual activities without informed or valid consent, e.g. where the individual may have insufficient mental capacity to have full understanding and appreciation of the activity. This form of abuse includes coercion into the activity due to the other person being in a position of trust, power or author-ity. Practice examples of non-contact activity can include exposure to pornography, voyeurism, exhibitionism, innuendo, harassment, teasing, and photography. Contact examples include touching of breasts, genitals, anus, mouth, masturbation, attempted penetration to full sexual intercourse (Brown and Turk, 1994).

Psychological and emotional abuse can involve fear through threats of force, intimi-dation, humiliation or emotional blackmail, bullying, swearing and any other form of mental cruelty or manipulation or exploitation that results in mental or physical dis-tress. Practice examples involve threatening an individual in a manner that is inappropriate to their age or cultural background, blaming, swearing, harassing, 'cold-shouldering', intentional isolation or confinement. It also includes the denial of basic rights, e.g. choice, dignity, privacy, self-expression and individuality.

Neglect is the repeated withholding of adequate care to achieve important daily activities of living which can be either intentional or unintentional. It also involves acts of omission, e.g. the failure within the context of a duty of care intervention to prevent harm of an individual, who may be considered not to have sufficient capacity to appreciate risk, poor or outdated manual handling techniques. Practice examples sometimes involve failure to provide food, heating, medical care, basic hygiene, appropriate personal and mouth care, basic pressure-area care, clothing, inappropri-ate use of prescribed medication.

Self-neglect alone may not necessarily warrant adult protection investigation unless the situation involves a significant act of omission by someone else with established responsibility for caring. Care management assessments and review procedures (including risk assessments) may often be a more appropriate response and interven-tion to consider in regard to situations of self-neglect. However, if an individual is mentally incapacitated, under the Mental Capacity Act there is a duty to intervene.

Financial abuse is the denial of access of the individual to money, property, posses-sions, valuables or inheritance, improper or unauthorised use of funds via omission, exploitation or extortion through threats. Perpetrators of financial abuse frequently hold positions of trust, confidence or power (see the research summary in this chap-ter). Practice examples include forcing sudden changes to a will, stealing, preventing access to or misappropriating money.

Institutional abuse occurs in care settings when individual service users' needs and wishes are sacrificed in favour of the organisation's agenda, staff regime or externally imposed performance targets. Practice examples can include arbitrary monetary limits to care plans waived as soon as there is a complaint, inflexible routines established around the needs of care staff rather than individual service users. Examples include fixed menus with no alternatives or choices offered, having to eat together at set times, rigidly enforced bedtime or toilet regimes, limited bathing times designated to suit staffing levels, no doors on toilets. Behaviour is generally cultural in origin and not specific to certain members of staff and is often as a consequence of inadequate leadership, poor management and staff training (see Chapter 10).

Discriminatory abuse exists when values, beliefs or culture result in the misuse of power that denies opportunities to some individuals or groups. This can include the exclusion of an individual from mainstream opportunities, e.g. education, health, employment, justice, civic status and protection. This form of abuse also incorporates discrimination based upon age, gender, race, disability, religion and sexuality. Practice examples may include unequal treatment, inappropriate use of language, slurs, harassment and intentional exclusion.

(Adapted from ADSS, 2005, and Sussex Multi-agency Policy and Procedures for Safeguarding Vulnerable Adults, 2007).

As the UK prevalence survey (Comic Relief and Department of Health, 2007) identified, abuse is more widespread than is often assumed by the public and the perpetrator is often someone the person would hope to trust.

RESEARCH SUMMARY

UK prevalence survey
Comic Relief and the Department of Health (2007) commissioned a two-year UK study of abuse and neglect of older people which involved 2,000 people aged over 66 years living at home in their own households including sheltered accommodation. Key findings were as follows.

It estimated that 4 per cent or 342,000 people aged 66 or over are neglected or abused each year.

Perpetrators were 51 per cent partners; 49 per cent were family members; 13 per cent were care workers; and 5 per cent were close friends.

The types of abuse reported were: neglect (1.1%), 11 people in 1,000; financial (0.7%), 7 people in 1,000; psychological (0.4%), 4 people in 1,000; physical (0.4%), 4 people in 1,000; and sexual (0.2%), 2 people in 1,000. Six per cent of people reported two different types of abuse.

Women were more likely to say that they had been mistreated than men (3.8 per cent women and 1.1 per cent men). Abuse was more prevalent among those who lived in rented housing compared with owner-occupiers.

Prevalence of mistreatment increased with being female, declining health status (e.g. those with a long-term limiting illness), suffering with loneliness or depression and likely to be in receipt of (or in touch with) services. Higher incidents of abuse were reported for those people who were separated or divorced (9.4 per cent) than for those who were widowed (1.4 per cent).

RESEARCH SUMMARY *continued*

Neglect was the most predominant type of mistreatment, followed by financial abuse. This is in contrast to the commonly assumed notion of abuse as physical violence.

Risk of interpersonal abuse was higher for women aged 66–74, men who felt lonely or depressed. Perpetrators lived in the same household in two-thirds of cases and in two-fifths of cases the respondent was providing care for them.

How do you assess seriousness?

Having outlined key categories of adult abuse it is important to recognise that within a practice setting, the seriousness of abuse is often not initially clear. It is vital that it is treated with an open mind and in a systematic, consistent person-centred approach in terms of assessing seriousness. In determining how serious or extensive abuse is, a useful starting point is to refer back to the concept of significant harm defined earlier (p11). This is essential to enable you to identify the appropriate response and intervention to a potential adult protection referral.

Be mindful of your own personal views and how these may impact upon your practice, e.g. personal anxiety in terms of individual professional accountability. Always consult with the investigating manager during the information-gathering investigation stage and utilise either individual or group supervision by adopting a critically reflective approach.

ACTIVITY **1.1**

In determining seriousness, what key questions would you need to consider in terms of intervention thresholds with regard to abuse?
1. *What ethical dilemmas might you struggle with in assessing seriousness?*
2. *What personal feelings or emotions may you need to be aware of in assessing seriousness?*

COMMENT

Assessing seriousness provides a useful exploration of the precise nature and degree of risk and harm of the person, which can often be discovered by the context in which the alleged abuse took place; the views and wishes of the victim; the impact upon the person and others; the level of capacity to protect themselves from significant harm; the level of threat to the person's independence, well-being and choice. These are all key areas that will require further exploration.

In addition, has there been a breach of trust, in the duty of care or in law (e.g. civil, criminal or family)? Other significant factors which must be considered are: What is the likelihood of repeated risks to the person or others from the same abusive individual or service? What internal and external factors may be contributing toward the abuse? Is the person suffering harm or exploitation? Does the person suffering or causing harm or exploitation meet the NHS and CC Act 1990 and/or the Fair Access to Care eligibility criteria? If not, what provision can be put in place to offer appropriate protection and monitoring? Is intervention in the best interests if the vulnerable adult is incapacitated or in the public interest? Is intervention lawful and is it in the interests of the individual, the professionals involved or the wider community and society? Asking such questions will enable investigating practitioners and managers to spot any vital triggers or abuse patterns in order to compile important chronological histories.

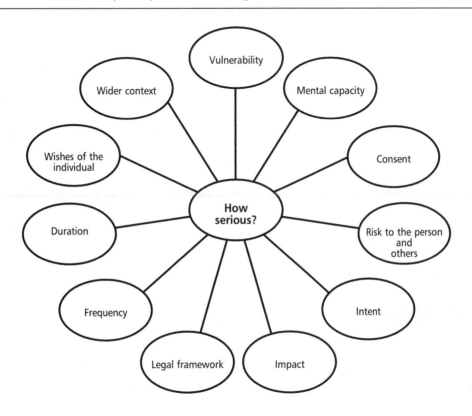

Figure 1.1 Assessing seriousness
Adapted from Hughes, J (2006) *Chairing multi-agency adult protection meetings.* Making Connections, Training and Consultancy

Figure 1.1 provides a basic tool for guidance in assessing seriousness and risk so as to determine the appropriate level of intervention. A positive approach to risk assessment, risk taking, risk ownership and management is the cornerstone of all safeguarding adults work and should be used to inform all decision-making (see Chapter 11). It helps clarify abuse by using a continuum based upon the context, frequency, consent and capacity, the intent, the perception and outcome. This provides you with a contextual framework to work within and clarify your thinking in terms of gauging the seriousness of the abusive incident. Crucially, it should ensure that responses are proportionate to the level of concern.

CASE STUDY

A social worker from the Community Team for People with Learning Disabilities reports to you, as a duty social worker for the Adult Area Team, that Robert (her service user) disclosed to his day centre key worker that he has hit and sworn at his frail mother, Joyce, when he gets frustrated and angry, following the death of his father a year ago. Joyce is Robert's primary carer and has since admitted to her home carer that on occasions Robert has knocked her over but she felt it was her fault as she nags him. Robert has lived with his mother for over 43 years. Neither Joyce nor Robert wants any further action to be taken or for them to be separated.

ACTIVITY 1.2

Having read through the case scenario, try to answer the following questions about common practice dilemmas that arise.
1. *Who is the adult at risk? Is this a case of abuse – if so, which categories? Should an adult abuse investigation take place? If so, what level of intervention should be considered?*
2. *What relevant policies, procedures and legislation might be helpful? Should any action have been taken before this situation was reached? If yes what should have happened?*

COMMENT

This case appropriately highlights that some perpetrators can be deemed in need or adults at risk themselves. It raises dilemmas in terms of what good practice measures may be required in working with Joyce and Robert; for example, impartiality, special measures to maintain the safety of both, allocation of separate workers and possible use of advocacy services. Awareness of capacity and unresolved loss and bereavement issues for both Joyce and Robert may also need sensitive exploration. Has Joyce been offered a carer's assessment or have they had their care needs reviewed, would this have alleviated their situation? Additional community services may be explored, e.g. respite, befriending services or sheltered work placement opportunities. Could Robert possibly have underlying challenging behaviour needs?

Why do people abuse?

Take a moment to think about why people may abuse. *No secrets* (2000) identified a number of key patterns of abusing behaviour. These patterns are not necessarily mutually exclusive and may be inter-related. The main abusing behaviours include the following.

Opportunistic – examples include theft when money or valuables are left lying around.

Long term – often set in the context of a family relationship; may include domestic violence between generations or when the power balance or caring responsibilities change.

Situational – can occur when pressure builds up, e.g. carer's stress, or when an adult at risk becomes challenging or difficult, along with alcohol and substance misuse.

Neglect – can be unintentional or intentional in its origins. Unintentional often occurs when carers have other pressures to deal with their own physical or mental health needs, or other equally competing caring demands, e.g. childcare responsibilities. For agencies, it can include failing to consult or access key primary healthcare services, e.g. community nursing services, dietician, podiatrist or dentist coupled with the lack of appropriate staff induction, training and development, monitoring or appraisal. Intentional may be linked to long-term or situational circumstances.

Unacceptable treatment or programmes – including punishments such as withholding food, drink, or imposing seclusion, unauthorised use of control or restraint and/or over-medication.

Institutional – lack of positive response to complex or diverse needs, rigid routines, inadequate funding, staffing and insufficient skills or knowledge base within the service.

Serial abuse – in which a perpetrator actively seeks out targets, befriends or grooms adults at risk. Sexual, emotional and financial abuses often fall into this category (*No secrets*, 2000, p17).

Kurrle (2001) highlighted that psychiatric illness and cognitive impairment were also significant characteristics of perpetrators.

Many of these factors are the same as in child abuse and it is not surprising that safeguarding adults has followed a similar, often piecemeal developmental path to that of safeguarding children.

The evolution of adult protection

Similar to child abuse, societal recognition of adult abuse is a relatively recent phenomenon. The 1970s saw physical abuse of older people hit the headlines with such phrases as 'granny bashing' (Baker, 1975). In the UK, formal recognition around adult protection arose in 1993 with the Department of Health guidelines. The sexual abuse of adults with learning difficulties became a particular focus of attention (Brown and Turk, 1993). There appeared to be little recognition of other areas of abuse until the mid-1990s when additional categories were at least noted (e.g. emotional and financial abuse). Research tended to concentrate upon those with learning difficulties and older people, neglecting other groups such as the physically disabled, those with sensory loss and people with mental health needs, possibly due to the link between mental incapacity and perceived vulnerability.

Professional terminology has much in common with safeguarding children (see Chapter 5) and Brown (2006) highlights research links between child protection and domestic violence within families, which in later life often gets redefined as spouse abuse (see Chapter 6). Sadly, as with child protection, the evolutionary process of policy development has been driven by subsequent inquiries or scandals (see below).

RESEARCH SUMMARY

Serious case reviews and adult abuse inquiries

Beech House (1993): mistreatment of older people living at Beech House, St Pancras Hospital, London, 1993–96.

Longcare Inquiry Buckinghamshire County Council (1998): 54 people with severe learning difficulties were placed in two private-sector residential care homes and were subjected to years of sexual, physical and emotional abuse, ill-treatment and neglect.

Sheffield City Council (2004): Director of Sheffield Social Services requested a serious case review following the death of a 79-year-old woman suffering from mental health problems. She sustained 49 injuries after she moved from sheltered housing into her son-in-law's home and died five weeks later. Living conditions were found to be poor. An open verdict was recorded and no one was ever charged.

Harold Shipman Inquiry (2005): published its final report in January 2005; this official inquiry concluded that this GP had murdered 215 patients over a 25-year period – the majority being older women.

Cornwall Partnership Trust (2006): investigation examined two treatment centres, four children's units and 46 houses occupied by small groups of people with learning difficulties (ex-NHS in-patients). The report highlighted years of abusive practices within the trust, coupled with a failure of senior executives to tackle these practices. Examples include physical abuse and misuse of people's money. Evidence of institutional abuse was also apparent, e.g. withholding food, individuals given cold showers and the imposition of tenancies despite lack of capacity to contract for tenure. The investigation also discovered an over-reliance on medication to control behaviour plus prolonged and illegal use of restraint.

Sutton and Merton (2007); NHS provision for people with learning difficulties – highlighted a catalogue of sexual, physical and emotional abuse of residents.

Adult serious case reviews (similar to child abuse inquiries) provide a retrospective analysis where patterns, factors and combined indicators of abuse are examined. Inquiries inform and revise future practice in terms of spotting triggers, highlighting problems of professional ignorance, incompetence and lack of accountability, multi-agency collaboration plus operational problems with procedural processes which may not have been understood or followed. Inquiries provide a watershed in terms of social policy influence regarding guidance and procedures for incorporation into future legislation; for example, the Lord Laming Inquiry (2003) regarding Victoria Climbié's death and its influence upon the subsequent Children Act 2004. Such a catalogue of adult inquiries raises fundamental questions regarding the robustness of external regulatory and inspection mechanisms coupled with practitioners' failure to 'whistle-blow' (see below) on systematic institutional abuse. Unlike child protection, however, legislative change has been limited.

Adult social care law – a need for reform?

Adult social care law has been dominated by piecemeal development. Such an evolutionary process has resulted in overlapping and conflicting obligations, for example, traditional service-led provisions versus self-directed support.

The last 60 years of social policy have witnessed rapid and fundamental changes, in terms of demographic trends, conflicting generational expectations and demands for social care. The scope of some of this legislation now encompasses outdated definitions, language and concepts.

One of the main objectives for adult social care law reform is to provide a clearer, more coherent legal framework through simplification, consistency, transparency for practitioners, service users and carers. However, it aims to be resource neutral, while embracing modern twenty-first century 'consumerist' expectations of adult social care.

At the time of writing, the Law Commission (an independent body responsible for the development of law in England and Wales) published a consultation in 2010 proposing adult social care reform (but not including mental health legislation or the Vetting and Barring Scheme) and intends on drafting a Bill in July 2012. It remains unclear as to whether the Coalition Government have the political desire to grant parliamentary time for adult legislative reform.

What legislation do practitioners currently use to investigate adult abuse?

Currently, no legislation exists in England, Wales and Northern Ireland explicitly relating to the investigation of abuse of adults, therefore investigations tend to draw upon the following legislation.

NHS and Community Care Act 1990, s.47 Assessment. This can be implemented in order to consider an adult's needs for services and thereby consider any risk factors present at the time of assessment. Assessment and commissioned services can support people who have been abused or can prevent abuse from recurring.

National Assistance Act 1948 s.29. The act deals with the welfare of people with disabilities and states that *the local authority shall make arrangements for promoting the welfare of persons blind, deaf or dumb or who suffer from a mental disorder of any description or who are substantially and permanently handicapped by illness, injury or congenital deformity or other disabilities*. This gives power to provide services arising out of an investigation under the 1990 Act above.

National Assistance Act 1948 s.47 Compulsory Removal from Home. This empowers a local authority with approval from the community physician to apply to a magistrates' court for an order for the compulsory removal of persons to hospital or into residential care. The grounds to warrant consideration under this section are that an individual must be *suffering from grave chronic disease, or being aged, infirm or physically incapacitated, are living in insanitary conditions: and unable to devote to themselves, and are not receiving from other persons, proper care and attention.*

Section 47 is rarely resorted to because of the perceived draconian nature of its use, but it is there to protect people from their own incapacity and other people from the consequences of living near such people.

Developing a legal perspective

As Mandelstam (2009) highlights, for an intervention to take place, a legal under-pinning of some sort is often essential. However, the law does not necessarily provide a magic solution in this respect but serves as an additional (often essential) tool with which to intervene. Law can be viewed as having a preventative, ameliorative, remedial or punitive function.

Preventatively speaking, for example, an assessment of an adult at risk and their carer by a local authority under existing community care legislation may result in social services providing assistance and reducing the stress or crisis of a fraught caring situation which may have been the tipping point into possible abuse or neglect.

If a situation has already deteriorated, perhaps a compulsory (ameliorative or reme-dial) intervention may be necessary e.g. under the Mental Capacity Act 2005, if a person lacks capacity to take relevant decisions to protect themselves from significant harm. However, if the situation results in a criminal offence being committed, then criminal law may provide a punitive measure in response as a consequence of fraud, assault or wilful neglect being proven.

Legal definitions

It is important to clarify fundamental legal definitions often used interchangeably but frequently misunderstood. Most social work areas of responsibility defined by legisla-tion can be categorised as either duties or powers. Local authorities (LA) are constrained by central government legislation in two ways.

- Acts which impose a duty, e.g. local authorities have no choice in whether to do something as it is imposed by law. No allowance for shortfall of resources is acceptable, although professional discretion may inform the manner in which the duty is informed. Generally, where 'shall' appears in legislation, it suggests an imperative and a duty is imposed. Any breach of a duty could result in an application for judicial review, e.g. the duty to carry out an assessment for com-munity care services under s.47 of the NHS and Community Care Act 1990.

- Those which bestow power, e.g. local authorities may do something if they choose to and will be guided by central or local government policies and targets. When a power is provided, there is an element of professional discretion in the decision whether or not to act at all, and a much greater amount of discretion to decide how to act, e.g. in paragraph 16 of Sch. 2 to the Children Act 1989 in respect of children looked after by an LA.

Legislation is often followed by regulations, or directions and guidance, which further clarify and assist in the interpretation of certain aspects of the Act. Directions are mandatory in nature and must be complied with in the same way as the original legislation. Guidance is not mandatory but failing to have regard to it at all can lead to a judicial review. None of these instruments gets the same amount of parliamentary scrutiny as primary legislation.

The broader notions of human and civil rights remain fundamentally important in the drafting and interpretation of recent legislation: an example is the Mental Capacity Act 2005, transparently based on concepts of autonomy, protection and procedural fairness. Human and civil rights are explored in more depth in Chapters 2 and 3.

Current policy and the legal framework

As mentioned, the legal framework surrounding safeguarding adults within England, Wales and Northern Ireland currently remains somewhat fragmented but it should not be presumed that there are no legal powers to intervene in a case of suspected abuse. For example, key principles combating discriminatory abuse are embodied in legislation such as the Race Relations (Amendment) Act 2000 and the Disability Discrimination Act 2005. The Human Rights Act 1998 and Mental Capacity Act 2005 have significant implications for safeguarding adults; these are considered in Chapters 2 and 3. It should also be highlighted that the legislative situation is different in Scotland, where the Adults with Incapacity (Scotland) Act has existed since 2000 and the Adult Support and Protection (Scotland) Act 2007 was introduced in March 2007 (see Chapter 4).

No secrets: Guidance on developing and implementing multi-agency protection of vulnerable adults (Department of Health, 2000)

This was an important and significantly influential document in the evolution of safeguarding adults practice as it provided the first governmental guidance on developing and implementing policies and procedures to protect vulnerable adults from abuse. Issued under s.7 of the Local Authority Social Service Act 1970, it must be acted under, by all local authorities, and case law has clarified that this requires having conscientious regard to it, although it is not binding in every single case.

> *The first priority should be to ensure the safety and protection of vulnerable adults. To this end it is the responsibility of all staff to act on any suspicion or evidence of abuse or neglect and to pass on their concerns to the responsible person or agency.*

> (*No secrets*, 2000, s.6m, p26)

This guidance set in place the foundation for the ADSS's later practice recommendations *Safeguarding adults*. It promoted and created a culture for a multi-agency approach to intervention, with social services being the lead co-ordinating agency. It led to the creation of adult protection committees and co-ordinator posts. It emphasised the need for local procedures, co-ordination, collecting and monitoring data, identified categories of adult abuse and the government's commitment to tackling adult abuse and the need for staff training, while raising the profile of adult protection especially within NHS, PCT and registered care-provider settings. Fundamentally, it highlighted the need to consult vulnerable adults and carers regarding the implementation of policy and procedures.

Safeguarding adults (ADSS, 2005)

The Association of the Directors of Social Services (ADSS) document provided a national framework of standards for good practice and outcomes in adult protection work, aiming to provide guidance and support to the aspirations of *No secrets*. It highlighted the need for proportionate and measured responses to abuse and neglect of adults who may need community care services. ADSS acknowledged the importance of robust guidance for serious case reviews and agreed guidance on developing local protocols with PCT and NHS trusts. The ADSS document identified six key developmental areas:

1. *Legislation* ADSS acknowledged developments made regarding the Domestic Violence, Crime and Victims Act 2004, recognising the crime of familiar homicide, and the Mental Capacity Act 2005. The ADSS also supported Action on Elder Abuse's campaign for specific legislation to protect vulnerable adults regarding duties to act, investigate, and share information, and powers to enter domestic premises.

2. *Prevention* ADSS encouraged closer work with crime-reduction partnerships with health, housing associations, independent and voluntary organisations, e.g. Trading Standards prosecutions regarding rogue traders.

3. *Performance indicators* ADSS encouraged CSCI to create and focus Performance Assessment Framework indicators (PAFs) on safeguarding adults outcomes across all related partnerships, e.g. police and NHS.

4. *Policies and procedures* ADSS advised all authorities to review policies and take into account lessons learnt from children's services. For instance, ensuring safeguards are in place for new initiatives such as the extension of direct payments and individual budgets.

5. *Resources* ADSS acknowledged the need to strengthen partnership working, funding for joint training and ownership of revised multi-agency policies. It recommended central government funding to assist authorities implementing new policies and procedures.

6. *Workforce issues* ADSS recommended research into future workforce training needs of a large diverse workforce, and joint training initiatives via local safeguarding partnerships.

No secrets review 2009

Between October 2008 and January 2009, the Department of Health consulted numerous key stakeholders, involving some 12,000 participants. There was a strong backing for adult protection legislation from some key stakeholders, including Action on Elder Abuse and the Association of Directors of Adult Social Services (ADSS) wanting adult safeguarding to be given the same legislative framework as safeguarding children, stating that it was the only way it received equivalent priority, for example, consideration for Adult Safeguarding Boards to be given statutory footing.

The ADSS, at the time, highlighted that adult safeguarding lacked a clear legislative framework resulting in many local authorities continuing to *'work in a vacuum'*. It was claimed that social workers needed to have the right to enter homes and settings (overseen by a magistrate) where abuse is suspected, seize incriminating material and if necessary bar alleged perpetrators or remove alleged victims from the place, even overriding the latter's wishes if necessary.

Understandably, some user groups, such as Scope and MIND, expressed concerns that (if granted) such powers would undermine service user freedoms. The Department of Health indicated that it required more time to evaluate the impact of the Scottish legislation (see Chapter 4) and how it was actually working, stating that similar powers (granted in Scotland) were hardly used (Samuel, 2008).

Gary FitzGerald (AEA Chief Executive) stated that much could be achieved by simply revising the existing safeguarding guidance, policies and procedures coordinated by local authorities. It could start to address the ongoing lack of engagement of the NHS and GPs in particular, in local adult protection arrangements, while some agencies continue to fail in co-operating in adult protection inquiries or sharing information.

Revised policies and procedures should specify timescales for responding to referrals and reporting on investigations (Ahmed, 2009).

It remains uncertain whether the current Liberal Democrat Conservative Coalition Government have the political desire to grant parliamentary time for adult legislative reform in the area of adult safeguarding. In light of their determination to scale back what was perceived by some as the Labour Government's intrusive vetting and barring scheme, the coalition Government want to roll back unwarranted state intrusion into private lives, so have subsequently drafted the Freedoms Bill.

> **CASE STUDY**
>
> *Steven Hoskin was a 39-year-old man with learning difficulties who was imprisoned, tortured and drugged before plunging to his death from a viaduct in St Austell in July 2007, after being falsely accused of being a paedophile.*
>
> *Hoskin was placed in a housing association bedsit by adult social services in April 2005 and was allocated two hours of help each week. Hoskin chose to cancel this service in August and by September his case was closed. Hoskin then lost control of his own life when his tormentor (a petty drug dealer) and his girlfriend moved in and began to abuse*

CASE STUDY continued

him. Before his death Mr Hoskin contacted the police 12 times in nine months regarding Darren Stewart (his main tormentor). Hoskin had been assessed as having low–moderate needs under the fair access to care criteria (DOH, 2003), resulting in Hoskin being on the edge of social care eligibility criteria in terms of time and resources.

Cornwall Social Services Department were later criticised by the judge for allowing Mr Hoskin to be bullied to death. A serious case and internal management review published in December 2007 revealed that 40 opportunities to protect Mr Hoskin had been missed, while highlighting the information-sharing failings between numerous agencies. The review agreed that Hoskin's human rights had been breached. Hoskin's three tormentors were convicted of his murder and manslaughter in August 2007 in Truro Crown Court.

ACTIVITY 1.3

1. What actions do you think should have been taken to protect Steven Hoskin?
2. What do you think are the implications for future multi-agency risk-assessment threshold training in terms of identifying similar adults?

COMMENT

Reflecting national economic trends, many local authorities have chosen to prioritise adult social care for those with critical or substantial needs only, although assessment is triggered by the knowledge that someone may be in need of anything coming within the definition of community care services. Key agencies failed to view Steve Hoskin as a vulnerable adult in his own right and instead viewed him as being involved in and surrounded by anti-social behaviour. The lack of co-operation between key agencies meant that the danger Steve Hoskin was in was not detected. Crucially, Steve Hoskin's decision to end his contact with social services was not reviewed, investigated, explored and was not seen as indicating incapacity, and risk-assessed as part of that assessment, when he cancelled his service. Possible preventative low-level services such as befriending, floating support or advocacy provided by a voluntary agency might have provided Hoskin with more accessible support and alerted the local authority sooner.

Other relevant legislation

The Care Standards Act 2000 reformed the regulatory system for care services in England. It created new standards in social care work, education and training of social workers. Part 1 established the new independent regulatory body for care services, formerly the Commission for Social Care Inspection (CSCI) now the Care Quality Commission (CQC), which regulates, registers and monitors all registered social care services and some nursing and healthcare services. It sets out indicative National Minimum Standards for domiciliary care, care homes, independent hospitals, clinics and nursing agencies. Standard 18 sets as its outcome that *service users are protected from abuse.*

The Care Homes Regulation 2001 Reg. 37 instructs the registered person (usually the registered manager) to give notice orally and in writing to CQC without delay of any occurrences of a service user's death, infectious disease, serious illness or injury, theft, burglary or accident in the care home. CQC inspectors can closely examine records, care plans, medicine administration, staff recruitment records and accident books during inspections (see CQC Regulation changes later in this chapter).

The Rehabilitation of Offenders Act 1974 enables some criminal convictions to become *spent, or ignored, after a rehabilitation period*. A rehabilitation period is a set length of time from the date of conviction. After this period, with certain exceptions, an ex-offender is not normally obliged to mention the conviction when applying for a job or obtaining insurance, or when involved in criminal or civil proceedings. There are exceptions to this basic civil liberty, for those applying for jobs involving contact with children and vulnerable adults, and sex offenders.

The Data Protection Act 1998 ensures data protection regimes are in place to ensure data held on individuals are treated correctly giving due regard to the privacy of the individuals. It requires that when personal details are obtained they are processed fairly and lawfully: are only disclosed in appropriate circumstances; are accurate, relevant and not held any longer than necessary; and kept securely.

The Freedom of Information Act 2000 places a duty on public authorities to release information to the public on request unless legal exemptions to disclose apply. In most safeguarding of adult situations, the information is likely to fall within these exemptions, e.g. local authorities' investigation proceedings, personal information provided in confidence.

Whistleblowing policies essentially allow staff to bypass internal systems if they feel the overall management is engaged in collusive improper conduct and is not addressing bad practice or abuse. Policies arose following several public and internal inquiries within health and social care settings regarding employees' failure to report perceived abuses, with an inability of practitioners to blow the whistle coupled with agencies' or public bodies' unwillingness to respond to known abuses to staff, users or patients. Such policies led to the Act below.

The Public Interest Disclosure Act 1998 prevents employers from treating employees who may disclose abuses in a detrimental manner, by providing protective measures to prevent unfair dismissal or victimisation. It aimed to encourage a culture of openness; however, employers are not required to have a policy on disclosing abuses of power by their own employees, nor are there any rules about preventing employers from refusing employment on the grounds that someone was a whistleblower in a previous employment.

Despite this provision there is still reluctance to blow the whistle for fear of redundancy and future employment. For example, Simon Bellwood (a UK social worker) was sacked in September 2007 after raising legitimate complaints about a 'Dickensian' system in a secure unit where children were routinely locked up for 24 hours or more in solitary confinement. His whistleblowing helped spark the major inquiry into children's services in Jersey amid widespread concerns about child protection on the island.

The vetting and barring scheme review

Following the general election in June 2010, Teresa May (Home Secretary) suspended the Vetting and Barring Scheme and ordered a review. The Vetting and Barring Scheme had been established following a recommendation made by the Bichard Inquiry 2006 (as a consequence of the employment errors that enabled Ian Huntley to gain employment as a school caretaker, which resulted in the murders of Soham schoolgirls Holly Wells and Jessica Chapman).

In February 2011, the Coalition Government published their review findings and agreed to implement its key recommendations.

- To merge the Criminal Records Bureau (CRB) and the Independent Safeguarding Authority (ISA) to form a streamlined new body providing a proportionate barring and criminal records check.

- The number of positions requiring checks will be restricted to those working closely and regularly with children and adult at risk.

- Teachers will continue to be vetted – but those who do occasional, supervised volunteer work will not.

- The portability of criminal records checks between jobs to cut down needless bureaucracy.

- Job applicants will also be allowed to see their CRB results before their prospective employer so 'mistakes' can be corrected.

- An end to the need for those working with vulnerable groups to register with the vetting and barring scheme and be continuously monitored by the ISA.

The Coalition Government has confirmed that until all the appropriate legislation has been introduced (to be included in the Protection of Freedoms Bill) and the new arrangements are established, the existing responsibilities of employers and the ISA will remain. These include:

- A person who is barred from working with adult at risk (and children) will be breaking the law if they work or volunteer, or try to work or volunteer with those groups.

- An organisation which knowingly employs someone who is barred to work with those groups will be breaking the law.

- If a regulated activity provider (e.g. care home, hospital, day centre, hostel) who provides care for adult at risk (and children) dismiss or remove a staff member (or volunteer) because they have harmed an adult at risk (or child), or they would have done so had they not left, must continue to inform the ISA.

Although some of the recommendations do reduce delay and duplication they are also considered high risk and controversial. Former police detective and child protection expert, Mark Williams Thomas, claims that cutting legislation will give offenders more opportunities to gain access to children and adults at risk. He claims that these reforms are simply about saving money and nothing to do with empowerment and greater safeguarding. He states that some serial perpetrators can be calculating so will seek out activities and opportunities where checks are not required (BBC News, February 2011). It remains to be seen how this common sense and less bureaucratic scheme will evolve operationally, especially when located within the wider policy context of David Cameron's 'Big Society' agenda.

A new system of regulation

The Care Quality Commission (CQC), the health and social care regulator for England, produced guidance in March 2010 for all providers of health and adult social care to comply with the Health and Social Care Act 2008 (Regulated Activities) Regulations 2010 and the Care Quality Commission (Registration) Regulations 2009.

The new system focuses on outcomes rather than systems and processes, and places the views and experiences of people who use services at its centre. The CQC focuses upon 16 regulations (out of 28) that fall within Part 4 of the Health and Social Care Act 2008 (Regulated Activities) Regulations 2010.

Safeguarding adults from abuse remains one of the major components of the new registration regulations (Regulation 11, Outcome 7) which aims to ensure that the 'registered person' must make suitable arrangements to ensure users are safeguarded from abuse, or the risk of abuse, and their human rights are respected and upheld. Regulation 11, Outcome 7 focuses upon:

- systems that support the rights of people to live life free from abuse;
- arrangements to identify and prevent abuse;
- responding appropriately to allegations;
- use of restraint;
- staff recruitment and vetting.

It has resulted in many local authorities revising their multi-agency policy and procedures for safeguarding adults at risk in terms of revised guidance on incident reporting and alerting of levels of safeguarding investigation in terms of thresholds, alerting and incident reporting relating to low or 'one off' incidents.

Some local authority commissioners, contract departments and user groups have raised concerns that this new form of regulation appears very 'light touch' enabling the majority of care providers the freedom to self-assess their own provider compliance assessments with little external surveillance, monitoring compliance visits undertaken by CQC inspectors.

This has created some tensions between some care providers and local authority contract departments when they have existing concerns over 'poor' or 'inadequate' providers based upon local intelligence obtained from commissioning social workers undertaking reviews, partner agencies, monitoring visits, complaints from users and their families.

RESEARCH SUMMARY

The extent of financial abuse

In January 2007 Action on Elder Abuse (AEA), a national UK charity, published a study relating to the extent and prevalence of financial abuse. Over 471 incidents were analysed over a 12-month period. Data were based upon all calls to the charity's helpline during 2006 relating to financial abuse of older people in their own homes. The audit revealed the following.

- *Of theft, fraud and deception which take place within a domiciliary setting, 53 per cent were committed by the victim's own sons or daughters aged 41–60 years.*
- *A minimum of £2m cash was reported as stolen or coerced from older people.*
- *18 houses were sold or taken without consent; a further 13 houses were given away without the full awareness of the owner or after significant pressure, e.g. emotional blackmail.*
- *Almost half (49 per cent) of victims were women aged 81 years or over.*

The Health Select Committee Inquiry into Elder Abuse (2004) made two recommendations regarding financial abuse:

Recommendation 18 stated: we recommend that the prevention, detection and remedying of financial abuse should be included as specific areas of policy development by adult protection committees.

Recommendation 20 stated: we further recommend that the regulatory bodies of health and social care increase their surveillance of financial systems including the use of powers of attorney and, in care homes, the use of residents' personal allowances.

ACTIVITY *1.4*

1. *What safeguards could local authorities put in place to protect those who have savings above local authority thresholds but are still subject to financial exploitation or abuse?*
2. *With increased expansion of individualised budgets across statutory adult services, can you think of any practice dilemmas for practitioners monitoring or reviewing such cases in relation to these AEA findings?*
3. *What practical mechanisms could banks and building societies put in place to protect older customers?*

COMMENT

This summary concisely outlines key financial abuse factors. Investigations frequently reveal that it is often those in positions of trust or in a caring role who illegally attempt to protect what they see as their rightful inheritance. In addition, it often manifests in the deliberate disposition of financial assets before a family seeks local authority funding assistance towards 24-hour placement care provision.

Some possible legal remedies regarding financial abuse could be the Theft Act 1968 e.g. obtaining or taking money by deception, but proof may be difficult to obtain if a person is confused or forgetful; the Court of Protection in terms of Deputyship or the removal of the same; the creation of a Lasting Power of Attorney whilst the donor is still capacitated, or the removal of same if abuse is suspected. One may want to consider a criminal prosecution e.g. under the Fraud Act 2006. Alternatively, one may want to consider the removal of an Appointee via written communication with the Department of Work & Pensions or by way of supersession through Deputyship via the Court of Protection. The role of the Independent Mental Capacity Advocate may alert authorities to abuse. Alternatively, the Banking Code (British Bankers Association, 2008) sets transparent standards in terms of protecting customers' accounts, supported by an internal complaints procedure and the external Financial Ombudsman Service. (Adapted from Schwehr, 2006, Legal and Training Consultant)

Putting policy into practice

All adults are entitled to live in a manner they wish and to accept or refuse support, assistance or protection as long as they do not harm others and are capable of making decisions about these matters.

(McKenzie, 2000, p9)

All adults should receive the most effective, but least restrictive and intrusive form of support, assistance or protection when they are unable to care for themselves or their assets.

The *least restrictive and intrusive* principles are key intervention values enshrined in the Mental Health Act 2007, the Human Rights Act 1998 and the Mental Capacity Act 2005 and remain key social work values which underpin the GSCC Codes of Conduct and the BASW Code of Ethics (2002). Practitioners need to bear these fundamental principles in mind with regard to safeguarding adult work. As stated earlier, all key statutory agencies need to ensure that their responses are proportionate to the level of mental capacity, concern and risk.

Figure 1.2 provides a personalised diagram showing the processes an adult protection referral usually takes, covering key stages of how a safeguarding adult referral should appropriately be managed and processed by the co-ordinating lead agency (the local authority social services department). However, it does not replace practitioners consulting with investigating managers or referring to copies of their multi-agency safeguarding adults procedural manual, which can now be accessed via local authority

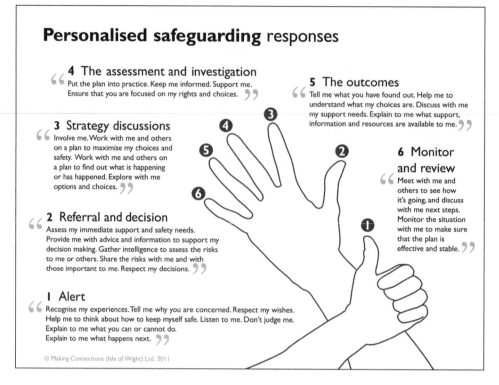

Figure 1.2 Personalised safeguarding responses
Making Connections (Isle of Wight) Ltd, 2011

websites so practitioners obtain detailed and specific operational practice information and knowledge.

Stevenson (1996) alerts us to the dangers of *over-proceduralisation* occurring within safeguarding adults when compared with child protection. It is important to highlight that procedures alone do not always immediately assist new practitioners or managers as they tend to focus upon procedural guidance and not on the professional skills required, e.g. legal and operational knowledge, practice experience, confidence to assertively question, enquire and challenge allied professionals' assumptions or care providers with regard to capacity, risk, malpractice, poor standards of care and areas of discrimination.

Lead agency responsibilities

It is predominantly the role of local authority social services to assess the level of seriousness, determine the most appropriate level of investigation, then make a decision about vulnerability and the victim's mental capacity in conjunction with exploring the level of risk, agree the proportionate level of investigation required to carry out and co-ordinate the investigation by appointing an investigation officer and manager. As part of the information gathering it is vital to liaise with other agencies and co-ordinate contributions from other professionals or services, ensure necessary links are made to other procedures (e.g. criminal or child protection investigations), convene, chair, record strategy discussions, case conferences and to devise a safeguarding plan as part of the care management process. Criminal investigations take precedence over adult protection investigations, so in certain circumstances, the police may well lead major criminal safeguarding investigations.

Inter-agency consultation

Key agencies have an enhanced duty to ensure staff involved in adult protection work are committed to attend case conferences, participate in sharing written reports, contribute to a shared decision-making process and follow through with agreed action plans. For inter-agency adult protection work to remain effective it continues to require ongoing co-operation commitment and communication between and within professional groups and care providers. Recently this has become more challenging due to fundamental and widespread restructuring across both primary care trusts and social service departments.

NHS and social care managers and practitioners need to maintain local collaborative networks and practice forums to maintain vital links to share good practice and to remain updated (see Chapter 10). The Practitioners Alliance Against Abuse of Vulnerable Adults (PAVA), founded in 1997 by Jacki Pritchard and Mervyn Eastman, strives to establish collaboration with practitioners in statutory, voluntary and private sectors to develop practice-based interventions and generate positive outcomes in safeguarding adults.

Adult protection case conferences

These conferences aim to share and evaluate the information gathered from the investigation, while considering new information that may have arisen within a legal context. They aim to ascertain the level of risk – now and in the future (see Chapter 11). A case conference also needs to consider the wishes of the adult at risk and identify key personnel and agree a framework for multi-agency working, clarify roles and responsibilities at individual, agency and provider levels. Its crucial task is to make recommendations and agree an adult protection plan while setting in place agreed arrangements for monitoring and reviewing within designated timescales.

Debriefing, feedback and evaluation

This is a crucial final stage which sometimes gets postponed or forgotten due to competing operational demands. It is extremely useful in terms of establishing ongoing practice and audit links with local policy and best practice forums, e.g. PAVA, Adult Protection Chairs and Adult Safeguarding Boards. It can also identify a need to commission preventative services (e.g. Steven Hoskin's case), or revise and review protocols. A reflective debriefing evaluation can identify training and development needs for staff, agencies or related professionals and, most importantly, improvement outcomes for adults at risk.

Intervention and assessment outcomes

Depending upon the severity of risks, the context, the complexity, degree and nature of the abuse, there can be several possible outcomes. A social work assessment can sometimes resolve isolated incidents following an assessment aided by the care management review and monitoring process if services are commissioned. Alternative outcomes may result in a disciplinary investigation via a professional body, e.g. GSCC, NCM, an individual referral to the Vetting and Barring Scheme; a local authority's contracts department investigation can suspend or terminate a contract. The Care Quality Commission (CQC) may impose conditions upon registration, suspend or cancel registration following statutory enforcement. Finally, it may result in a police or criminal investigation and prosecution, a civil prosecution and ultimately imprisonment.

CHAPTER SUMMARY

This chapter critically reviewed key social policy and legislation which has influenced the evolutionary nature of safeguarding adult policy. Currently, there is no consolidating piece of legislation in existence within England, Wales and Northern Ireland similar to the Adult Support and Protection (Scotland) Act 2007. However, different pieces of legislation supplemented by policy guidance do exist which practitioners can consider for a range of abuses and responses. Action on Elder Abuse and the Association of Directors of Adult Social Services have lobbied for adult protection to be given the same legislative status as child protection so vulnerable adults will receive equivalent legislative priority and resources. Policy history has shown that Scottish legislation on occasions informs the approach of Parliament, so the legislative developments discussed in Chapter 4 should be considered.

Practitioners operating within safeguarding adults aim to prevent abuse, and also to enhance well-being and maximise individual choice and social inclusion. Legislation and policy can provide guidance, but will never be able to provide all the answers in these complex and emotive situations.

FURTHER READING

Journal of Adult Protection (Pier Publication)
A straightforward and accessible journal full of innovative evidenced-based research by practitioners, with viewpoints and commentary on current policy in this important field.

Mandelstam, M (2009) *Safeguarding vulnerable adults and the law*. London: Jessica Kingsley.
A comprehensive legal text that focuses upon a complex framework which currently surrounds adult safeguarding policy and practice. Essential reading for any local authority practitioner, voluntary organisation, trainer or research, in this rapidly changing field.

Pritchard, J (ed) (2009) *Good practice in the law and safeguarding adults*. London: Jessica Kingsley.
Provides an accessible and up-to-date summary of the key legislative framework, developments and best practice, relevant for social care practitioners, researchers, educators and care provider managers involved in adult protection in England, Wales and Scotland.

Penhale, B and **Parker J** (2008) *Working with vulnerable adults*. Abingdon: Routledge.
This skills-based text provides essential information and knowledge for practitioners and students interested in this growing field.

www.pavauk.org.uk Practitioners alliance against abuse of vulnerable adults
PAVA strives through collaboration with practitioners in the statutory, voluntary and private sectors to develop practice-based interventions and to generate positive outcomes in working with the abuse of vulnerable adults.

www.elderabuse.org.uk Action on elder abuse
AEA is a national charity which aims to protect against and prevent abuse of vulnerable older people. It raises awareness, encourages education, information and support to those in need and runs a national freephone helpline number.

www.safeguardingadultsforum.co.uk
An accessible up-to-date independent website for England. Provides a useful resource for all safeguarding developments plus a forum and debating platform for those involved in this field of work.

Chapter 2

Human rights and wrongs: The Human Rights Act 1998
Andy Mantell

A C H I E V I N G   A   S O C I A L   W O R K   D E G R E E

This chapter will help you to meet the following National Occupational Standards.

Key Role 1: Prepare for, and work with, individuals, families, carers, groups and communities to assess their needs and circumstances.

- Inform individuals, families, carers, groups and communities about your own, and your organisation's duties and responsibilities.
- Assess and recommend an appropriate course of action for individuals, families, carers, groups and communities.

Key Role 3: Support individuals to represent their needs, views and circumstances.

- Assess whether you should act as an advocate for the individual, the family, carer, group and community.
- Assist individuals, families, carers, groups and communities to access independent advocacy.
- Advocate for, and with, individuals, families, carers, groups and communities.

Key Role 6: Demonstrate professional competence in social work practice.

- Review and update your own knowledge of legal, policy and procedural frameworks.
- Use professional assertiveness to justify decisions and uphold professional social work practice, values and ethics.

It will also introduce you to the following academic standards set out in the social work benchmark statement.

5.1.2 The service delivery context.

Introduction

The Human Rights Act 1998 has been seen by some as a 'whinger's charter' and been condemned by some elements of the tabloid press who have bayed for its revocation (*Daily Mail*, 2007). Dismissing the Human Rights Act 1998 reflects taken-for-granted assumptions about our rights and our ability to enforce those rights. However, guaranteed rights are particularly important for those who lack power or who are denied a voice, those who have been excluded or marginalised within our society. Let us be clear, when we talk about safeguarding adults we are fundamentally talking about human rights.

No secrets, the Department of Health guidance on adult protection, was unequivocal: *Abuse is a violation of an individual's human and civil rights by any other person or persons* (Department of Health, 2000).

The centrality of human rights in the protection of people from abuse was underlined in the Association of Directors of Social Services (2005) National Framework on Safeguarding Adults:

> *All persons have the right to live their lives free from violence and abuse. This right is underpinned by the duty on public agencies under the Human Rights Act 1998 to intervene proportionately to protect the rights of citizens.*

> (ADSS, 2005, p4)

This chapter considers the relevance of the Human Rights Act 1998 (HRA 1998) to safeguarding adults. You will be introduced to the context and guiding principles behind the HRA 1998. We will then explore the articles and guiding principles of the Act in relation to safeguarding adults and practice situations. This discussion will highlight the tension between competing rights and the significance of the concept of proportionality.

Background to the Human Rights Act 1998

Following the atrocities committed during the Second World War, in 1948 the United Nations established a Convention on Human Rights. This has helped to challenge abuse at the macro level (see Chapter 1) by setting standards, such as the Convention on the Rights of the Child, against which the policies and practices of governments can be judged and failings highlighted.

The European Convention on Human Rights 1950 provided direct redress for European citizens. It was implemented by the UK government in 1951, but it was incorporated into international, rather than domestic, law. This meant that UK citizens had to go to the European Court of Human Rights in Strasbourg if their rights were infringed. The Labour Party pledged to rectify this situation in their 1997 Manifesto. The HRA 1998 was implemented in the UK in 2000, at last incorporating these rights into domestic law.

However, the Conservatives have proposed that it be replaced with a Bill of Rights and the Liberals have called for a 'Freedom Bill' (EHRC, 2010, online). If the coalition government does introduce new legislation it will still need to be compatible with the ECHR to avoid an increase in cases being taken to Strasbourg.

The Equality and Human Rights Commission came into being under the Equality Act 2006 and took over the roles of the Commission for Racial Equality, the Equal Opportunities Commission and the Disability Rights Commission in 2007. At its inception it was envisaged that: *a human rights commission, probing, questioning and encouraging public bodies, could have a real impact in driving forward the development of a culture of respect for human rights* (JCHR, 2010, p5). However, they recognise that they have currently failed to have achieved that mandate (JCHR, 2010) and given the change in government and current budgetary cutbacks it will be interesting to see if it survives and if so in what form. The EHRC remains committed to preserving and expanding human rights protection in the light of the coalition government's plans to replace the current legislation (EHRC, 2010, online).

Guiding principles

Reinterpreting the law

The government in drafting all new legislation tries to ensure that it is compatible with the HRA 1998. Furthermore, the courts now have to interpret all legislation in a way that is compatible with the HRA 1998. They can overrule subordinate legislation, such as the Code of Practice to the Mental Health Act 1983 (amended by the Mental Health Act 2007), but not the Act itself, as this is primary legislation. In this case they can only issue a declaration of incompatibility and refer back to the government. This ensures that legislative authority still resides with Parliament. The minister responsible can make a remedial order to rectify the problem or the government may decide not to act. In the case of *JT v UK* (2000) the government recognised that a patient under the Act should have the right to apply to the court to change their nearest relative under the Mental Health Act 1983 (see below), but despite the issuing of a declaration of incompatibility it has taken several years to change the legislation. The Mental Health Act 2007 does now allow a patient to apply to the court to change their nearest relative, but only under limited grounds.

It is still possible to appeal to the European Court of Human Rights in Strasbourg (as occurred in the case of *JT v UK*), but in making its decisions the European Court of Human Rights recognises that domestic courts are best placed to make decisions and consequently allows them a margin of appreciation (i.e. a degree of leeway).

Many of the UK's courts' decisions are based on common law (i.e. previous case law). These precedents will now have to be gradually replaced with decisions that have taken into account the HRA 1998. This will include Strasbourg case law such as Herczegfalvy's case discussed below (p42). The Act is also a *living instrument*, that is its interpretation must alter over time to reflect changes in society. For example, the UK's policies towards gay and lesbian people have shifted significantly over the last 50 years from labelling their behaviour as deviant to enabling them to undertake legally recognised civil partnerships.

Public authorities

The HRA 1998 applies to public authorities, rather than private organisations or individuals. A public authority is not acting unlawfully if it is acting in accordance with primary legislation. For example, if an approved mental health professional compulsorily admits someone to a psychiatric unit they are breaching that person's right to liberty, but this is allowed because they are acting under primary legislation, i.e. the Mental Health Act 1983, as amended by the Mental Health Act 2007.

While the HRA 1998 focuses on the actions of public authorities there is also a positive obligation upon public authorities to protect people from the acts of other people which may breach their human rights.

The Act defines three categories of public authority: the courts and tribunals; core public authorities who are wholly within the public spheres, such as local authorities and the police; and functional public authorities, which have a mix of public and private functions such as Network Rail. In this third category only the public functions fall within the Act. What constitutes a public authority has been the subject of much contention.

CASE STUDY

A local authority social worker places Mrs Handsworth, who has dementia, in a care home run by Omnicare, a well-respected national company. She has limited funds and her care is paid for by social services. Her daughter, Linda, was initially very pleased and relieved at the placement as she was concerned for her mother's safety. The care home is set in large grounds and her mother has always liked walking in gardens. However, Linda becomes concerned that her mother is never allowed out. When Linda asked the manager about this, she replied that it was because of the risk of her mother wandering.

ACTIVITY **2.1**

Is Omnicare *a public authority?*
Does the Human Rights Act 1998 apply in Mrs Handsworth's situation?

COMMENT

If the social worker had placed Mrs Handsworth in a care home run by the local authority it would be considered to be a public authority, but until recently despite her placement being funded by the local authority, Omnicare would not have been viewed as a public authority (see legal case study below).

It should not be assumed that because a care home is private their residents have less protection of their human rights. In *R (Johnson and others) v Havering Borough Council* (2007) EWCA Civ 26, Ms Johnson was a resident in a council care home which was transferred to private ownership and it was proposed that she would have to leave the home. Proceedings were taken on her behalf, arguing that her rights would be less protected by this transfer of ownership and her right to a family and private life breached by having to move home. The court ruled that her rights were maintained, because if she suffered cruel or inhuman treatment she would still have the same recourse to the criminal courts and her social worker would have to act to protect her under section 21 of the National Assistance Act 1948.

In Ms Johnson's and Mrs Handsworth's cases the care home would be bound by the regulations of the Care Standards Act 2000, which has to be interpreted to be compatible with the Human Rights Act 1998. In Ms Johnson's case the courts argued that the Care Standards Act 2000, supervised by the Commission for Social Care Inspection (now the Care Quality Commission), provided protection in excess of that offered to protect private and family life under the HRA 1998.

If a public authority such as social services becomes aware that a person's rights may have been breached, they have a positive obligation under the HRA 1998 to preserve those rights. Even where there is no involvement by a public authority the courts are required to act in a manner that is compatible with the Act and to interpret all legislation in a similar manner.

CASE STUDY

YL v Birmingham Council (2007) UKHL 27

YL was an 84-year-old woman who was suffering from Alzheimer's disease and was admitted to a care home run by Southern Cross Health Care Ltd. Southern Cross Health Care Ltd sought her removal, but legal proceedings were instigated, on her behalf, arguing that to move her would breach her right to life, her right to freedom from cruel and inhumane treatment and her right to a private and family life.

The House of Lords ruled that a private care home providing care and accommodation under contract to the local authority was not exercising functions of a public nature and was not therefore a public authority. Consequently the claim that YL's rights had been breached was rejected.

COMMENT

This ruling was consistent with an earlier ruling in favour of the Leonard Cheshire Foundation (R (Heather) v Leonard Cheshire Foundation (2002) EWCA Civ 366). The view that the courts were taking that private care homes were not public authorities, yet local authority care homes were, placed residents in an iniquitous position. This was most starkly highlighted by Ms Johnson's case (above) where at the point the care home was privatised she ceased to receive care from a public authority despite her care not changing.

As we have already seen, the court did not consider Ms Johnson's rights would be significantly affected by this change. However, there was clearly a different quality of protection. For example, in YL's case, although Birmingham Council would certainly try to act to ensure her right to life and freedom from cruel and inhumane treatment, they would not be able to avoid her right to a private and family life being infringed by her moving to new accommodation.

The Joint Committee on Human Rights (2004, p56) commented that this situation leaves real gaps and inadequacies in human rights protection in the UK, including gaps that affect people who are particularly vulnerable to ill treatment. In effect a care home 'stands in the shoes of the State and yet does not have responsibilities under the Human Rights Act' (Joint Committee on Human Rights, 2004, p16). Consequently, under section 145 of the Health and Social Care Act 2008, where a person is placed in a care home under statutory provisions then the home is now viewed as exercising a public function and must comply with the Human Rights Act 1998. In England and Wales that would mean the person having been placed under Part III of the National Assistance Act 1948,

COMMENT *continued*

in Scotland section 12 or 13a of the Social Work (Scotland) Act 1968 and in Northern Ireland articles 15 and 36 of the Health and Personal Social Services (Northern Ireland) Order 1972. However, those who are not placed in this way, for example, those who pay privately, still remain less protected.

Absolute, limited and qualified rights and their derogation

Some rights have been classified by the Act as absolute, meaning that there can be no derogation (i.e. exemption from them). The right to life and the right to protection from torture are examples of absolute rights.

Limited rights allow for specific exceptions expressed within the Act, for example, the right to liberty is limited to allow for the incarceration of criminals.

Qualified rights allow for a range of exceptions, but only if the following rules are met:

- the interference has a basis in law;

- the interference is to achieve a permissible aim, for example, the protection of public health;

- it is necessary to achieve a pressing social need, pursue a legitimate aim and is a proportionate action (see below).

An example of a qualified right would be the right to respect for private and family life. Within this right a person has a right to confidentiality, but an exception to that right would be if that person was physically abusing their partner.

A partial derogation exists from Article 5, the right to liberty, and in May 2007, the then Home Secretary, John Reid, suggested that it might become necessary to derogate from other aspects of the HRA 1998 due to the emergency threat posed by terrorism (Ford et al., 2007).

Proportionality

Proportionality is a crucial concept at the heart of any acceptable interference with a person's human rights. To be legitimate any action must be the minimum necessary to gain the aim and not be arbitrary or unfair. This concept tries to preserve people's rights as much as possible and ensure that public authorities do not act in an excessive manner. For example, if a hospital patient with an acquired brain injury is aggressive towards another patient, it would not be a proportionate response to continuously, heavily sedate them. A more proportionate response might be to move them to a single room.

Your rights

Listed below are your rights, enshrined within articles of Schedule One of the HRA 1998.

- The right to life (Article 2).
- The right to freedom from torture and degrading treatment (Article 3).
- The right to freedom from slavery and forced labour (Article 4).
- The right to liberty (Article 5).
- The right to a fair trial (Article 6).
- The right not to be punished for something that wasn't a crime when you did it (Article 7).
- The right to respect for private and family life (Article 8).
- The right to freedom of thought, conscience and religion (Article 9).
- The right to freedom of expression (Article 10).
- The right to freedom of assembly and association (Article 11).
- The right to marry or form a civil partnership and start a family (Article 12).
- The right not to be discriminated against in respect of these rights and freedoms (Article 14).
- The right to own property (Protocol 1, Article 1).
- The right to an education (Protocol 1, Article 2).
- The right to participate in free elections (Protocol 1, Article 3).

There is not space to explore all these articles so we will focus on a few pertinent examples with reference to case studies and the case law, to illustrate the HRA 1998's relevance to safeguarding adults.

Article 2: The right to life

The right to life must be at the heart of safeguarding adults. This is an absolute right and as with all legislation it is important to carefully consider the wording; it is a right to life, not a right to death. Consequently when Dianne Pretty, who was dying from motor neurone disease, sought to ensure that her husband would not be prosecuted for assisting in her suicide, her wishes were declined (*R v DPP, ex parte Dianne Pretty and Secretary of State for the Home Department (Interested Party)* 18/October 2001).

ACTIVITY 2.2

Do you agree with the court's ruling?

COMMENT

Mrs Pretty was trying to establish that her husband's behaviour would be in her best interest rather than abusive. However, such a decision would have established a precedent in euthanasia that the court was not happy to accept. The Mental Capacity Act 2005 (see Chapter 3) is clear that people may refuse treatment even if this may then result in death, but they cannot demand treatment that will kill them. There is a blurred area for medical practitioners between the provision of pain relief medication which could result in death and pain relief medication which is likely to kill the patient, the so-called 'Brompton cocktail'. Dr Shipman's well-documented murders provided a cautionary tale as to why safeguards are necessary even with those professions that we trust most.

As the result of Debbie Purdy, in a subsequent case (R (on the application of Purdy) v Director of Public Prosecutions), appealing to the House of Lords, the Law Lords required the DPP to publish guidance on when a prosecution would be sought under section 2(1) of the Suicide Act 1961 (see DPP, 2010). The DPP aimed to distinguish between helping someone to kill themselves and ending their lives:

> someone acting out of compassion, to help a terminally ill patient with a *clear, settled and informed wish to die*, was unlikely to face the courts. But persuading or pressuring the victim to kill themselves, or benefiting from their death, would encourage prosecution.
>
> (Seddique, 2010, online).

Article 3: Freedom from torture and cruel, inhuman or degrading treatment or punishment

While Article 3 covers many of the most common forms of abuse within households (see O'Keefe et al., 2007, for prevalence), you might not expect it to occur within public authorities. However, the Cornwall abuse inquiry (CSCI and Healthcare Commission, 2006) highlighted how people with learning difficulties were punished and treated in degrading and cruel manners. This is just a recent example of numerous inquiries into abuse in hospital and institutional care. Institutional cultures can provide a breeding ground for such practices to flourish (see Chapter 9).

Treatment against a person's wishes would generally be viewed as a breach of Article 3. It is therefore unsurprising that compulsory detention and treatment under mental health legislation is a particular point of contention.

ACTIVITY **2.3**

A mental health patient is handcuffed to a bed and forced to have food and medication. Do you think that this is a breach of Article 3?

These events occurred to Herczegfalvy (Herczegfalvy v Austria (1992) 15 EHRR 437) and he argued that he was subjected to inhuman treatment. However, the court decided that as long as the treatment is proven to be a therapeutic necessity then it is permissible. The court also considered that the way in which the treatment is administered is a key component in distinguishing treatment from abusive behaviour.

It can therefore be seen that while Article 3 is an absolute right, what constitutes freedom from torture and cruel, inhuman or degrading treatment or punishment is open to interpretation.

While Articles 2 and 3 are both absolute rights, it would be possible for them to come into conflict. Denying a person such as Mrs Pretty treatment could be viewed as a breach of her Article 2 right to life, but the provision of treatment could be viewed as a breach of her Article 3 right to freedom from inhuman or degrading treatment. In such a situation, where the person lacked capacity, you and the multidisciplinary team would need to be guided by what was in their best interest (see Chapter 3).

Article 5: Right to liberty and security of person

Liberty is a fundamental right yet it is frequently abused in the name of protection. I was once asked to see a woman with learning difficulties who was due to be admitted to hospital for a hip operation. She was very concerned about her son whom she cared for. Her son, who also had learning difficulties, was in his early thirties and had been diagnosed with schizophrenia when he was 18. Since then his mother had kept him in their house in her attempts to keep him safe and protect other people. He was well looked after but had been in effect detained by his mother for more than ten years, because of her fears about his mental health problems. The woman had her hip operation and her son was successfully helped to move into supported accommodation. No criminal action was taken against the mother.

Under Article 5 everyone has the right not to be detained. There are two exceptions to this rule: those who have committed a crime and people of 'unsound mind' who are a danger to themselves or others. While unsound mind is not defined by the European courts, they have been clear that it does not include those whose views deviate from the prevailing norms in a society. Such safeguards help to defend against the manufacturing of spurious disorders as a form of social control. For example, the Union of Soviet Socialist Republics recognised a condition known informally as 'Solzhenitsyn's disease'.

'Solzhenitsyn's disease'
The Serbsky Psychiatric Institute, in Moscow, diagnosed political dissidents as having 'slow-developing schizophrenia'. Delusions of reconstruction and reformation *or* Solzhenitsyn's disease *was described by one of their psychiatrists as:*

The patient thinks it is necessary to reform the system of government control in this country. He thinks that he himself is capable of undertaking leadership; that it is necessary to review theoretical problems of social science and that he himself is capable of explaining the theory and practice of Soviet industry and reconstruction. His ideas are so essential (he believes) that he should leave the Soviet Union and disseminate them in all the countries in the world.

(Wing, 1978, p189, cited in Olsen, 1984, p88).

After the collapse of the Soviet Union the Institute acknowledged that there was no such condition (Glasser, 2002).

For a person of unsound mind to be detained, with the exception of an emergency, reliable evidence must be put before a competent authority, for example, a court. This evidence must show that the person has a mental disorder established by someone with medical expertise and that it is of a nature or degree that warrants detention. This is to avoid the possibility of arbitrary detention, a criticism which has been levelled against the Mental Health Act 1983 for its administrative rather than judicial approach to detention. The amendments contained within the Mental Health Act 2007 do not seem to have gone far enough to assuage these concerns and it will be interesting to see if legal challenges develop on this basis.

CASE STUDY

Johnson v UK *(24 October 1997) (1999) 27 EHRR 296*
From June 1989 to January 1993 Mr Johnson was detained in Rampton Hospital, a secure hospital in Nottinghamshire. A Mental Health Review Tribunal had found that he was no longer suffering from mental illness, but placed a condition on his release that he must reside in a hostel. Since no hostel was available he remained in hospital and took his claim for freedom to court. The European Court acknowledged that the absence of the mental disorder did not necessarily warrant immediate and unconditional release. However, the condition that was imposed was not within the tribunal's power to guarantee within a reasonable time frame. Consequently the court found that Mr Johnson's Article 5 rights had been breached and awarded him £10,000 in damages.

Mr Johnson's case highlights that just because an action is taken with the best of intent, it does not mean that its effect may not be abusive and oppressive upon the individual.

If we reconsider the first case study, Mrs Handsworth's inability to leave the unit could be seen to be a breach of her right to liberty. The rights of mentally disordered people who lack capacity and are not detained under the Mental Health Act 1983 as amended by The Mental Health Act 2007, or by declaratory relief from the Court of Protection, are of great concern. There are currently thousands of people in care homes in England and Wales, particularly people with dementia or learning difficulties, who risk deprivation of liberty by staff's attempts to protect them. In the Mental Health Act 2007 the government amended the Mental Capacity Act 2005 to provide safeguards to those who lack capacity and may be deprived of their liberty (discussed in more detail in Chapter 3). However, some uncertainty remains as to the point at which a person is being deprived of their liberty.

Article 6: Right to a fair and public trial within a reasonable time

People have a right to an objective, independent hearing within a reasonable amount of time. While this relates primarily to people who have committed a criminal offence, it does have a wider application. In relation to people who are detained under mental health legislation it is important that people are told the grounds for their detention, how long it is likely to be for and their rights to appeal. This provides the person with the information and means to refute the evidence used for their detention.

The covert or forced administering of medication where someone has the capacity to consent can be tantamount to detention and a breach of Article 6, as well as Articles 3 and 5. The ongoing sedation of a person effectively deprives them of their liberty without recourse to a court. Macdonald et al. (2004) found that 43 per cent of non-specialist care homes covertly provided medication, for example, by hiding it in food. It is indicative of wider oppression and the persisting lower societal status of older and disabled people that their views and opinions are still often ignored (see Chapter 7).

Article 8: Right to respect for private and family life, home and correspondence

The other articles explored above address the issues that people tend to think of when they think of adult abuse. Article 8 by comparison seems innocuous, yet anecdotally I have found it a prominent issue in practice. In the Mental Health Act 1983, for example, there was a duty upon approved social workers (now approved mental health professionals) to consult with an individual's nearest relative when undertaking an assessment. The nearest relative is a prescribed list within the Act rather than necessarily the patient's choice. Imagine a situation where a woman has suffered sexual abuse from her father, which subsequently leads to her developing depression and attempting to commit suicide. Despite the fact that she wants nothing to do with her father, under the Mental Health Act 1983, he would have had to be contacted. As we have seen already in the case of *JT v UK*, the inability of the patient to be able to apply to court to replace their nearest relative led to the issuing of a declaration of incompatibility with the HRA 1998. Whilst the Mental Health Act 2007 did not amend the 1983 Act to allow patients to choose their nearest relative they can now apply to court for their nearest relative to be changed ('displaced') if they are 'an unsuitable person to act', for example, due to abusive behaviour.

Our home and family life are central aspects for many of us to our sense of being. Yet social workers frequently have to intervene in family life, for example, moving an older person from her home of 40 years to a safer care home. Such decisions are too complex to reduce to simply applying the principle of proportionality to ensure that her absolute rights are maintained.

Article 14: Prohibition of discrimination

Social work has always prided itself on its anti-oppressive stance and with the HRA 1998 it gained a considerable tool to combat discrimination. Article 14 states that the rights of the convention should not be limited by discrimination, for example based on age, sex, race, colour, language, religion, political or other opinion, national or social origin, association with a national minority, property, birth or other status.

Disabled and older people have found that services for them have been rationed. For example, I once worked with a man with learning difficulties who had been refused a heart operation based on a doctor's assumptions about his quality of life. Such societal attitudes that denigrate people's worth encourage institutional cultures in which abusive behaviour thrives as permissible (see Chapters 7 and 9).

CASE STUDY

Alice Powder, aged 40, has Huntington's disease, a rare, inherited, neurological condition that affects a person's motor coordination, their cognition and their mental health. People tend to become symptomatic in their late thirties to forties and have a life expectancy of approximately 20 years from onset. Alice was admitted to hospital following a fall and was found to have very poor nutrition and personal hygiene. She lived on her own and had occasional contact with her widowed mother. She had received home care support daily but they found her mood volatile; at times she would hug them as they came through the door but often she refused to let them in or she became aggressive.

Alice's speech was very unclear but she reluctantly agreed to enter a care home. Initially she settled in well, but after four months she stopped washing. When asked she said that she had just washed and seemed oblivious to the deteriorating state of her hygiene. She started to refuse to change her clothes and to not allow staff into her room. She still had an impulsive tendency to hug people and staff were concerned that her poor hygiene was becoming a health risk to herself and others. She was assessed under the Mental Health Act 1983, but not found to meet the criteria. She was, however, viewed to lack capacity to understand the implications of her not washing.

The care home served notice on her and requested that the local authority found her a new placement. Social services were unable to find a placement willing to take her and in the meantime her hygiene deteriorated further and a nurse became concerned that she might have head lice. After consulting with social services, the primary care trust, the GP and her mother, it was agreed that Alice would be asked to have a wash and if she refused she would be forcibly washed, her room cleaned and her clothes laundered. She refused and she was washed once a week for three weeks and then she resumed washing herself again. She was caused considerable distress by this process and was subsequently moved to another home.

ACTIVITY 2.4

Do you think any of the above articles could have been breached in Alice's case? What would you do in this situation?

COMMENT

Alice's treatment could arguably be seen as a breach of Article 3, as degrading treatment, Article 5, security of person; and Article 8, respect for private life. On the other hand, it could be argued that no article has been breached as her treatment was therapeutically necessary. In the past such action would have been under common law, but would now be considered acts in connection with care and treatment of someone who lacks capacity, within the Mental Capacity Act 2005 (see Chapter 3). These actions must still be in the best interest of the person. If the staff had not acted it could be argued that they would have failed in their duties towards the other residents, in particular Article 3, by housing them in unsanitary conditions, and Article 8 by not respecting how they would like to live their lives.

While there was a case for intervention, it is the manner of intervention that needs further exploration as it must be proportionate. The approach above is quite confrontational. An alternative approach might be to change the focus of the intervention. One care home I worked with provided a menu of pampering activities; the residents could choose from a list of experiences, such as having a bath which has aromatherapy oils and rose petals, relaxing music and a glass of wine. This different tack may not work, but it is important to explore all options before force is considered.

CHAPTER SUMMARY

This chapter has introduced you to the centrality of the Human Rights Act 1998 in any consideration of safeguarding adults. After an overview of the rights contained within the Act it has focused in particular upon those articles that in practice tend to be the source of most concern. We have also seen that articles should not be viewed in isolation. Adult abuse will frequently breach several articles or present a conflict between articles. When considering an incident or your decisions, you need to consider if a person's rights have been affected and if that interference is legitimate.

In exploring the practical and ethical dilemmas raised by the Human Rights Act 1998 I have also sought to raise your awareness that what is considered a breach of human rights and abusive is not always as clear-cut as it may initially appear. We have seen the important role played by the principle of proportionality in balancing different rights and reconciling the competing rights of individuals and the significance of best interest where a person lacks capacity (discussed in Chapter 3).

While the Human Rights Act 1998 has been demonstrated to be particularly relevant to public authorities, it can be seen through its effects on all legislation and the activities of the courts to offer safeguards to everyone. It is not, however, a panacea, providing an immediate remedy and a course of action for those working to safeguard adults. Instead it serves more to provide a framework informing best practice in this most complex of fields.

FURTHER READING

WEBSITES

Daw, R (2000) *The impact of the Human Rights Act on disabled people*. London: Royal National Institute for Deaf People and the Disability Rights Commission.
This book provides an accessible introduction to the applicability of the HRA 1998 to disabled people.

Johns, R (2011) *Using the law in social work.* 5th edition. Exeter: Learning Matters.
Johns's book considers the issues raised by the HRA 1998 in relation to social work practice.

www.doh.gov.uk/publications/index.html
Lists government circulars and letters.

www.bma.org.uk/ap.nsf/Content/HumanRightsAct
The British Medical Association's guide to the HRA 1998 explores some interesting practical implications of the Act.

www.dca.gov.uk/peoples-rights/human-rights/pdf/act-studyguide.pdf
The Department of Constitutional Affairs guide to the HRA 1998 (3rd edition).

www.yourrights.org.uk
Liberty's guide to the HRA 1998.

Chapter 3

Making choices: The Mental Capacity Act 2005
Andy Mantell and *Alex Clark*

A C H I E V I N G   A   S O C I A L   W O R K   D E G R E E

This chapter will help you meet the following National Occupational Standards.

Key Role 1: Prepare for, and work with, individuals, families, carers, groups and communities to assess their needs and circumstances.

- Inform individuals, families, carers, groups and communities about your own, and your organisation's duties and responsibilities.
- Assess and recommend an appropriate course of action for individuals, families, carers, groups and communities.

Key Role 3: Support individuals to represent their needs, views and circumstances.

- Assess whether you should act as an advocate for the individual, the family, carer, group and community.
- Assist individuals, families, carers, groups and communities to access independent advocacy.
- Advocate for, and with, individuals, families, carers, groups and communities.

Key Role 5: Manage and be accountable, with supervision and support, for your own social work practice within the organisation.

- Carry out duties using accountable professional judgement and knowledge-based social work practice.

Key Role 6: Demonstrate professional competence in social work practice.

- Review and update your own knowledge of legal, policy and procedural frameworks.
- Use professional assertiveness to justify decisions and uphold professional social work practice, values and ethics.

It will also introduce you to the following academic standards set out in the social work subject benchmark statement.

5.1.2 The service delivery context.

5.1.4. Social work theory.

Introduction

This chapter will start with an exploration of how certain individuals and social groups have been perceived within our society as less capable of making choices and decisions. It will be argued that these perceptions have contributed to the social construction of notions of 'vulnerability' and risk, which are key concerns within safeguarding adult policy and practice. The second section of the chapter will consider the Mental Capacity Act 2005 (MCA 2005). The third part of the chapter will explore the implications of the Act in relation to anti-oppressive practice. It will be argued that you, as a professional, need to adopt a critical and reflective approach when applying the MCA 2005. The social context in which the individual lives and the nature of power relations in the professional–client relationship need to be acknowledged and explored.

Capacity, choice and difference

Consent is a significant distinguishing feature between safeguarding adults and safeguarding children. For adults, informed consent is often a pivotal factor in determining whether an action is abusive. Yet the distinction between those of us who are deemed to have or lack capacity is not always clear or absolute. Informed consent is determined in relation to age (adult v. child) and mental faculty in relation to people with learning difficulties and mental health problems.

However, *Gillick v West Norfolk and Wisbech Area Health Authority* (1985) established the principle that a child under 16 can give consent for treatment in their own right provided that they had achieved sufficient understanding and intelligence to enable them to understand what is proposed. Those who are 16 and 17 can consent to treatment, but until the Mental Health Act 2007 parents could overrule a 16- or 17-year-old person's refusal to admission or treatment for a mental disorder (Dimond, 2008). Even now the High Court can act in their best interest to overrule their wishes if they refuse life-sustaining treatment, which is why you have to be over 18 to be able to make an advance decision to refuse treatment (see below).

The level of mental faculty required for capacity is also made more confusing by the law requiring different thresholds for different activities. For example, you require more capacity to make a will than get married, yet marriage annuls previous wills.

It is therefore important to note that while this chapter often refers to capacity, capacity or incapacity are not viewed in global terms but in relation to the specific decision at the time it needs to be taken. So a person may not have the capacity to manage their finances, but they may be able to choose what food they would like.

Pyles (2006) argued that capacity is a socially relative and ambiguous concept. Although legally I have adult status and am judged to be able to make decisions and choices in relation to my life, it could be argued that the actual choices which I can engage in are finite and shaped by circumstances and the influences of others.

ACTIVITY **3.1**

Think about the last time you made an important decision or choice; for example, buying a car or where to go on holiday.
What factors influenced your decision?
How did the decision you made differ from your ideal choice?

COMMENT

You may well have focused on the availability of resources (financial and time) which shaped your decision-making, as well as the actual range of options that were available. If you reflect on the process in a little more depth you might also recognise your knowledge base (what information you had) and previous experience also influenced what you finally decided. You may also have been influenced by the views of other people, such as your partner. In essence your capacity to make a choice was contextually related and to some extent limited. Therefore, while we may theoretically be autonomous individuals able to give objective consent, the reality is that we are enmeshed within social and environmental influences. Our capacity is constrained by subjective and emotional considerations, which result from our culture, and social relationships, as well as our economic freedom. These restricting factors can be particularly influential in abusive situations (see situational capacity below).

The notion of incapacity has been argued to be linked as much to social differences which are culturally constructed, as to being innate (Drake, 1999). Difference is constructed around ideas, assumptions and perceptions of individuals and groups. Goffman's (1964) classic work on stigma argued that individuals who were physically different or whose behaviour was perceived to be different, were categorised as being of less social worth and deviant. Barnes et al. (1999) link these social processes, in the case of disabled people, with the infantilisation of individuals and groups; the idea that they never grow up, inherently lack capability and need to be looked after. The development of medical science led to the socially accepted belief that individuals who were defined as having certain characteristics (physical difference) and behaviours and intellectual traits could be defined as being biologically different (physical impairments, learning difficulties and mental health problems). Allocation to such groupings was constructed as being rooted in biology and the natural rather than the social world (Annandale, 1998). In addition, membership of one of these 'abnormal' groupings demanded that the individual be not only cared for, but also protected and looked after (Marks, 1999). The professional becomes the expert and the patient is relatively powerless and dependent (Drake, 1999). Membership of such a group or category has often been viewed as synonymous with being unable to make suitable and acceptable choices.

RESEARCH SUMMARY

In 1992 Jenny Morris researched into disabled people's experiences of receiving social services. She found that the need for practical assistance with everyday living was frequently linked to the notion that an individual was vulnerable and lacking capacity. Morris argued that Western culture assumes that there is a link between physical and practical dependency and mental capacity. She advocates that we need to stop conflating 'independence' with mental autonomy and capacity. Disabled people should be supported to counter the internalised oppression that flows from this social construction of dependency (Morris, 1992).

In considering the application of the MCA 2005 it is therefore essential to be sensitive to your perceptions of groups within society and to acknowledge their experiences which influence how they act and how they are influenced by others.

The Mental Capacity Act 2005

The MCA 2005, implemented in October 2007, aimed to ensure that the rights of disabled people were safeguarded, that those who are incapacitated are protected and to provide better protection to those who provide care. The MCA 2005 makes it a crime to ill-treat or wilfully neglect someone who lacks capacity.

The Adults with Incapacity (Scotland) Act has been in effect since 2000, but it has taken much longer for the rest of the UK to acquire similar safeguards for incapacitated adults. Until the MCA 2005 the general medical care of incapacitated individuals was governed by common law (i.e. case law), care for mental disorders came under common law or the Mental Health Act 1983 (see the 'Bournewood gap' case study later in this chapter) and the managing of financial affairs came under the Mental Health Act 1983. The MCA 2005 evolved from the consultation document (Green Paper) *Who decides?* (1997), to try to develop a more coherent approach to the management of the needs of those who are incapacitated.

Capacity lies at the heart of the government's strategy for health and social care provision as well as its policy on safeguarding adults. The Green Paper *Independence, well being and choice* and subsequent White Paper *Our health, our care, our say* emphasised the importance of respecting and responding to the individual's views. Previously, the government's *No secrets* (Department of Health, 2000) guidance for managing adult protection was reliant upon community care policy for the implementation of packages of care to support the person (see Chapter 1). *Safeguarding adults* (ADSS, 2005) can be seen to be reasserting the link to the new welfare policy, with the same emphasis on independence, well-being and choice:

> *By its very nature abuse – the misuse of power by one person over another – has a large impact on a person's independence. Neglect can prevent a person who is dependent on others for their basic needs exercising choice and control over the fundamental aspects of their life.*
>
> (ADSS, 2005, p4)

The capacity to consent

The MCA 2005 defines a two-stage test of capacity:

1. *The diagnostic test*   Does the person have an impairment of the mind or brain, or is there some other sort of disturbance affecting the way their mind works?

2. *The functional test*   If so, does that impairment or disturbance mean that the person is unable to make the decision in question at the time it needs to be made?

It is important to note that the impairment does not have to be permanent; it only needs to affect the individual at the pertinent time.

Deciding if a person is unable to make a decision is itself determined by a four-stage test referred to by Bennett (2010) as the UWRC (understand, weigh, retain and communicate) test.

1. Does the person have a general understanding of what decision they need to make and why they need to make it?

2. Does the person have a general understanding of the likely consequences of making or not making the decision?

3. Is the person able to understand, retain, use and weigh up the information relevant to this decision?

4. Can the person communicate their decision?

ACTIVITY **3.2**

Informed consent

It is important to note that consent needs to be 'informed'. What information do you think a person needs in order to make an informed decision about whether to accept a medical intervention?

COMMENT

In providing a person with information to enable them to make a decision it is important that they have all the pertinent facts, but in working with someone with cognitive difficulties it is also important not to overload them with details. This can be a difficult balance to achieve. For example, a doctor may neglect to mention that the side-effect of a medication may be weight gain, but the individual may be very concerned about their body image.

Particularly important points to cover are:

- *What will happen without the intervention?*

- *What is the prognosis, short and long term, with the intervention and what are the likely side-effects?*

- *What are the other options for treatment, their side-effects and likely outcomes?*

Think about the last time you saw a doctor and received treatment. Were all those points covered? The average GP consultation is under ten minutes. This is a process which is reliant on your trust in the expert model and can be seen to be at odds with establishing informed consent.

Guiding principles

Five principles are enshrined within the MCA 2005. Their application can be demonstrated in relation to 'John', a fictitious person based on real experiences.

> ### CASE STUDY
>
> *John is a 25-year-old man who lived in a house share and worked as an estate agent. He suffered an acquired brain injury in a road traffic accident and is now receiving rehabilitation in hospital. He has a right-sided weakness and is unable to walk and has severe cognitive difficulties. He finds it hard to concentrate and he is distressed by noise. His girlfriend has not visited in the eight months he has been in hospital, but his parents visit daily. He can have problems understanding what people say and he now finds it hard to say or write his thoughts.*

Principle 1: Assumption of capacity –

A person must be assumed to have capacity unless it is established that he lacks capacity (MCA, 2005, section 1(2)). This principle enshrines the previous common law concept. In emphasising that people are assumed to have capacity it provides a challenge to the stereotyping of groups within society, such as people with learning difficulties, as lacking capacity. It was not uncommon in the past for patients such as John not to be included in meetings to plan their future care.

In assessing capacity, practitioners have sometimes mistakenly placed the onus on patients like John proving that they have capacity.

Principle 2: Enable people to make decisions –

A person is not to be treated as unable to make a decision unless all practicable steps to help him to do so have been taken without success (MCA, 2005, section 1(3)).

> ### ACTIVITY 3.3
>
> *List what steps you think may be necessary to enable John to make a decision about where he will live in the future.*
>
> ### COMMENT
>
> *Think about John's situation. How would you feel? He has suffered trauma and loss. He may feel very isolated, lonely and abandoned by his girlfriend. While as a social worker you may be charged with planning for his discharge, it is important to be aware that he may not share this priority; he may be fearful of facing his future. He may require help to explore his feelings before he is able to consider where he will be living.*
>
> *It is important to ensure that John is seen somewhere that is quiet and without distracting stimuli such as other activities occurring around him. Is he comfortable? It can be extremely difficult to concentrate if we are in pain. Communicating clearly, in short sentences, pacing your delivery and the amount of information will avoid overwhelming him. Visiting placements and using pictures as a reminder can help to keep different options clear in his mind.*
>
> *He may be assisted in communicating by the use of equipment, such as light writers or an alphabet chart. Seek advice from other multidisciplinary team members such as nurses,*

COMMENT *continued*

speech and language therapists, occupational therapists and psychologists. Having someone present whom he is comfortable with and who is attuned to his speech may help. However, be wary that the person may also influence his views. He may have difficulty recalling what was discussed in the meeting and so would benefit from a record of what occurred. Chapter 8 explores these issues in more detail.

Principle 3: Capacity does not necessarily mean wisdom

A person is not to be treated as unable to make a decision merely because he makes an unwise decision (MCA, 2005, section 1(4)).

ACTIVITY 3.4

What is an unwise decision?
Think about a time you have made an unwise decision. What were your reasons?
How would you feel if you were never allowed to make unwise decisions?

COMMENT

In considering what is wise we need to make a distinction between our own view and other people's. For example, you may think it is unwise to climb a rock face without a rope (or at all), but I may be an experienced rock climber whose joy comes from the freedom and exhilaration this produces.

It can be seen from this example that risk of harm can play a significant factor in our consideration of wise decisions. In John's circumstances the professionals working with him may feel a tension between advocating for his rights to take risks and wanting to protect him. It is also all too easy for our views to become clouded by defensive practice concerned with protecting our own careers. These issues are discussed in more detail in Chapter 11.

Principle 4: Best interests

An act done, or a decision made, under this Act for or on behalf of a person who lacks capacity must be done, or made, in his best interests (MCA, 2005, section1(5)). As Johns (2007, p560) dryly observed: *Those who take over decision-making powers are under an obligation to make wise decisions; service users are not.*

When John first had his accident, he was in a coma and decisions had to be made for him. He was provided with care, nutrition and medication to aid his recovery. However, what if he had stayed in a coma? At what point is it not in his best interest to continue to sustain his life? Jocelyn Hurndall (2007) provided a heart-rending insight into this process. Her son Tom was shot by an Israeli soldier while acting as a human shield in Gaza and was in a coma for nine months before the decision was made to cease further medical intervention.

The code of practice to the Mental Capacity Act 2005 (Department for Constitutional Affairs, 2007, p71) provided the following guidance when deciding what is in someone's best interests:

> *Take into account all relevant circumstances and do not make the decision simply based on the person's age, appearance, condition or behaviour.*
>
> *Make every effort to encourage and enable the person to take part in making a decision.*
>
> *If there is a possibility that the person will regain capacity, can the decision be delayed until then?*
>
> *The person's past and present wishes, beliefs and values should be taken into account and the views of those who are close to them should also be considered.*
>
> *The process used to define a person's best interests should be carefully recorded and reviewed regularly as what is in the person's best interests may change over time as may an individual's decisions and choices.*

While this guidance is helpful, *Ashley* (Pinder, 2007) illustrated the extreme complexity of such decisions.

CASE STUDY

Ashley's treatment

Ashley is a nine-year-old girl with severe encephalopathy who lives with her parents in the USA. Her condition is incurable and she has severe physical and mental impairments. Her parents, in conjunction with a medical board of ethics, decided that it would be in Ashley's best interests to suspend her physical development. Her breasts and womb were removed and she was given hormone treatment to limit her weight to 75lbs. This will avoid her going through puberty, and make it easier for her parents to continue to provide her with care for as long as possible. Some carers and professionals have supported this decision as a pragmatic way of maintaining her quality of life and avoiding her experiencing unnecessary suffering. Disability groups have been outraged and threatened by this action.

ACTIVITY 3.5

Do you think the actions taken were in Ashley's best interests?

COMMENT

Ashley's situation raises points at the micro and macro levels. At the micro level her circumstances highlight the difficulty in distinguishing between her and her parents' best interest. At the macro level the issues are about human rights – a disabled person's right to go through the life course, to physically develop into a woman. Her situation raises concerns about creating a precedent for the treatment of other disabled people. Her circumstances highlight the distinction between different perspectives: the medical model, which focuses on her treatment; and the social model, which explores how society can change so that her care is not problematised.

In the UK it would be expected that any similar decisions would be referred to the courts for a decision (see below).

Principle 5: The least restrictive intervention

Before the act is done, or the decision is made, regard must be had to whether the purpose for which it is needed can be as effectively achieved in a way that is less restrictive of the person's rights or freedom of action.

(MCA, 2005, section 1(6))

If, for example, John became aggressive due to his distress at the noise on the ward it could become necessary to restrain him, but this would be an immediate measure rather than an ongoing solution. It would not be appropriate to lock him in a room or chemically sedate him. It would be more appropriate to move him to a single room away from the noise. This notion of the least restrictive response has been adopted from the Mental Health Act 1983 and can be seen to have resonance with the concept of proportionality in the Human Rights Act 1998 (see Chapter 2). It is a particularly important consideration in any circumstances where a person may be deprived of their liberty (see below).

Making decisions

The MCA 2005 established a range of ways decisions can be made by or on behalf of a person. They are ranked here in order from least to most restrictive. It is important to note that the more directly the authority comes from the individual, the more likely it is to 'trump' other forms of authority, for example, advance decisions take precedence over lasting powers of attorney. Where the individual is acting on a person's behalf, they must always bear in mind the five principles stated above.

Informed consent by the individual

This is the usual way in which an action affecting a person is achieved. Going against a person's wishes can be abusive and risks criminal and/or civil prosecution. There are, however, exceptions – for example, stopping a person committing a crime. Common law also places a duty of care upon us all to intervene where a person is an immediate risk to themselves or others. Primary legislation (see Chapter 1), such as the Mental Health Act 2007, can also override the wishes of the individual.

Advance decisions to refuse treatment

In the past the terms 'advance refusals' and 'advance directives' have been used, but the new phrasing is very precise. This only relates to refusing treatment. It does not relate to other aspects of the person's life and the person can not enforce what treatment they would like, although any such views should be taken into consideration. Advance decisions to refuse treatment have to be in writing and witnessed if referring to life-sustaining treatment, but in other circumstances they can be verbal refusals. Verbal refusals run the risk of their meaning being altered, intentionally or unintentionally, by others.

The MCA 2005 emphasises that the advance decision to refuse treatment must be valid (i.e. the person must be over 18 and have capacity at that time) and applicable to the current circumstances. Applicability raises its own dilemmas: if the wording is too general they may be applied in circumstances that you would not want, but if they are too specific they may never be applied. For example, a person may state that if they are ever in a coma they would not want life-sustaining treatment. Does this mean if they are in a coma for a day, a month, a year?

An advance decision to refuse treatment does not generally apply to people who are liable to subject compulsory admission under the Mental Health Act 2007. The exception is where the advance decision to refuse treatment relates to electro convulsive therapy. However, even in this case it can be overridden in an emergency (Hale, 2010).

Lasting Powers of Attorney (LPA)

LPAs are legal documents which enable someone else to manage your affairs. They are registered with the Office of the Public Guardian which oversees LPAs and supervises deputies (see below). They are similar to the old Enduring Powers of Attorney, but can relate to a person's welfare as well as their property and affairs. They must be registered with the Office of the Public Guardian before they can be used and it is important to note that an LPA in relation to welfare cannot be used until a person has lost capacity, but a property and affairs LPA can be used unless prohibited in the LPA. All these authorities could be invested in one person or you could choose different people to manage your welfare and your finances.

LPAs can be seen as a more flexible approach than advance decisions to refuse treatment, but mark a shift from your expressed words to trusting another person to accurately represent your views.

Acts in connection with the care or treatment of someone who lacks capacity

The MCA 2005 provides the authority to carry out activities related to a person who lacks capacity. These may be related to their personal care, their healthcare or treatment. This authority is quite broad and may include paying for goods or services from their money, although formal authority would be required to access their bank accounts or sell their property.

The Court of Protection and deputies

The Court is the final arbiter of all matters related to a person's capacity, the validity of advance decisions to refuse treatment and LPAs.

The Court can also make declarations or decisions or appoint a deputy on financial and welfare matters. A deputy is similar to a receiver (prior to the MCA 2005) but could, if authorised by the Court, act in relation to health and welfare as well as financial matters. However, relatively few Personal Welfare Deputies have actually been appointed. Existing receivers have now become deputies, but remain limited to considering issues related to finances.

Restraint

Welfare LPAs, those undertaking acts in connection with the care or treatment of a person who lacks capacity and care, and welfare deputies have authority to restrain a person who lacks capacity. However, until the implementation of the Mental Health Act 2007 they were unable to detain the person due to the 'Bournewood gap'.

CASE STUDY

The 'Bournewood gap'
HL, a man with learning difficulties, was informally admitted to a psychiatric hospital in the Bournewood NHS Trust. He lacked the capacity to consent to treatment and so could not be a voluntary patient but he was not compulsorily detained. When his carers wanted to visit him, they were denied access on the basis that he would want to go home with them and would consequently need to be formally admitted. His carers went to court seeking his release and in October 2006 the European Court of Human Rights overturned a House of Lords ruling and decreed that HL's right to liberty (Article 5 of the Human Rights Act 1998) had been breached.

ACTIVITY 3.6

What do you think should have happened in this situation?

COMMENT

A key principle in the Mental Health Act 1983 (and the MCA 2005) was the principle of the least restrictive intervention. By informally admitting HL the Bournewood Trust was avoiding his compulsory detention and the stigmatisation that can accompany formal admission.

However, this meant that his care was governed by common law. His care lacked the safeguards, such as formal appeals and reviews, that were inherent in the Mental Health Act 1983. Significantly, it also highlighted a discrepancy between practice and the Human Rights Act 1998. Only primary legislation or the direction of the High Court (including the Court of Protection) in what is called declaratory relief, could lawfully allow a person's right to liberty to be breached. The MCA 2005 did not allow such practice and detention under the Mental Health Act 1983 was not always appropriate. Common law provides a defence from prosecution for restraining a person at immediate risk to themselves or others but no power to deprive them of their liberty. Significant numbers of people with dementia, for example, have been cared for in this manner. To complicate matters further, what constitutes deprivation of liberty will depend to a large extent on the individual. For example, if a door to a care home has double handles or a key pad, one person may understand that they can ask staff for help to leave, but another may feel trapped. Concerns about this situation led the government to amend the MCA 2005 in the Mental Health Act 2007 to provide deprivation of liberty safeguards for people who are mentally disordered and lack capacity.

The deprivation of liberty safeguard

Schedule A1 of the amendments to the MCA 2005 allows for the detention of an individual for up to 12 months. The managing authority, i.e. the care home or hospital looking after the person, must apply to the supervisory authority, who will assess whether the detention is permitted. In England the supervising authority is the local authority for care homes and the primary care trust for hospitals. In Wales the supervising authority for hospitals is the National Assembly.

Six areas are assessed:

- Age – Is the person 18 or over?

- Mental health – The person must be suffering from a mental disorder as defined under the Mental Health Act 2007.

- Mental capacity – The person must lack the capacity to decide to reside in the accommodation and receive the appropriate treatment.

- Best interests – This will consider three criteria:
  1. The person is or is going to be detained.
  2. This detention is in the person's best interests.
  3. The detention will prevent harm to the person (note that it does not include harm to others).

- Eligibility – The person must not be subject to the Mental Health Act 2007.

- No refusal – No LPA or deputy appointed by the court has refused the decision.

The assessment process encourages multidisciplinary practice, with the expertise of a range of professionals able to be drawn upon within the six assessments. As a minimum the mental health assessment must be conducted by a different person than the best interests assessment. The mental health assessment is conducted by a doctor who is approved under the Mental Health Act 1983 (amended by the Mental Health Act 2007) or who has at least three years' post-qualifying practice in the diagnosis and treatment of mental disorder. The best interests assessment may be carried out by an

approved mental health professional, a registered social worker, occupational thera-
pist, first level nurse or a chartered psychologist.

The person must also have a personal representative or an independent mental capacity advocate (IMCA) and will be entitled to reviews and appeal to the Court of
Protection.

Independent mental capacity advocates (IMCA)

In situations where a person who lacks capacity does not have family or friends to
advocate on their behalf and a decision needs to be made regarding serious medical
treatment, a change of accommodation or deprivation of liberty safeguards, then
local authorities and NHS bodies have a duty to appoint an IMCA. In safeguarding
adults procedures local authorities and NHS bodies have the power to appoint an
IMCA where they consider that this would benefit the individual.

The IMCA will ensure that the requirements of the MCA 2005 have been followed; in
particular, that the person's capacity in relation to the decision has been assessed and
that their views are, if possible, ascertained and taken into account. Where the person
is unable to indicate their feelings then the IMCA acts as a *non-instructional advocate*
(Brown and Barber, 2008, p64). The IMCA is concerned with ensuring that the person's interests and rights remain at the centre of the decision-making process (Lee,
2007).

Mental capacity in practice

The simplistic dichotomy between people being deemed to have or lack capacity fails
to acknowledge the complexity of the decision making process. Even the positive
principle of the assumption of capacity could place people at risk. For example, people
with severe traumatic brain injury often sustain a degree of cognitive impairment
(Todd et al., 2004) which may not be immediately obvious. In such cases it may be
negligent to assume capacity without having undertaken an assessment.

People may be considered to have borderline capacity under the UWRC test, but be
strongly subject to the influences of other people, who may be benevolent or mal-
evolent in their motivations and actions.

The interface between the mental capacity test and the principle of best interests

In practice, we are always striving to act in a person's best interests, whilst respecting
their wishes. Where a person lacks capacity then the Mental Capacity Act 2005
enshrines that, where it becomes necessary, acting in the person's best interest
takes precedence over their views. What is less clear is the role of this principle within
the process of assessing capacity (Scheepers, 2010). Consider a person who meets the
diagnostic requirement of the Act and has borderline capacity on the functional test
of capacity. They may choose to act unwisely, but as we know from the third principle

this does not mean they lack capacity. However, what if we are gaining clear evidence that they are consistently acting to their detriment? Do we reach a point at which this becomes evidence that they lack capacity to manage that issue?

Bennett (2010) argues that in such cases an assessment of the person's best interests may be necessary. The mental capacity test applies to a specific issue at a specific time, but assessing best interests enables us to consider a much broader context in relation to the individual. This can be particularly important where a person is viewed as vulnerable to abuse. However, there is a risk here that in our concern to protect an individual we may view their not agreeing with our perspective as evidence of lack of capacity. In such cases, where best interests become the deciding factor in determining if a person has capacity then the view of the Court of Protection should be sought to ensure that their rights and the other principles of the MCA are not inadvertently breached.

The protection of the vulnerable decision maker is more fully addressed in Scottish legislation by the Adult Support and Protection (Scotland) Act 2007. In the rest of the UK, adults at risk who are viewed to have capacity may fall within the jurisdiction of the Court of Protection as a result of the decision in SA [2006] EWHC 2942 (Fam). The Court of Protection ruled in this case that it was possible for a person who has capacity to suffer situation incapacity (see case study below).

CASE STUDY

Situation Incapacity (SA [2006] EWHC 2942 (Fam))
SA was an 18-year-old woman who lived with her Muslim, Pakistani family, but was a ward of court until she was 18. She was profoundly deaf and communicated by British Sign Language and could lip read English, but her family's first language was Punjabi. She had an intellectual age of 13–14 and a reading age of 7–8. Her parents wanted to take her to Pakistan for an arranged marriage and the local authority applied to the Court of Protection to prevent this happening.

Justice Munby considered that although she was now over 18 she and any other vulnerable adult could come under the jurisdiction of the Court of Protection. Whilst SA had the capacity to decide whether to marry or not, in this situation she was deemed incapable of making this decision. The Court of Protection defined three types of 'situation incapacity', all of which applied in SA's case:

(i) Constraint   curtailment of freedom of activity.
(ii) Coercion or undue influence   particularly based on affection, duty, obligation or social, cultural or religious beliefs.
(iii) Other disabling circumstances   which 'may so reduce a vulnerable adult's understanding and reasoning powers as to prevent him from forming or expressing real and genuine consent, for example, the effects of deception, misinformation, physical disability, illness, weakness (physical, mental or moral), tiredness, shock, fatigue, depression, pain or drugs. No doubt there are others' (see Leslie, 2008, for further discussion).

Whilst this ruling offers protection to a group who are particularly vulnerable to the actions of others, the breadth of the circumstances that could cause situational incapacity are extremely wide. It will be interesting to see how such cases are interpreted in future case law.

Mental capacity and anti-oppressive practice

Thompson's (2006) PCS analysis of anti-oppressive practice and Braye and Preston-Shoot's (1995) model of consultation, participation and partnership (see Chapter 7) allow us to identify strategies for empowering clients to manage the challenges associated with expressing informed consent (also see Chapter 8).

Knowledge and information

It is important that clients who are being empowered to make decisions have the knowledge base to inform their decision-making. To transform information into knowledge it must be formatted in a way that the person understands. Gharichi (1996) uses the term *information deprivation*, which reflects the fact that people or groups are relatively powerless because they lack access to information on which important choices which potentially impact on their lives could be made.

Experience

All of us engage in decision-making with a sense of skill and mastery as we engage with the experience of making decisions; like most things in life, the more we do it the more confident and able we are to do it again. This may include making mistakes, but this is also an important part of how we learn and develop our likes and dislikes. Consequently, as the MCA 2005 states, we must promote and encourage people's participation in all decisions that affect them.

Support and encouragement

People who use services may frequently need a degree of practical and emotional support in relation to decision-making. This may involve the professional helping people who use services to explore choices and the potential consequences of each of them, or simply encouraging individuals to make a decision. You could also remind people of the decisions which they have already successfully engaged in as means of reassuring and developing a sense of confidence. Documentary evidence of decision making is also particularly helpful where a person has memory problems.

Resources

The availability of resources, or lack of them, may well constrain individuals in relation to decision-making and exercising choice. The decision to live independently, for example, may not seem feasible if accommodation and a weekly budget are not available. Therefore the social worker can develop the choices open to an individual by checking whether they are claiming the social security benefits which they are entitled to and exploring possible housing options with local housing associations. Keeping up to date with new developments such as Homeshare, where tenants gain free accommodation in return for providing care, are crucial to developing creative responses within a climate of rationed resources. Individual budgets may provide the flexibility to enable people to live their lives as they would wish. However, groups such as those with mental health problems (MIND/NFRC, 2009) remain underrepresented and budgetary threats to the progress of personalisation (Dunning, 2010) make this currently unlikely to change.

Support networks

Most of us informally consult others (friends, partners and families) when we have an important decision to make. By helping people to build social contacts and networks we allow them to develop support in relation to decision-making. Voluntary organisations, buddy systems and circles of support can provide advocacy, peer advocacy and social support promoting social inclusion (Jay, 2007). See Chapter 7 for further discussion of advocacy.

Family members managing direct payments or individual budgets may form an essential and empowering part of the person's network, but there is also the risk that they may become overly protective, stifling the person's potential for independence.

Engaging with people who use services

Recent policy within social care has argued that the promotion of choice is central to services which are responsive to people's needs, circumstances and wishes. Individual budgets will allow service users to not merely receive services which are responsive to their individual needs, but also to actively participate in the design and delivery of the services they receive. There is also a clear emphasis on the promotion of choice for all service users, with support and encouragement being provided to those whose personal circumstances or cognitive condition make choice a complex or difficult act.

The process of enabling people to exercise choice, as has already been suggested, is complex and takes time. Braye and Preston-Shoot (1995) suggest that relations should be based upon consultation (incorporating users' views and wishes into professional decision-making), participation (where there is some degree of service user involvement), partnership (where there is a sharing of power and thus decision-making) and control (where the service user has a tangible sense of autonomy).

Consultation can be a formative stage in the process of engaging in decision-making. Participation might involve the person being able to choose from a range of options or to decide how and when a decision is implemented. The partnership stage would offer the opportunity for the person to experience a degree of authority and control in relation to decision-making, while also receiving your support.

The MCA 2005 is aiming for a control model of engagement in which people enjoy the normal challenges, benefits and stimulation of making the decisions which shape their lives. Braye and Preston-Shoot's (1995) model, although clearly formulated in terms of distinct stages, could be used with a sense of fluidity and adapted to meet the context of circumstances of the situations; differing levels and demands of decision-making could be based upon different models depending upon the legal requirements and professional judgements by the social worker.

CHAPTER SUMMARY

The capacity to consent and make informed choices is at the heart of determining if an act is abusive and ensuring that our subsequent support and care plans are empowering rather than victimising.

The MCA 2005 goes a long way to counter assumptions of global incapacity based on the social categorisation of people, for example, as having learning difficulties. It, at last, provides a clear framework to ensure that where possible, people's wishes are respected and to protect those who lack capacity in relation to a matter.

However, it is down to you as a practitioner to ensure that the spirit rather than simply the letter of the law is followed. Your practice will enable people to be at the centre of decisions about their future. I recently heard of a person with mental health problems who chaired their own review meeting – now that is empowering practice!

FURTHER READING

In looking at the MCA 2005 it is important to consider it in conjunction with the code of practice which is currently being produced.

For a basic introduction to the Scottish legislation on mental capacity see *Scottish Government (2008). A short guide to the Adults with Mental Incapacity (Scotland) Act 2000.* Available from **www.Scotland.gov.uk**

The following series of training packs provides excellent general and environment specific knowledge, illustrated with case studies.

Department of Health (2007) The MCA 2005: Core Training Set.
www.dh.gov.uk/en/Publicationsandstatistics

Department of Health (2007) The Mental Capacity Act 2005: Community Care and Primary Care Training Set.
www.dh.gov.uk/en/Publicationsandstatistics

Department of Health (2007) The Mental Capacity Act 2005: Acute Hospital Training Set.
www.dh.gov.uk/en/Publicationsandstatistics/

Department of Health (2007) The Mental Capacity Act 2005: Mental Health Training Set.
www.dh.gov.uk/en/Publicationsandstatistics

Department of Health (2007) The Mental Capacity Act 2005: Residential Accommodation Training Set.
www.dh.gov.uk/en/Publicationsandstatistics

The Office of the Public Guardian provides an informative website for those requiring detailed information about the activities of the Court of Protection:
www.publicguardian.gov.uk/

Further information about the role of IMCAs, including a booklet, can be found at:
www.dh.gov.uk/en/Policyandguidance/Healthandsocialcaretopics

For a general reader on the MCA 2005 see:
Brown, R, Barber, P and Martin, D (2009) *The Mental Capacity Act 2005: A guide for practice.* Exeter: Learning Matters.

For a more detailed exploration of mental capacity see:
Dimond, B (2008) *Legal aspects of mental capacity.* Oxford: Blackwell.

Chapter 4

Adult protection: The Scottish legislative framework
Kate Fennell

A C H I E V I N G   A   S O C I A L   W O R K   D E G R E E

The chapter relates to the standards for professional practice detailed in the Scottish Social Services Council Code of Practice for Social Service Workers. These are:

4.1 Recognising that service users have the right to take risks and helping them to identify and manage potential and actual risks to themselves and others.

4.2 Following risk assessment policies and procedures to assess whether the behaviour of service users presents a risk of harm to themselves or others.

4.3 Taking necessary steps to minimise the risks of service users from doing actual or potential harm to themselves or other people.

6.7 Recognising and respecting the roles and expertise of workers from other agencies and working in partnership with them.

Learning Outcomes

This chapter should allow you to:

- understand the relationship between the social work role in adult protection and the relevant legislation in the Scottish context;
- have a knowledge of the Adults with Incapacity (Scotland) Act 2000 and the Adult Support and Protection (Scotland) Act 2007 and the relationship between these two pieces of legislation;
- understand the roles of appropriate agencies and professionals within the framework of adult protection in Scotland.

Introduction

The purpose of this chapter is to describe the legal context in which the protection of adults operates in Scotland. It will outline the duties and powers provided by the Adult Support and Protection (Scotland) Act 2007 which was implemented in October 2008 as well as the protective measures available under the Adults with Incapacity (Scotland) Act 2000.

Background

In the first 10 years of its existence the Scottish Parliament implemented three pieces of progressive legislation which tackle the complex issues involved in the protection of adults. The Adults with Incapacity (Scotland) Act 2000, the Mental Health (Care and

Treatment) (Scotland) Act 2003 and more recently the Adult Support and Protection (Scotland) Act 2007 provide a more modern, inclusive and flexible approach to managing situations of risk. At the heart of this triad of legislation are fundamental principles which recognise people's right to be at the centre of any decision making process, to be heard, to participate and to be empowered. These principles reflect the tenets on which the Human Rights Act 1998 (see Chapter 2) is based and provide an ethical guide for those acting within these laws.

One of the significant factors which produced the impetus for the introduction of the Adult Support and Protection Act was the events that became known as the Scottish Borders Inquiry (see Research summary).

RESEARCH SUMMARY

The Scottish Borders inquiry

The inquiry was jointly conducted by the Social Work Services Inspectorate and the Mental Welfare Commission for Scotland. These are central government agencies with responsibility, respectively, for the oversight of social work services and the care and treatment of people with mental health problems. Their joint report begins:

> In March 2002, a woman was admitted to Borders General Hospital with multiple injuries from physical and sexual assault. A police investigation revealed a catalogue of abuse and assaults over the previous weeks and possibly much longer. Three men were convicted of the assaults later in 2002.

> The woman was considered to have a learning disability. A series of events had led to her being cared for by one of the convicted offenders. Over many years, there were events and statements in records held by social work, health services and the police that raised serious concerns about this person's behaviour towards this woman.

> (Scottish Executive, 2004)

The details of the case were extremely disturbing but even more shocking to many was that numerous concerns had been raised at various points over time without any direct response or action. The report goes on:

> Other individuals were receiving care under the same circumstances. They had varying degrees of learning disabilities, physical disabilities and mental health needs, which were largely neglected, to the point of becoming potentially life-threatening for some.

> Health and social work records contained numerous statements of concern about their care, including allegations of serious abuse and exploitation. These had not been acted upon. From late 2000, the lives of these individuals became increasingly chaotic. They were neglected, lived in unsuitable and unsanitary conditions and were financially and sexually exploited.

The joint inspection report identified 29 failures in the efforts to protect these individuals and made 42 recommendations that would improve the ways in which people could be protected.

Of the 42 recommendations the inquiry made regarding adult protection, one was directed at the Scottish Executive (now known as the Scottish Government). This was to provide comprehensive adult protection legislation as a matter of urgency. The legislation that was developed was the Adult Support and Protection (Scotland) Act 2007.

The Scottish Borders Inquiry identified that there was a lack of clarity within agencies about their roles in relation to adult protection and a lack of understanding of the roles of other agencies. Poor communication and information sharing between organisations were also highlighted as issues.

ACTIVITY **4.1**

Please consider the following case scenarios.

1. *George, 92, has lived on his own since his wife died. His family live a distance away. George employs a housekeeper. She is very domineering and has gradually taken over control of all of George's affairs. She actively discourages contact from his family. He is always anxious to please her and do as she says. Recently, she has arranged for him to rewrite his will and leave all his estate to her when he dies. George believes he couldn't possibly survive without her.*

2. *Heather, 25, lives in a care home for people with learning disabilities. A new worker, John, has started in the unit. He has built up a close relationship with Heather and encourages her to go on outings and spends time with her. At first Heather enjoyed the attention from him, but she has become withdrawn and anxious. She keeps asking staff who is going to be on duty at night. When asked about it she tells another worker that one night last week he came into her bedroom and touched her breasts. Heather was terrified. He warned her not to tell anyone that he was her special friend. If she did, he would lose his job. He promised her that he would bring her a special present the next night that he was on duty.*

Decide which of the two cases causes you the more concern. Consider the choice you have made. What personal and professional values may have influenced your choice? Now try to consider the cases again from the viewpoint of a police officer and then of a nurse.

COMMENT

A variation of this exercise is regularly used on multi-agency adult protection training. It illustrates how different professional outlooks influence our actions. Mostly people agree that Heather's situation is the more concerning. A serious crime has been alleged in an environment where it could happen again or to another service user. George's situation is often of more concern to police officers than other professionals as they tend to have experience of such a scenario leading to a crime.

Both situations require to be investigated on a multi-agency basis to determine the facts of each case. This requires that criminal investigation, assessment of social care and health needs be conducted in a collaborative manner. Without such a framework, the danger is that the adult may not receive a co-ordinated response or one agency may believe they have no role and assume that another agency is dealing with the situation.

ACTIVITY 4.2

Please consider the following statement: It is a fundamental human right not to suffer abuse and all adults require the same level of protection to prevent this abuse.

Does this seem correct to you? Are some people more likely to be abused and neglected than others? If someone were abusing you in some way, what sort of protection or assistance would you want to be given? And by whom?

COMMENT

A condition or a disability may make some adults more vulnerable to being harmed than the rest of the population. However, the presence of a condition does not automatically mean that someone may be harmed. It is the entirety of a person's circumstances which may mean that they are less able to safeguard their welfare.

The principles of adult protection legislation underline the need for people to be treated equitably. A person's disability should not preclude them from seeking and receiving justice.

Procedures and guidance are required for these kinds of situations so that all agencies have a framework for considering and addressing risk and harm. Most importantly agencies need to have protocols for sharing information and concerns about adults and they need to work together to form coherent protection plans.

Multi-agency Adult Protection Guidelines were developed in 2003 by five local authority areas, including Scottish Borders Council, and the National Health Service Trusts and police force that served these areas (Edinburgh, Lothian and Borders Chief Executive Group, 2003). In October 2009, the Guidelines were re-launched as *Adults Support and Protection: Ensuring rights and preventing harm*. The Guidelines had been revised to take account of changes introduced by the Adult Support and Protection (Scotland) Act 2007. The purpose of these guidelines is to provide information and advice for those working to protect adults.

Many local authorities and care agencies in Scotland have their own Adult Protection operational procedures which provide directions for staff in how to meet their legal responsibilities.

Adults who lack capacity

The purpose of this section is to consider the current legal framework of adult protection.

ACTIVITY 4.3

Please consider the following statement: It is a fundamental human right to choose to remain in an abusive situation.

In your personal life have you known someone who was in an abusive relationship and chose to remain in it? Under what circumstances would intervention by an outside agency be appropriate and legitimate in such a situation?

COMMENT

In Scotland, the legislation which relates to adults unable to make decisions regarding their welfare or finances is the Adults with Incapacity (Scotland) Act 2000 (AWI Act).

It is against the law for a person to be in an abusive situation if one of four circumstances applies.

- *Elements of the relationship breach the criminal law, such as if a physical assault or sexual crime occurs.*

- *The relationship poses a risk to the general public.*

- *The relationship is between an adult and individual who must conform to some form of professional code of practice such as a doctor, nurse or professional carer.*

- *The adult does not have the capacity to provide informed consent to the relationship.*

RESEARCH SUMMARY

The Adults with Incapacity (Scotland) Act 2000

The AWI Act provides a hierarchy of measures to allow others to act or make decisions for an adult who lacks the ability to do so for themselves, in relation to their financial affairs, health and personal welfare.

- *Financial (Continuing) and Welfare Powers of Attorney – an arrangement that can be put in place whilst the adult still has capacity. (This is similar to Lasting Powers of Attorney in England – see Chapter 3.) Powers of Attorney have to be registered with the Office of the Public Guardian (for Scotland). There are certain safeguards built into the legislation which allow public bodies to take protective action where the Attorney is not acting in the best interest of the adult.*

- *Access to funds – a simple way of managing day to day funds.*

- *Authority for doctors and other health professionals to carry out examinations and treatment.*

- *Intervention and Guardianship Orders (not to be confused with Guardianship under the English and Welsh mental health legislation).*

An Intervention Order (Financial or Welfare) is appropriate for a once off decision or action and a Guardianship Order gives authority to act and make certain decisions over the long term. Anyone with an interest in the adult can make a Guardianship application, accompanied by medical reports to the Sheriff Court. The sheriff is the equivalent of a judge in England and Wales but the Sheriff Court, unlike the Family Court or indeed the Court of Protection, deals with the vast majority of civil law in Scotland and as such is a generic court.

Where it is necessary and when there is no-one else to do so, the local authority has a duty to apply for a Guardianship Order. The Chief Social Work Officer can be appointed as Welfare Guardian but in respect of Financial Guardianship powers, the local authority will usually nominate a solicitor.

A person may only require Access to Funds for the management of their funds but may need Welfare Guardianship to authorise a major change in care arrangements.

All interventions under the AWI Act and any person acting as a proxy decision maker must act in accordance with the principles of the Act. These are that any intervention must:

- *be of benefit to the adult;*
- *be the least restrictive measure possible;*
- *take into account the adult's past and present wishes;*
- *take into account the views of relevant others;*
- *encourage the adult to maintain their skills.*

The Adult Support and Protection Act (Scotland) 2007 places a duty on councils to make inquiries and conduct investigations to establish whether or not action is required to stop or prevent harm occurring. These actions may include legal measures under the Adults with Incapacity Act 2000 such as Welfare Guardianship.

ACTIVITY **4.4**

Please consider the following case study.

Yasmin is a 17-year-old Pakistani woman who has a learning disability. She attends a day centre and the staff have observed a number of occasions when she has attended in dirty clothes. She is losing weight and her hair is often dirty. Staff have observed that she has head lice and have contacted her doctor with regard to this. They have taken these issues up with her parents but they have been unwilling to discuss them or to come in to review meetings. Yasmin's parents have phoned to say she will not be returning to the centre as the family are going to Pakistan as part of the process of Yasmin taking part in an arranged marriage.

You are Yasmin's social worker. How would you proceed? What kind of assessments would you require and from whom? If you decide to take any actions under the AWI Act, how would you ensure that they were in keeping with the principles of the Act?

> **COMMENT**
>
> *Initially, this situation should be considered within adult protection process and on a multi-agency basis. Yasmin's self-care issues may be the result of deliberate neglect or because her family are finding it difficult to provide the appropriate level of care. They should be offered a carer's assessment. Health services should be involved to establish Yasmin's level of capacity to enter into a marital or sexual relationship and understand the implications of this. An advocacy worker should be provided for Yasmin to ascertain her views independently. The police should be contacted to establish if she or her family are known to them. A case conference may have to be called to decide if an application should be made under the AWI Act for guardianship to ensure that Yasmin gets the services she requires to protect her welfare. It may be that powers will also be sought to limit Yasmin's opportunity to travel. All of these steps have to be conducted in a manner that is ethnically sensitive. This will include the provision of interpreters and obtaining of social care and health services with workers from the same ethnic group if possible, in order to help ensure the co-operation of the family.*

Two things are essential in considering the use of the AWI Act in adult protection. Firstly, the adult's capacity to decide to make decisions about their situation must be established. Secondly, any intervention in the situation must be in accordance with the principles of the AWI Act (2000). Compliance with principles may require actions that seem contradictory. An adult with dementia who has been physically abused by a member of their family may still wish to have contact with them. In such a case a Guardianship Order may be required to enable the adult to live in a manner that prevents the abuse but allows the adult to have supervised visits to the family member.

The task of establishing capacity can be complex (see Chapter 3 for further discussion). Capacity is the ability to understand the information relevant to a decision and the consequences of making that decision. Such decisions can be significantly affected by circumstances and the influence of others.

ACTIVITY 4.5

Please consider the following case study.

Annie is 74 years old. She has moderately severe chronic obstructive pulmonary disease (this causes difficulty breathing and she therefore struggles with tasks that require exertion), aortic valve disease, ischaemic heart disease, atrial fibrillation (heart disease, which similarly gives rise to difficulty in carrying out tasks that require exertion, including problems with mobility), and suffers from anxiety. Annie has been assessed by a psychiatrist and she does not have any form of mental disorder or communication deficit and therefore is seen as having capacity. Her main carer is her son Henry, who lives with her.

Annie has been admitted to accident and emergency on several occasions with bruises to her face and upper body. She has told nursing and medical staff that Henry has been verbally aggressive, and physically assaulted her on a number of occasions in the past. However, she is adamant that she wishes her son to continue to live with her. She will not consider alternative accommodation such as residential care, nor respite. She forbids

ACTIVITY **4.5** *continued*

the staff to call the police or social work services, saying she will not repeat what she has said if they do.

The hospital staff considers it is their duty to contact the social work department and the police. From both agency records it emerges that Henry has a long criminal record, mostly involving aggression and violence. This includes a five-year custodial sentence for stabbing someone.

You are the hospital social worker on this case. How would you proceed? Would you consider a case conference? Who would you want to invite? What would you want to discuss?

COMMENT

From the outset of this case it is likely that you are limited to informal measures of protection, that is, measures that would be acceptable to Annie and perhaps Henry. If Annie will not give evidence to the police it is unlikely that they will be able to proceed, as there will be no corroborative evidence and Henry's actions do not constitute a threat to the public interest. It might be advisable for them both to be interviewed by the police in any event to rule out these possibilities and to establish if this is a case that involves domestic abuse procedures. Annie is known to be capable of making the decision to continue living where she is, despite the risks involved, so action under the AWI Act is not possible. However, given her level of vulnerability and the repeated physical assaults a case conference should be called to pull together a multi-agency risk-management plan for Annie. This would have to involve all the health, social care and police services that may be required to support Annie at home. As part of this a 'lifeline' contact number should be developed for Annie so she can summon assistance and receive support should she wish to change her decision. A carer's assessment should also be completed for Henry. The plan should also address how workers who visit to provide support to Annie and Henry can do so safely and without fear of aggression.

The above situation highlights what has been seen as a major deficit in the legislative framework within which adult protection was conducted. If an adult had capacity, there were no appropriate statutory measures of legal protection that could be sought for non-criminal acts. Suppose that Annie does not believe she can make a different decision. Suppose she is making this decision because Henry has convinced her that her wishes do not mean anything. Under these circumstances is it acceptable that those agencies who wish to protect her have no recourse to legal action?

The Adult Support and Protection (Scotland) Act 2007

The above Act came into force in October 2008 and was designed to address the issues discussed in this chapter. In particular, where the adult has capacity but is disempowered by other people or situations. The new Act:

- provides principles to underpin the work of all agencies and individuals involved in adult protection;

- requires that all local authority areas establish a multi-agency adult protection committee to ensure that adult procedures are in place and regularly reviewed. These committees are similar to Adult Safeguarding Boards in England and Wales;

- introduces national definitions to underpin adult protection;

- gives local authorities duties in relation to adult protection and the opportunity to apply to court for the statutory powers necessary to perform these duties.

- places a duty on specific public bodies to cooperate with investigations into situations of harm.

The Act relates specifically to adults at risk. It defines an adult at risk as someone who is 16 or over:

- who cannot safeguard their own well-being or property; and

- who is affected by disability, mental disorder, illness or infirmity and is more at risk of being harmed than other adults who are not so affected; and

- another person's conduct is causing or is likely to cause the adult harm.

The term *harm* has been used instead of *abuse* as it was noted during the consultation process that abuse is often seen as a one-off dramatic incident. What appears as minor but repeated acts against an adult can, over a period of time, cause considerable harm to an individual.

Wherever it occurs, in an institution or in the community, harm involves a power imbalance and exploitation. It can involve acts of omission and commission and it is not the intent but rather the impact of harm that is crucial.

The principles of the Act are:

- Any intervention in an adult's affairs will provide benefit to the adult.

- Any intervention will be the least restrictive option possible.

- Any intervention will take into account the wishes of the adult, both past and present.

- Any intervention will take into account the views of people who are important to the adult.

- Any intervention will involve the adult's participation as much as possible.

- Any intervention will not result in the adult being treated less favourably than someone who is not an adult at risk.

- Any intervention will take into account the adult's abilities, background and characteristics (including the adult's age, sex, sexual orientation, religious persuasion, racial origin, ethnic group and cultural and linguistic heritage).

Under the Act the local authority has powers to:

- investigate suspected harm;

- carry out assessments of the adult and their circumstances;

- examine health, financial and other records to determine if an adult is at risk of harm.

The local authority may also apply to the court for an order to protect the adult at risk. These include:

- an Assessment Order to take the adult to a specified place for a period of not more than seven days to establish if they are an adult at risk of harm;

- a Removal Order to take the adult to a specified place to prevent the adult from being seriously harmed;

- a Banning Order to prevent a specified person from having contact with the adult to prevent harm. Conditions can include a banning order which may, for example, allow access to family members on a supervised basis. This will respect people's rights to have a family life.

The court can grant a protection order only if the adult at risk agrees, unless:

- the court believes the adult at risk has been unduly pressurised to refuse consent; and

- that there are no steps which could reasonably be taken with the adult's consent which would protect the adult from the harm which the order or action is intended to prevent.

The court may believe the adult at risk has been unduly pressurised if:

- the harm which the order is intended to prevent is being, or is likely to be, inflicted by a person in whom the adult at risk has confidence and trust;

- the adult at risk would consent if the adult did not have confidence and trust in that person;

- 'undue pressure' can also be applied by those whom the adult fears.

The legislation means that statutory measures of protection can be applied for in relation to people who are capable but seen as being subjected to 'undue pressure'. This has significant implications for increasing the numbers of adults who require protection from abuse and harm.

ACTIVITY **4.6**

Please go back and re-read the case study in relation to Annie (Activity 4.5). Reconsider the questions within the framework of the Adult Support and Protection (Scotland) Act 2007. If you decided to apply for an order, which order would it be? What evidence

ACTIVITY **4.6** *continued*

would you provide to show that Annie was an adult at risk? If she did not agree with the order, what evidence would you provide to argue she was under 'undue pressure' not to cooperate?

COMMENT

There is ample evidence that Annie is affected by her disability and infirmity. Medical evidence could be given to show she would not be in a position to defend herself from attack. Equally it could be shown she is suffering harm, by detailing the various wounds she has received at home.

A number of orders could be applied for. It might be least restrictive to apply for an order that bans Henry from the house unless someone else is there. Consideration would need to be given as to how that could be enforced, especially if Annie is not in agreement with such an order. An application could be made for Annie to be removed to a setting where she was safe and could receive the support she required, while still having the chance to see Henry.

Providing evidence that Annie is subject to undue influence and pressure is likely to be the biggest challenge. If evidence existed of his having exerted such influence in front of health or care staff, this might be admissible, as could evidence of Henry's having attempted to isolate Annie from others.

The Adult Support and Protection Act 2007 in practice

The number of protection orders granted in the first two years of the Act has been quite low. This is in spite of the fear in some quarters that the Act would be overly intrusive with protection orders used to compel people to do what public agencies regarded was in their best interest. However, the Act was designed in such a way that there are sufficient checks to protect the human rights of the adult. In keeping with the spirit of the Act, protection orders will only be used as a last resort with alternative measures of support and protection considered in the first instance.

Only a handful of removal orders and assessment orders have been granted. However, banning orders have been successfully used to prohibit alleged harmers from specified places. These places have imaginatively included bus routes and community resources such as medical centres and shops.

Now consider how banning orders could be used in the following scenarios:

A man with learning disability lives independently in the community with the support of a housing worker and day centre placement. He is being targeted by misguided youths who he believes are his friends because they have told him so. He is unhappy, however, when they begin using his flat as a drug den, taking his money and his food. He is disempowered and unable to ask them to leave.

The son and daughter-in-law of an 80-year-old man are financially, emotionally and physically harming him. Whenever he tries to resist their demands for money, the son physically assaults him which, on more than one occasion, results in a hospital admission. The man has medical and nursing needs and would benefit from a nursing home placement. He has told the hospital social worker that he would be relieved to move into a care home but that he knows that his son will remove him from there to save money.

The Act hasn't altered the way that social work or health practitioners deliver services nor has it changed what is professional good practice. It does, however, provide a statutory structure in which situations of harm can be investigated on a multi-agency basis and it provides additional legislative tools to protect adults.

CHAPTER SUMMARY

Within Scotland, there are a range of legal and civil tools to safeguard adults. The duty of public agencies to cooperate is now enshrined in law and local protocols and procedures have been developed to enhance inter-agency communication and collaboration.

- The Adults with Incapacity (Scotland) Act 2000 provides measures of protection for those adults who are at risk of abuse and neglect because they are incapable of making the decision to remove themselves from this situation because of a mental disorder or inability to communicate.
- It does this by allowing for others to become their proxy decision maker or guardian including the Chief Social Work Officer.
- The Adult Support and Protection (Scotland) Act 2007 has the potential to provide, alongside other civil and criminal laws, measures to protect adults who are temporarily incapacitated by someone or circumstances.
- Agencies should interpret their duties under the law according to the principles of these Acts, not least that any action should be the least restrictive and be seen to provide benefit to the adult.
- Social work practitioners will continue to play a crucial role in responding to the challenges of balancing risk and rights, protection and self-determination with ethically sound practice that emphasises the inclusion, empowerment and the dignity of the individual.

FURTHER READING

Baillie, D, Cameron, K, Cull, L, and West, J (2003) *Social work and the law in Scotland.* Basingstoke: Palgrave Macmillan.
An excellent guide to how various aspects of the law in Scotland relate to social work principles and practice.

Calder, B (2010) *A guide to Adult Support and Protection (Scotland) Act 2007.* Dundee University Press.
Bert Calder's accessible guide is written primarily for social workers by a social worker.

Patrick, H and Smith, N (2009) *Adult protection and the law in Scotland.* London: Bloomsbury Professional.
Hilary Patrick and Nicola Smith make sense of the legislative framework for adult protection in Scotland. The issues are teased out for the reader in a very clear and helpful manner.

Patrick, H (2007) *Mental health, incapacity and the law in Scotland.* Haywards Heath: Tottel Publishing.
The most comprehensive text on all legislation in Scotland relating to mental disorder and incapacity.

PART 2
EMPOWERING PRACTICE

Chapter 5

Learning from safeguarding children
Sam Baeza

A C H I E V I N G   A   S O C I A L   W O R K   D E G R E E

This chapter will help you meet the following National Occupational Standards.

Key Role 2: Plan, carry out, review and evaluate social work practice with individuals, families, carers, groups, communities and other professionals.

- Unit 9: Address behaviour which presents a risk to individuals, families, carers, groups and communities.

Key Role 4: Manage risk to individuals, families, carers, groups, communities and colleagues.

- Unit 12: Assess and manage risks to individuals, families, carers, groups and communities.

It will also introduce you to the following academic standards set out in the social work subject benchmark statement.

5.1.2 The service delivery context.

Introduction

This chapter will look at the way that social policy and practice with respect to safeguarding children have evolved and moved forward, and to see what lessons this has for the safeguarding of adults (see Penhale, 1993). The first part focuses on those issues learnt through the tragic death of children at the hands of their carers. This is because the pathway of child protection has been one where government changes in legislation and practice have always tended to follow on from a series of well-publicised specific instances of abuse which have resulted in pressure to reform. The main question to be addressed here is whether the safeguarding of adults will need to follow the same tortuous path of abuse, pressure, enquiry and legislation or whether proactive reform can be instigated without this. And indeed, given the present-day continued recurrence of high-profile child abuse cases, whether in fact legislative change is the right way forward in achieving change in the adult sector.

Issues of abuse can lead to very emotive reactions and some of the effects of these on policy and practice are looked at in the first part of the chapter. This is just one area among many where information gleaned from child abuse policy and practice can usefully be applied to safeguarding adults. Collins (2007), for example, notes that although studies of such things as resilience and emotion have mainly been client-focused on children and young people, some of their findings can equally be applied across the board to adults who similarly experience what he has called 'negative events':

> Clearly, social workers have to deal with many negative emotions when they encounter strong feelings of depression and/or aggression experienced by users coping with traumatic events, experiencing poverty, discrimination and living in areas of obvious deprivation, which lack appropriate resources. (p4)

In following through the processes within child abuse policy and practice those already established mechanisms of child protection will be highlighted as likely to be especially appropriate for adult practice. These include such innovations as child protection conferences, joint police and social worker investigations of suspected abuse, classification of abuse and the importance of including families and carers and family members at all stages of any protective process.

The emotive response to abuse

Before moving on to the examination of the evolution of policy and practice, it is important to address the reaction that knowledge of any form of abuse can bring about as this often has serious effects on outcomes. As with child abuse, the safeguarding of adults needs to be considered in the context of the situations in which they occur. Both lead to strong emotive feelings in the general public and in those dealing with the situation. This is even more the case when the abused is a child. In the field of child protection, for example, Collins (2007) has explored the deleterious effect on the victim of the apprehensive attitudes of those working on cases involving physical abuse. As is stressed in Chapter 6, the subject of violence has always been an extremely emotive one and none more so than when that violence occurs within a family setting as in domestic violence. After all, families are generally portrayed by society as a place where its members receive support and are safeguarded from harm, yet in reality they can also be very abusive environments.

CASE STUDY

Child abuse
Workers in child protection teams know only too well that children can be harmed and sometimes even killed by their own carers. This short excerpt from a child death inquiry brings the point graphically home:

> *He had lain in urine soaked bedding and clothes for a considerable number of days. Photographs taken after his death show burns over most of his body, derived from urine stain, plus septicaemia, with septic lesions at the end of his fingers and toes. In addition, he was suffering from severe pneumonia. It is impossible to imagine the level of suffering that this little boy experienced before his death slowly occurred. (The Bridge Child Care Consultancy, 1995, p7)*

ACTIVITY **5.1**

Having read this:

- *How does it make you feel?*
- *Who do you blame for his death?*
- *How might this affect a worker dealing with this case?*

COMMENT

Reading about abuse to children such as that suffered by the boy in this case evokes strong feelings. It is reasonable to feel sad, angry, disgusted, etc., when dealing with child abuse and it is sometimes easy to give in to the temptation to apportion blame. For this reason, when working with any form of abuse, it is important to keep an even mind and not rush to judgement. In other words, it is extremely important to be reflective (Knott and Scragg, 2007). Investigating abuse can bring up traumatic memories from our own past and likewise for other workers. The importance of good supervision cannot be overemphasised. At least one public inquiry has highlighted the importance of supervision and advised that team managers should not key work cases as this can compromise oversight of cases (London Borough of Greenwich, 1987).

CASE STUDY

Adult abuse
Abuse to adults is no less disturbing, as this short case study demonstrates.

When Gladys, a 69-year-old woman with the beginnings of senile dementia, was found by her son Paul, she was in a state of total panic and confusion. Peter, her husband and carer, was not in the house. After Paul calmed her down, he found a number of bottles of pills with prescribed drugs which Peter had given her in an effort to subdue her. Peter later said that he would over-medicate Gladys in order to go out.

ACTIVITY **5.2**

Having read this:

- *What discussion are you going to have with Peter and Paul?*
- *What support are you going to try to offer them?*
- *How are you going to deal with the emotions evoked by those involved in this case?*
  1. *Gladys*
  2. *Peter*
  3. *Paul*
  4. *Your own.*

83

Much like the previous case of child abuse above, this kind of work evokes strong feelings in people, including the workers involved. It would be important not to lose sight of Gladys, who is the victim in this case, and also to involve her husband and son who will need help if they are to continue to appropriately care for her.

Features and categories of child abuse

The categories of abuse for adults (see Chapter 1) mirror those for children, although financial abuse is more common in adult abuse. Experience of investigating child abuse has identified the following features to be aware of.

The characteristics of physical abuse of children are now well known. The manifestations include bruising, cigarette burns, fractures, intra-cranial haemorrhage and intra-abdominal injuries. Typically the child presents hours or days later than might reasonably be expected, given the nature of the injuries, and the history is incompatible with the findings. In some cases, the child has previously been well cared for and the abuse may represent a sudden loss of control by an exhausted, stressed parent. In others, there is evidence of long-standing abuse, with injuries of varying ages and, in many cases, signs of undernutrition, poor hygiene, emotional abuse and neglect.

Domestic violence between adult partners is often associated with child abuse (see Chapter 6). Sexual abuse may accompany physical abuse but often the features are more subtle. Although the public image of the perpetrator is focused on the 'stranger in the park', in reality the majority of those who sexually abuse children are considered to be respectable adults who are members of, or known to, the family. The abuse often develops over a long period of time, starting with inappropriate touching or other actions and only coming to others' attention much later as the child gets older and more willing to disclose what has happened.

More recently, professionals have had to respond to sexual abuse on the internet and the new technologies. This is a growing area of concern, which is emerging at a rapid pace (see Davidson and Gottschalk, 2011).

Emotional abuse always forms an aspect of all abuse, but can sometimes be found on its own. Unlike physical and sexual abuse, emotional abuse is more difficult to define. However, O'Hagan (1993) offers a useful starting point by pointing out that:

> *Emotional abuse is the **sustained, repetitive**, inappropriate emotional response to the child's expression of **emotion** and its accompanying expressive behaviours. (p28)*

A fourth category of abuse, which is also difficult to both define and place within a recognisable framework, is neglect. The current definition used by social workers is contained in *Working together to safeguard children: A guide to interagency working to safeguard and promote the welfare of children* (DfES, 2006, p38):

The persistent failure to meet a child's basic physical and/or psychological needs is likely to result in the serious impairment of the child's health or development. Neglect may occur during pregnancy as a result of maternal substance abuse. Once a child is born, neglect may involve a parent or carer failing to:

- *Provide adequate food, clothing and shelter (including exclusion from home and abandonment)*

- *Protect a child from physical and emotional harm or danger*

- *Ensure access to appropriate medical care or treatment*

It may also include neglect of, or unresponsiveness to, a child's basic emotional needs.

ACTIVITY 5.3

- *Do you think the above categorising of abuse is helpful to practitioners working with adults?*

- *If so, in what way(s) does it help them?*

- *Are the features of adult abuse different to those of children?*

COMMENT

The categorisation of child abuse has changed over the years and categories have been added and also removed as practice has moved on, but the use of common agreed definitions can assist in mapping unmet need or sudden changes and can help focus resources.

The evolution of child protection

Safeguarding children has been a dominant feature of social work practice for far longer than safeguarding adults, with developments in policy and practice arising largely as a result of tragedies and subsequent inquiries (DoH,1995).

Children have not always been seen as people who should be kept safe from harm. One only needs to look back at Victorian times to see that children were both an important economic asset and a drain on family resources. Children were seen as the property of their parents and in terms of discipline, as long as the child was not excessively punished, pretty much anything went.

Family life was not seen as the providence of the state, which kept silent on the issue of child abuse (Ferguson, 2004). Child abuse and neglect were seen as a problem of the 'lower classes' and although through time some child-focused legislation had been enacted (The Children Act 1948 and the Children and Young Persons Act 1963), it did not receive much attention until its rediscovery in 1962 by a group of

American paediatricians headed by Henry Kempe. It was they who coined the term 'the battered child syndrome' (Kempe et al., 1962) to describe abuse perpetrated on children by their parents. What is particularly significant is the fact that child abuse was seen almost as a disease which could be treated.

The definition of child abuse has changed as time has gone on and indeed the term 'child abuse' was replaced by 'child protection' and now has been superseded by 'safeguarding'. How we see the harming of children is dictated by how we as a society construct childhood and all that it entails (Daniel and Ivatts,1998; Parton, 2006). In effect the construction of childhood has meant that what is now seen as abusive may not have been seen as abusive in the past, and these changes have affected our practice. This construction also applies to adults and it is important for practitioners working in the field of adult safeguarding to be aware that practice has to keep pace with changes of view or definition. The view of ageing changes in time both in positive ways and in less positive ways and with it come changes in how the response to adult abuse is managed (see Johnson, 2005, for an authoritative and wide-ranging discussion of ageing).

Legislation changes

Although the first Act of Parliament for what was then termed 'child cruelty' was passed in 1889, it wasn't until after the Second World War that a real attempt to deal with physical abuse was made with the passing of the 1948 Children Act, which established a children's committee and a children's officer in each local authority. This change in the law was prompted, like many others since, by the tragic death of a child, in this case 13-year-old Dennis O'Neil, who was killed by his foster parents (Home Office, 1945). The physical abuse of children again gained national notoriety when in 1973, Maria Colwell (see below) was killed by her step-father. The death of Maria greatly influenced the drafting of the 1975 Children Act, which emphasised the needs of children as distinct from the rights of parents.

RESEARCH SUMMARY

In 1973 Maria Colwell was murdered by her step-father while under the supervision of the local authority. Maria had been previously removed from the care of her mother at the age of two as a result of concerns about her mother's parenting ability. While boarded out, she had been happily looked after by her aunt. The general view within social work and society in general at the time was that children should be looked after by their parents if at all possible and so the local authority supported Maria's mother's plans to resume her care. Maria died 13 months later, grossly undernourished and severely beaten by her step-father. The inquiry into her death which followed found that there had been a catalogue of errors and omissions (principally a lack of communication) by the professionals entrusted with her care.

What has clearly emerged, at least to us, is a failure of the system compounded by several factors of which the greatest and most obvious must be that of the lack of, or ineffectiveness of, communication and liaison. A system should so far as possible be able to absorb individual errors and yet function adequately.

(Department of Health and Social Security, 1974, para 240)

And more specifically:

Many of the mistakes made by individuals were either the result of, or contributed to, by inefficient systems operating in several different fields, notably training, administration, planning, liaison and supervision. (para 241)

The government of the time used the publication of the Maria Colwell Inquiry report in 1974 to issue a series of letters and circulars which laid the foundations of the system, which existed albeit with some minor changes until the introduction of the Children Act 1989. These included the establishment of area review committees (ARC), the institutionalisation of the case conference system and the establishment of child protection registers. The ARC, which later became Area Child Protection Committees, have since been overtaken by safeguarding children boards and children subject to child protection plans respectively.

The 1975 Children Act was very much influenced by the death of Maria but also by the death of another child, Susan Auckland, who was killed by her father, who had previously been convicted of the manslaughter of another of his children. The Act made two major changes.

1. It incorporated among the grounds for care proceedings the fact that a child was or might be living in the same household as a person who had committed offences under schedule 1 of the 1933 Children and Young Persons Act.

2. It required the appointments of guardians *ad litem* to act exclusively on behalf of the child. The guardian *ad litem* is charged to represent the best interests of the child which can differ from the position of the local authority as well as the interest of the parent or guardian.

Changes in child protection procedures continued apace, with the Department of Health continuing to issue advice and circulars after each of a number of child death inquiries (from 1973 to 1981 there were 26 such inquiries). The speed of changes slowed somewhat in the early 1980s with only three inquiries to 1984.

What all of these earlier inquiries noted was poor practice by the professionals and a lack of communication on their part. The year 1985 saw the publication of the Jasmine Beckford Inquiry Report (London Borough of Brent, 1985). Jasmine, aged 4, died in July 1984. She had been horrifically abused to death by her step-father, Morris Beckford, while still under the care of the local authority. The inquiry into her death highlighted what they saw as an unwillingness on the part of social workers to act in the interests of the child, by placing too much emphasis on trying to rehabilitate Jasmine back with her parents (just as the inquiry 20 years earlier had found in the case of Maria Colwell). The inquiry was extremely forceful in its call to social workers to use all their powers in order to protect children.

As a result of this inquiry the Child Review Committees were reframed and renamed as Area Child Protection Committees (ACPC), and child abuse registers were renamed Child Protection Registers. This in effect refocused local authorities to act whenever risk to children was identified. The result of these changes was that *the focus of attention was to be shifted to the protection of children first and to consideration of the needs and rights of parents second* (Corby, 2006, p44).

This inquiry was followed by a further two high-profile public inquiries after the death of Tyra Henry (London Borough of Lambeth, 1987) and Kimberley Carlisle (London Borough of Greenwich,1987). Both inquiries again found poor social work practice and a serious lack of communication between professionals. The inquiries called for changes in the training of social workers to include more input on the law and called on workers to intrude heavily into the life of families if this meant better protection for children.

All of this was set to change, when in 1987 the 'Cleveland affair' broke (Butler-Sloss, 1987).

RESEARCH SUMMARY

Allegations of child sexual abuse were being made by a paediatrician at a Middlesborough hospital. Using a novel technique known as reflex anal dilation, in 1987 she diagnosed 121 children as victims of sexual abuse. Once the diagnoses had been made, social workers who up to that point had been urged to act decisively removed the children from their families and placed them into care. This resulted in children being kept in hospital wards as there were insufficient places in either foster care or residential care to cope with the sudden influx of children. The children were kept away from their parents while forensic interviews took place so that their evidence was not influenced by their carers.

Initially public opinion favoured the doctor and the social workers but, as the number of cases increased, parents decided to hold a protest march from the hospital to the offices of the local newspaper, where they planned to tell their versions of events. The public slowly turned to support the parents and a public inquiry was held led by Dame Elizabeth Butler-Sloss. Cases involving 96 of the 121 children alleged to be victims of sexual abuse were dismissed by the courts.

The report of the inquiry levelled criticism at all the practitioners involved for not working together. Interestingly and in complete contrast to advice given to social workers in cases of physical abuse, practitioners were accused of acting in an overzealous manner. The report also said that greater rights should be given to parents so that they could be kept informed of decisions being taken by social workers. The Jasmine Beckford Inquiry only three years earlier had made a strong recommendation that parents should not be involved in case conferences. The Cleveland Inquiry, on the other hand, made an equally strong recommendation that parents should be involved and should be invited to all or part of the case conferences.

The inquiry had a wide-ranging effect on social work practice. At the time of the events the government was drafting what was to become the 1989 Children Act. As a result of the events in Cleveland the Act was hastily amended to include more rights for parents and children. The result of Cleveland was to emphasise parental participation, the use of voluntary approaches and the curbing of professional power.

The Children Act 1989 consolidated all previous children's legislation. The 1989 Act was greatly influenced by the notorious events in Cleveland, when the alleged sexual abuse of children took centre stage. This Act gave every child the right to protection from abuse and exploitation and the right to have inquiries made to safeguard their welfare. Its central tenet was that children are usually best looked after within their family. The Act came into force in England and Wales in 1991 and – with some differences – in Northern Ireland in 1996.

Although the Children Act 1989 is still very much in force today, policy in relation to children has been greatly influenced by the death in 2001 of Victoria Climbié and the subsequent inquiry into her death (Laming, 2003).

RESEARCH SUMMARY

Victoria was starved and tortured to death by her great aunt, Marie Therese Kouao, and her partner, Carl Manning, despite being known to four London boroughs, two hospitals, two police child protection teams and the National Society for the Prevention of Cruelty to Children. The inquiry uncovered that child protection staff missed at least 12 chances to save Victoria. It also exposed a complete breakdown in the multi-agency child protection system established in the wake of the murder of seven-year-old Maria Colwell in 1973. Health, police, housing charities and social services failed to work together effectively to protect the girl. Lord Laming's final report, published in January 2003, concluded that the child protection system failed as a result of a lamentable lack of 'basic good practice' by frontline staff and, most significantly, senior managers failing to take responsibility for the failings of their organisations.

The fallout from the inquiry is still being felt today. Local authorities have reorganised their education and children services into one department and specific responsibility for safeguarding children work is to be undertaken by the newly created Safeguarding Boards.

ACTIVITY **5.4**

Practice review

- *Why do you think that there was a different response to the inquiries in the cases of Maria Colwell and Jasmine Beckford to that of the cases in Cleveland?*

- *How does the poor practice identified by these inquiries resemble that described in the Scottish Borders Inquiry which was discussed in Chapter 4?*

> **COMMENT**
>
> *Sexual abuse was still seen as something which did not happen and certainly something that did not happen within families. Some of the children removed in Cleveland came from middle-class families which had greater power than the disadvantaged and marginalised families in the cases of Maria Colwell and Jasmine Beckford.*
>
> *The death of Victoria Climbié has again shifted the balance of power to create a situation where social workers are worried about the consequences of getting it wrong and are therefore more willing to take statutory action.*

In September 2003, the government published the *Every child matters* Green Paper alongside its formal response to the Victoria Climbié Inquiry Report (DfES, 2003). The Green Paper proposed changes in policy and legislation in England to maximise opportunities and minimise risks for all children and young people, focusing services more effectively around the needs of children, young people and families. Most recently, the government introduced the Children Act 2004, the overall aim of which is:

> to encourage integrated planning, commissioning and delivery of services as well as improve multi-disciplinary working, remove duplication, increase accountability and improve the coordination of individual and joint inspections in local authorities. The legislation is enabling rather than prescriptive and provides local authorities with a considerable amount of flexibility in the way they implement its provisions. (www.dfes.go.uk/ publications/childrenactreport)

ACTIVITY 5.5

The Children Act 2004 places a duty on children's services to ensure that every child, whatever their background or circumstances, has the support they need to:

- be healthy;
- stay safe;
- enjoy and achieve through learning;
- make a positive contribution to society;
- achieve economic well-being.

Should the government insist that the five points above apply to the adult population? How do you think the points above could be included in a charter to safeguard adult at risk?

COMMENT

Legislative changes have not followed a smooth transition. This is important in terms of safeguarding adults as one would hope that service providers would learn from the mistakes and advances of safeguarding children. A great number of the legislative changes have come about after the tragic deaths of children.

Safeguarding adults and children: Similarities and differences

Fundamentally, adults are presumed to have the mental capacity to make choices, and the right to make their own decisions. Consequently there are limited powers to intervene as adults are deemed able to draw upon civil and criminal law to protect their rights.

Children, on the other hand, are usually presumed to lack capacity and so need protection. Adults who are considered to lack capacity have greater protection, for example, the Mental Capacity Act 2005, but not to the degree that is afforded to children (see Chapters 3 and 6). There remain clear links to past child abuse and re-victimisation as adults. Messman-Moore and Long (2000) identified a clear overlap between individuals abused as children, mental illness symptoms and a greater propensity to being reabused as adults. Safeguarding adults is set within a wider framework of care management and needs assessment, fair access to care eligibility. Currently there is no emergency protective legislation for adults equivalent to emergency protection orders (EPOs) in the Children Act 1989. Inter-agency co-operation and communication both between and within professions is just as crucial in adults as it is in child protection work. However, the need for ongoing specialist work and support to continue after an investigation can often be neglected in both child and adult protection work.

How current practice has developed

Practice and legislative changes in child protection can be summarised using Figure 5.1.

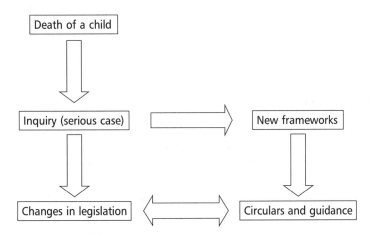

Figure 5.1 Changes in child protection

How can these changes and history help when safeguarding adults?

The recommendations of a number of inquiries highlight a number of themes which seem to be repeated each time, such as the lack of communication between professionals and the lack of co-ordination between agencies. Some of these issues also seem to be present in inquiries regarding vulnerable adults (Norfolk, 2004)

The inquiries into the deaths of children have also brought with them changes in procedure, which have been adapted for work with the safeguarding of adults. An example of these is child protection conferences.

Child protection conferences are multi-agency meetings used to discuss any harm suffered or likely to be suffered by a child. At such meetings, which are attended by representatives of all agencies involved with the child as well as parents, decisions are made as to how best to protect the child from harm. The resulting care planning makes agencies focus on specific areas of concern, and it leaves carers in no doubt as to what those concerns are.

Many local authorities are taking on board the experience of child protection, often gained at the cost of tragic deaths of children, and putting in place for safeguarding adults procedures similar to those found in childcare. There is no reason to suspect that protection structures such as safeguarding boards and tools such as protection conferences will not help in the protection of adult at risk, and the introduction of guidance such as that proposed by the *No secrets* (DoH, 2000) paper and *Safeguarding adults* (ADSS, 2005) are to be welcomed (see Chapter 1).

The Children Act 1975 also introduced the concept of a children's guardian *ad litem*. This allowed for an independent person to focus on the child. It will be interesting to see the extent to which independent mental capacity advocates (IMCA) are able to fulfil a similar role for adults (see Chapter 3). What is important is not to get caught up in the prevention of risk at the expense of providing support. This was graphically shown by a number of studies after the 1989 Children Act had been in force for some time (DoH, 1995).

The court process

What has always been problematic in safeguarding children and is also problematic in safeguarding adults is how to empower children or adults who have been abused (Smith and Tilney, 2007). This is most vividly present when children have to give evidence in court. Generally, the adversarial system requires witnesses to give their evidence in open court. However, some witnesses may be anxious at the prospect of confronting the defendant and others may be intimidated by the court atmosphere. Many of the measures that have been introduced to make court appearances less terrifying for children could be adopted for adult at risk, including:

- removal of wigs and gowns;

- presence of a support person;

- use of screens so that the witness cannot see the defendant;

- video links and videotaped evidence.

However, although all these measures help in making the process of giving evidence a less daunting experience, these come into play only once the case has gone into court. The process before court can be just as difficult, if not more so, in that professionals have to strike the right balance between gathering and preserving evidence and not traumatising the person further. One of the problems with gathering evidence is the importance of not 'tainting' the evidence by repeated questioning. This issue of repeated questioning has been used in court by defending solicitors to render children's evidence as inadmissible by arguing that children have been coached if they have received therapy. This means that professionals have to weigh the value of obtaining a conviction against the inability to offer much-needed therapeutic help to children before the case comes to trial. This is a serious consideration given that this wait can last for months.

CHAPTER SUMMARY

This chapter has provided a brief history of the many legislative changes which have accompanied advances in the safeguarding of children. Tragically many of these advances have come about as a result of high-profile public inquiries into the deaths of children, usually at the hands of their carers. There are a number of lessons which can be used in the growing field of adult safeguarding. Chief among them is the need to listen to and involve families in a process which places the victim of abuse at the centre of our thinking. In short, this chapter argues that adult safeguarding needs to learn from the mistakes made in child protection and not just repeat them.

FURTHER READING

Two good texts of current thinking around child protection are:

Corby, B (2006) *Child abuse: Towards a knowledge base.* Maidenhead: Open University Press/ McGraw-Hill.

Ferguson, H (2004) *Protecting children in time: Child abuse, child protection and the consequences of modernity.* Basingstoke: Palgrave Macmillan.

WEBSITES

It is always useful, although sometimes harrowing, to go back to the actual reports of the inquiries of the children involved such as the ones I have referred to above.

A useful website with up-to-date changes is the DfES website, which has details of the *Quality protects* and *Every child matters* projects.
www.dfes.gov.uk

Chapter 6

Domestic violence: Understanding the connections
Gill Butler

Introduction

This chapter highlights the importance of recognising areas of overlap between domestic violence and the abuse of vulnerable adults. It will begin by briefly summarising current understandings of the nature and extent of domestic violence in England. The prevalence figures that will be discussed below indicate that domestic violence is most commonly perpetrated by men, hence this will be reflected in the terminology used in this chapter. However, the importance of an open approach that recognises that women also abuse and that violence may take place in same-sex relationships always needs to be held in mind.

The work of McDonald (2005) will be used to provide a framework for analysing our understanding of and responses to domestic violence. Examples from practice will be used to demonstrate the impact that the different ways of understanding the issues will have on the work undertaken by practitioners. The framework will then be used to help you to reflect on your practice when safeguarding adults.

The chapter will then draw on research studies that have explored women's views about what has been helpful for them and on my own research into a local outreach service. These studies challenge stereotypical assumptions about women who have experienced domestic violence and will be used to inform the wider discussion of the design and delivery of services to safeguard adults. The chapter deliberately prioritises the views of women who have experienced domestic violence, in an attempt to challenge approaches that pathologise and define women by their experience of abuse, rather than recognising their expertise in identifying solutions.

This chapter will help readers to:

- review their assumptions about the experience of domestic violence;

- consider the links to other forms of adult abuse;

- challenge models of practice that reinforce notions of individual pathology;

- think creatively about their approaches to safeguarding adults.

Defining domestic violence

ACTIVITY 6.1

Before reading the following sections, pause for a moment and consider:
What is domestic violence? What is adult abuse?
In what ways are they similar? How do they differ?
Make a note of your thoughts.

COMMENT

The language that we use to categorise situations can have a significant impact on the way we respond. It is important therefore to reflect carefully on why particular terms are used, whether they are appropriate and whether or not they add to our understanding of how to respond helpfully.

Definitions of domestic violence and the appropriateness of the terms 'domestic', which arguably trivialises the issues, and 'violence', which may be seen as too narrow, rather than 'abuse' have been the subject of considerable debate which can be explored further in Mullender (1996, pp8–10); Hanmer and Itzin (2000) and Calder (2004, pp14–20).

For the purposes of this chapter the current government definition will be adopted:

Any incident of threatening behaviour, violence or abuse (psychological, physical, sexual, financial or emotional) between adults who are or have been intimate partners or family members, regardless of gender or sexuality. This includes issues of concern to black and minority ethnic (BME) communities such as so called 'honour based violence', female genital mutilation (FGM) and forced marriage.

www.crimereduction.homeoffice.gov.uk

Domestic violence thus sits as a clearly defined area within the wider definition of abuse given in *No secrets* (DoH, 2000), where abuse is defined as *a violation of an individual's human and civil rights by any other person or persons.* If someone has been abused, we should then also be considering whether this is as a result of domestic violence. If they also meet the definition of a vulnerable adult (ADSS, 2005), the application of safeguarding adult procedures needs to be considered. It is important to note that while there is no entitlement to any statutory service provision in relation to domestic violence, it may be that as a result of the impact of the physical or mental trauma caused by domestic violence, a woman may then be eligible for a service.

There is a considerable amount of research which can be used to assist our understanding of domestic violence in the general population, which is outlined below. Additionally there is a small amount of research specifically looking at the impact of domestic violence on disabled women and a study focusing on older women in Canada that can also contribute to our understanding. The model of practice developed by the Duluth Domestic Abuse Intervention Project (DAIP) was developed by women in Duluth, Minnesota, who had been abused by their male partners and were attending women's education groups. The model that they developed was thus designed to illustrate men's abusive behaviours towards women. The Project adopts an approach based on a structural analysis of the issues, while also seeking to promote women's empowerment. The model identifies domestic violence as a process designed to maintain power and control (Figure 6.1) and illustrates the wide range of strategies and behaviours that abusers may use to exercise and maintain control.

It is important to recognise this as a process, rather than to focus on individual incidents (Calder, 2004; Wilcox, 2006). An attack or threat may be effective in maintaining control for years after the time at which it happened. The all-pervasive nature of the controlling behaviours helps to explain why it is so difficult for women to leave and, indeed, leaving is extremely dangerous as this may result in an increase in violence (Hanmer and Itzin, 2000, p19). It is also important to be aware that abusers may threaten women with the involvement of social workers and other professionals, on the basis of their alleged shortcomings, which they claim will result in dire consequences, such as sectioning under the Mental Health Act, or removing the children (Mullender, 1996; McGee, in Hanmer and Itzin, 2000).

ACTIVITY **6.2**

Make a list of the possible threats that might be made to control people.
What impact might this have on their relationship with you, or a social worker?

COMMENT

It can be easy to underestimate the very real fear and anxiety that people may experience in a situation where they are being abused. Building confidence and trust in such situations will take time and will entail helping the person to recognise that the power of the abuser can be successfully challenged.

Figure 6.1 Power and control wheel
Reproduced by permission of Duluth Domestic Abuse Intervention Project

RESEARCH SUMMARY

How widespread is domestic violence?
Prevalence is difficult to establish, as inevitably the social taboos surrounding domestic violence and difficulties with definitions will result in some degree of uncertainty. However, analysis of ten separate domestic violence prevalence studies revealed consistent findings which are accepted by the Home Office and cited on the Crime reduction website. They conclude that one in four women experience domestic violence over their lifetime and approximately two women per week are killed by current or former partners (www.crimereduction.homeoffice.gov.uk).

Few domestic violence prevalence studies to date have focused on women who face the 'double jeopardy' (Cockram, 2003, p6) of being disabled and being female. However, in the interim report from a study in England, which focused on disabled women, Hague et al. (2007) summarise findings that indicate that as many as one in two disabled women may experience domestic violence in their lifetime.

> RESEARCH SUMMARY *continued*
>
> *A further limitation is that prevalence studies so far have mostly focused on women of child-bearing or child-rearing age, so little is known about the experience of older wo-men (Walsh et al., 2007). Similarly, studies to date have not focused on prevalence in relation to women with learning disabilities. Nor do we know anything about the pre-valence of domestic violence in relation to vulnerable men.*
>
> *Walsh et al. argue for the importance of recognising the complex interconnections be-tween different forms of family violence, while recognising that there may be qualitative differences between younger and older women's experience resulting from socialisation processes. Thus they contend that older women are more likely to be submissive and regard domestic violence as a private matter, unlikely to emerge as a public issue. This point may be equally valid in relation to disabled people receiving care from others, who may be expected to be grateful to their carers and not to complain.*

Who are the abusers?

Research by Strauss and Gelles in the 1980s found that in self-report surveys women carried out almost as many assaults as men. However, this survey did not adequately define the severity or outcomes of assaults, nor did it identify who initiated the assault (Mullender, 1996, p13).

A study carried out by the Home Office found that in more than a third (41 per cent) of cases brought to the courts under the Protection from Harassment Act 1997, the suspect had previously had an intimate relationship with the complainant; 33 per cent of the suspects were ex-partners, 4 per cent were relatives, 1 per cent a current partner and 4 per cent were friends. In situations where the suspect previously or currently had an intimate relationship with the victim, 94 per cent of the suspects were men (Harris, 2000). This picture of abuse being predominantly perpetrated by men is also reflected in census research cited by Stanko, which found that 81 per cent of reported domestic violence cases were of female victims attacked by male perpe-trators; 8 per cent were male victims attacked by female perpetrators; 4 per cent were female victims attacked by female perpetrators; and 7 per cent were male victims attacked by male perpetrators (Stanko, 2000).

Findings from the self-completion module of the 2001 British Crime Survey cited by Walby and Allen (2004) indicate that the outcomes of violence by men are substan-tially more serious than those by women:

> *During the worst incidents of domestic violence experienced in the last year, 46 per cent of women sustained a minor physical injury, 20 per cent a moderate physical injury, and six per cent severe injuries, while for 31 per cent it resulted in mental or emotional problems. Among men, 41 per cent sustained a minor physical injury, 14 per cent a moderate physical injury, one per cent severe injuries and nine per cent mental or emotional problems.*

Sandra lives with her husband Robert, who works as a banker, and three children, Sam 6, David 8 and Trish 10. Three years ago they moved away from her family in London when Robert gained promotion, to a detached country cottage. Shortly after they moved, Sandra had a car accident and wrote off the car. Robert was very angry and as a result she no longer drives. Sandra has a history of depression that started shortly after they moved. She has at times become suicidal and has been detained under the Mental Health Act 1983 on two occasions. Each time she has received electro convulsive therapy (ECT). She is currently very depressed but fearful that she may be admitted to hospital and receive ECT. Sandra cannot understand why she is depressed; she does not have to work and she has a perfect house. She does find it difficult to get Trish to school, as she is always making excuses to stay at home with her mum. Sandra feels worthless as Robert says the only things she has to do are look after the children, keep the house tidy and have a decent meal on the table when he comes home, but she cannot even manage to do that. Robert likes everything to be exactly in the right place (including the cushions) and although people have commented that you would not know they had children as the house is so tidy, Sandra still does not seem to get it right for Robert. He gets very angry with her and has threatened to report her to social services for being such an incompetent mother, unless she pulls herself together.

ACTIVITY **6.3**

Using the power and control wheel (Figure 6.1), identify the means by which Robert exercises control.

Drawing on the research above, if you were a community mental health support worker, what questions would it be helpful to ask?

Make a list of the implications of these research studies for your practice in safeguarding adults.

COMMENT

While there are clearly difficulties in establishing the prevalence of domestic violence, the extent of the research available reveals that this is an issue that needs to be carefully considered in all our practice. Information in relation to prevalence among people who may be defined as vulnerable is limited, but the initial findings highlighted above indicate that prevalence is likely to be higher.

For many years practice in relation to safeguarding children failed to take adequate account of the prevalence of domestic violence. Similarly, practice in the family courts often failed to take adequate account of violent behaviour by men towards women when considering contact applications (Humphreys and Stanley, 2006; Radford and Hester, 2006). Recognising the connections between these discourses has been critical in ensuring that more appropriate decisions are made that incorporate a proper understanding of the risk posed by violent men. The importance of recognising complexity and interconnections is also highlighted by Littlechild and Bourke in Humphreys and Stanley (2006, p213). They argue that in relation to child care, if we:

incorporate our knowledge of the problems caused by such men's violence into child care policy and practice, rather than seeing domestic violence as a separate issue from the protection of children, we will be able to protect abused children, abused family members, and social work staff more effectively.

This is equally relevant in relation to policy and practice with vulnerable adults, where there is a need to incorporate our knowledge of the problems caused by domestic violence, rather than seeing this as a separate issue. At the same time, it is also important to recognise and draw on the research and expertise that have been developed in relation to domestic violence, in order to protect abused adults more effectively.

It is also important that the gendered nature of most domestic violence does not blunt our sensitivity to the abuse of vulnerable men, which has hitherto received little attention. It might be reasonable to work from the premise that disabled men may be twice as likely to be abused as non-disabled men, given that this appears to be the case for disabled women.

Understanding and responding to domestic violence

Various theories about the causes of domestic violence have been developed (see Calder, 2004, p23 for a useful summary), but the work of McDonald (2005) is particularly helpful as it provides a useful framework when analysing approaches to safeguarding adults. He argues that the ascendancy of neoliberalism in Australia has resulted in managerial service responses that individualise and pathologise domestic violence. He proposes four perspectives:

- victim blaming;

- pathologising;

- social movement;

- empowerment.

The relevance of this work to the UK context will be demonstrated with illustrations from practice and research. (I have modified this slightly following feedback from students, to provide a framework that can be used to analyse practice responses to domestic violence.)

Victim blaming. Responsibility for the violence is placed on the victim, usually the woman, who is seen as being in some way at fault. From this perspective domestic violence is largely a private, hidden matter, only becoming of interest to the state if there are children who may be at risk. Women may be judged negatively for failing to leave their partners and failing therefore to protect their children. Research into women's experiences of mental health services in England illustrates this approach:

They treated me terribly...I did hear a couple (medical staff) in the corridor saying 'There's an OD (overdose) case, domestic violence. She's been in before, just leave her. She'll be out by morning.'

(Humphreys and Thiara, 2003, p217)

Pathologising. Domestic violence is seen as a symptom of personal problems, an unhealthy relationship or family. The focus of attention tends to be on the perceived symptoms or deficits, which may be seen to contribute to the problem. The separation of symptoms from the experience of abuse may result in little attention being paid to the perpetrator, with intervention focusing on the need for personal change or the use of medication such as anti depressants. This approach has gained ground even with women's refuges as the increasing reliance on funding from statutory agencies is often contingent on requirements that require staff to work with women to identify individual problems/needs and then produce an individual support plan. While it is important to recognise the devastating impact that domestic violence can have and that such tools may be valuable when working with individual women, there is a danger that the focus is on individual deficits which are seen as existing in their own right, rather than as a result of the abuse. Similarly in social work agencies staff often find that in order to offer services, individual pathology needs to be established.

However, this portrayal of women as helpless victims paints a partial picture, which is challenged by Abrahams's (2007) research with women who have experienced domestic violence. She found that:

Women did not see themselves as powerless or passive within these situations. They took positive action to defuse tension to protect themselves and their children and utilised any opportunities that offered to maintain contact with others.

(Abrahams, 2007, p28)

Similarly, this quotation from a woman attending a group for women experiencing domestic violence provides a useful insight into the value of such services, while also demonstrating the importance of recognising the strength and resilience which may be fostered within such an environment.

I certainly didn't expect to find a room full of very strong and brave women, and there is certainly more fun and laughter in our sessions than I would have expected.

(Service user quoted in Havant Women's Aid Annual Report, 2006)

Structural (referred to as 'social movement' by McDonald). The use of violence as a means of asserting power and exercising control has traditionally been sanctioned by patriarchal societies and indeed in relation to war and the punishment of children may still be regarded as legitimate. This perspective thus sees domestic violence as arising from prevailing social norms and power structures, where it is legitimate for men to exercise control as they feel appropriate. It is thus seen as a structural problem that needs to be addressed through legal remedies and appropriate policies that ensure equality, proper redress and zero tolerance. Services need to be designed with and for women. Good examples of practice that seeks structural and social change are provided by Women's Aid, which has with some considerable success campaigned to increase awareness, improve legal remedies and improve services for women experiencing domestic violence. Commissioning research studies and promoting campaigns such as 'Zero tolerance' may all be seen as strategies that seek to change social attitudes and social structures. On a smaller scale, staff in women's refuges may provide training and education to raise the awareness of local agencies and improve their practice.

Coming from a feminist perspective, writers such as Mullender (1996) highlight the importance of structural issues and a shared recognition of the experience of women as vulnerable to the abuse of power. Hence effective responses have a different emphasis, which move away from pathologising women to focus on listening to the views of women and involving them in the design of services. Cockram (2003, p6) highlights the experience of disabled women who may experience abuse as an added layer of oppression as they may simultaneously be discriminated against on the basis of gender and disability. In some respects their experience of abuse may be identical, but in other ways it may be unique, as some disabled women may be dependent on others to meet basic needs. There are additional barriers to seeking help as services designed to support women who have experienced domestic violence are often ill equipped to provide appropriate support (Cockram, 2003; Hague et al., 2007).

Empowerment. This perspective has some similarities with the structural perspective in that domestic violence is seen to arise from power imbalances. However, the focus is on interpersonal relationships and the achievement of personal empowerment. This is crucial in order to counter negative, undermining messages that abusers often use in order to undermine women's sense of self-belief and self-esteem. Effective approaches to practice when working from this perspective include the use of narrative, providing women with the opportunity to be heard, to have their experiences recognised and to make connections with the experiences of others (Milner, 2001; Dalrymple and Burke, 2006). Solution-focused work (O'Connell, 2005) that builds on strengths is also effective. According to McDonald when using this approach a decision to stay with the abuser but refuse to accept the violence may be seen as a positive outcome, as the measure of success is the woman's empowerment. Group work is also highlighted by women survivors as particularly effective, as will be shown in the section outlining practice responses that women find helpful.

CASE STUDY

Brian is 65 years old. He has Parkinson's disease, which he says generally causes him few difficulties although he admits that he has recently had several falls as he is now finding it difficult to lift his left leg. He cares for his wife Annie, who has recently had a stroke, which has impaired her speech and resulted in early-onset dementia. Annie often accuses her husband and her children (when they occasionally visit) of stealing her things, in-cluding her purse. She says that Brian does this to stop her from being independent. Brian says she is just paranoid and forgetful. She tells you that no one visits, no one cares about her and that she never has a decent meal. She cannot remember when Brian last let her go out. Brian dismisses her comments as resulting from her poor memory. He says she has always been difficult and argumentative.

ACTIVITY **6.4**

Consider the relevance of McDonald's framework for understanding this case study.
Discuss with a colleague and list the issues that you need to consider.
What perspective might help you understand this situation?
What approach might you take in order to help?

COMMENT

Difficulties in interpersonal relationships may encourage us to focus on individual deficits and in this case to collude with Brian in blaming Annie. However, if we look at this situation from a structural perspective, we become more aware of their social isolation, practical difficulties and issues facing Brian as a carer.

Women's views about helpful responses

RESEARCH SUMMARY

The following summary is predominantly based on a major study carried out by Humphreys and Thiara (2003) into the views of 200 women and 14 children who had experienced domestic violence. The findings are complemented by research findings by Abrahams (2007), who interviewed 23 women who were either residents or ex-residents of women's refuges, and my own research in 2005 in focus groups with 12 women using an outreach group for women who had either previously experienced or were currently experiencing domestic violence. There was a high level of consistency in the findings.

In relation to the support that they gained from being with each other women high-lighted the following.

- *Contact with others, as isolation was a major issue for many.*
- *Quality time and the opportunity to talk.*
- *Friendship and mutual support:* I find that at my age, I don't have children and the caring part of me wasn't there. It's nice to have people you can care about, make cups of tea, etc. ... And they're grateful. There's so much love here.
- *Acceptance and understanding: no one judging them:* The only people that understand how we feel are the other people in this room. Friends don't understand.

RESEARCH SUMMARY *continued*

- *Encouragement.*
- *Practical support and assistance.*

High-quality practice by service providers shared similar characteristics:
- *Proactive approach to asking about abuse, enabling women to feel able to disclose.*
- *Lifting the blame and belief in women's accounts.*
- *A non-judgemental approach.*
- *Time to talk, on three levels: everyday conversation, supportive talk and healing talk.*
- *Support and understanding.*
- *Help with practical issues.*
- *Recognition of the need to ensure safety and help with safety planning.*

(Humphreys and Thiara, 2003; Abrahams, 2007)

Women highlighted the need for safety to take precedence and to be recognised as a separate issue to whether or not they stayed in the relationship. The importance of services being accessible, well publicised, and totally confidential was also highlighted. Services needed to be flexible and responsive to their individual circumstances. They wanted services that rebuilt their capacity to cope and enabled them to regain self-respect and confidence. Views about counselling services were mixed, although some found them helpful. Underpinning the various aspects of service provision outlined above is the importance of really listening, which is reflected in the following quotation from one woman who had been actively involved in planning a service:

If they listen to us it is just so good. It makes the services better, just much better. No one has ever listened to us before. And then suddenly those posh organisations are. It brings tears to my eyes just thinking about it.

(Hague, 2005, p195)

COMMENT

Analysis of the views expressed by the women in these studies reflects the importance of approaches that are predominantly based upon a perspective that recognises domestic violence as a widespread problem embedded within the social structures of society and thus seeks to address the issues on this basis. The support of other women was highly valued, empowering and reduced isolation. A proactive approach to asking about abuse, practical support and information provided by workers contributed to the process of empowerment by helping women to be more aware of possible choices and how to access them. If such an approach is not adopted, abuse may simply remain hidden.

My old GP did not ask the right questions. I feel I would have disclosed and got out of the situation much quicker. The CPN was unhelpful as she was always in a hurry and made me feel as though I couldn't take up her time.

(Humphreys and Thiara, 2003, p220)

COMMENT continued

It is noticeable that the provision of counselling and therapeutic approaches received a mixed response. The improvements that women note themselves in their mental health as a result of leaving the abuser and gaining support from other women indicates the need to be cautious about assuming that 'symptoms' indicate pathology.

Tensions in the social work role

The constraints of agencies whose resources are restricted to fulfilling their statutory duties result in serious tensions for social workers, whose only reason for being involved may be concerns about the welfare of children. It is thus unsurprising that some studies have revealed very mixed views about social workers, as the perception can be that the social worker is only interested in the child and sees the woman as culpable if she fails to leave the abuser and protect her child (Mullender, 1996; Humphreys et al., 2001; Tunbridge Adams, 2007). Additionally, as we saw above, resources available to social workers tend to be dependent on establishing individual pathology.

Links to safeguarding adults: Key points

The work outlined above in relation to domestic violence suggests that it may be helpful to consider the following points.

- Abuse is endemic and rooted within unequal structures in society. This enables us to move away from approaches to practice that pathologise or blame in any way the person who has been abused. However problematic an individual's behaviour, it is always those responsible for the abuse who must be held to account. This stance reinforces the importance of clear definitions, policies and procedures that enable us to identify and name abusive practices. It is also important to remember that while they are essential, they are only a starting point; the process of developing and implementing them in partnership with service users is critical, as we saw above in relation to the services valued by women who had experienced domestic violence.

- Domestic violence is very widespread, so this knowledge needs to be incorporated into approaches to practice in relation to safeguarding adults. It is important to be aware of the many subtle mechanisms used to maintain control and silence those who are being controlled.

- Research studies with adults to date indicate that abuse is gendered. We also need to be aware that additional sources of disadvantage create further vulnerability.

- There is a body of research into the experience of women who have experienced domestic violence and practice knowledge developed by those who have worked in this area. This has wider relevance and can be incorporated into practice to safeguard adults. This work highlights the important role of voluntary-sector organisations and community-based initiatives, where models of service delivery are less likely to be experienced as stigmatising.

Practice implications

Social work practice needs to address the structural issues that create the conditions where abuse can thrive. Such practice may include supporting the development of social networks to reduce isolation, advocacy, practical support, empowerment and education to establish a zero-tolerance approach to abuse and the promotion of equality within relationships. A helpful model designed to reassert equality and interdependence within relationships with carers has been developed by the Wisconsin Coalition Against Domestic Violence, from the 'equality wheel' (DIVP). This identifies the following characteristics of relationships as crucial:

- dignity and respect, positive communication;

- non-threatening behaviour;

- involvement – encouraging personal relationships and contact with others;

- honesty and accountability;

- responsible provision of services, equipment and medication;

- economic equality – access to money is not contingent on appropriate behaviour;

- choice and partnership, listening to the person;

- negotiation and fairness: discussing the impact of the caregiver's actions with the person, compromising and seeking mutually satisfying resolutions to conflict.

The dimensions identified above may provide a helpful framework for discussions both with those who have been abused and those who have abused others.

CHAPTER SUMMARY

During the last 40 years a considerable body of knowledge has developed in relation to the experience of domestic violence. Women survivors have identified particular approaches outlined above, which are helpful. It is noticeable that there were few differences in terms of the support that women gained from one another and that which they valued from service providers. In many ways these epitomise the notion of being 'ordinary', in 'extraordinary' situations (Jordan, 1990). It should also be noted that much of this support did not come from statutory agencies, as women normally only become eligible for services if there are childcare or mental health problems.

The more recent recognition of the need to safeguard adults is rightly leading to the development of detailed procedures designed to ensure that abuse is not tolerated in any setting, whether it is 'domestic' or institutional. What is important now is that the procedures do not just provide an effective managerial defence for beleaguered local authorities, in a culture that seeks to apportion blame rather than accept responsibility. This chapter is not arguing that the development of policy, definitions and detailed

CHAPTER SUMMARY *continued*

procedures is unimportant, rather that these must be developed and delivered in full consultation with service users and carers, recognising their strengths and expertise. The process is critical, otherwise services are likely to fall short of their intended aims and to focus narrowly on identification and investigation. We need practice that is bold and confidently based on the research evidence from service users. The following quotation from *Shaping our lives* (Beresford, 2007) reinforces the importance of approaches to practice that recognise structural issues and work with a model of empowerment:

> *People value a social work approach based on challenging the broader barriers they face . . . They place particular value on Social Work's social approach, the social work relationship, and the positive personal qualities they associate with social workers. These include warmth, respect, being non-judgemental, listening, treating people with equality, being trustworthy, open, honest and reliable and communicating well. Service users prioritise practice which is participatory in process and purpose.*

As we have seen above, there is remarkable consistency across the board about what is valued, so surely this should be the basis for practice.

FURTHER READING

Abrahams, H (2007) *Supporting women after domestic violence.* London: Jessica Kingsley.
This book provides practical advice for those working with women who have experienced domestic violence. It highlights the experience of loss and draws on the work of Maslow to provide a framework for practice. It draws on valuable research with women who have experienced domestic violence to identify what they identify as helpful responses.

Hanmer, J and Itzin, C (eds) (2000) *Home truths about domestic violence: Feminist influences on policy and practice.* Abingdon: Routledge.
This book provides an excellent foundation for those wanting to gain a greater understanding of the development of policy, research and practice in relation to current understandings of domestic violence.

WEBSITES

www.womensaid.org.uk
The Women's Aid Federation of England (WAFE) website is an excellent resource with sections for women and children who have experienced abuse, as well as for students. It includes sections on policy, law, research, contacts and practical guidance, plus links to relevant sections of other websites such as **www.crimereduction.homeoffice.gov.uk**

Chapter 7

Working with difference
Gill Constable

A C H I E V I N G   A   S O C I A L   W O R K   D E G R E E

This chapter will help you to meet the following National Occupational Standards.

Key Role 1: Prepare for, and work with, individuals, families, carers, groups and communities to assess their needs and circumstances.

- Prepare for social work contact and involvement.

Key Role 3: Support individuals to represent their views and circumstances.

- Advocate with, and on behalf of, individuals, families, carers, groups and communities.

Key Role 5: Manage and be accountable, with supervision and support, for your own social work practice within your organisation.

- Work within multi-disciplinary and multi-organisational teams, networks and systems.

Key Role 6: Demonstrate professional competence in social work practice.

- Contribute to the promotion of best social work practice.

Introduction

To get the most from this chapter you will need to reflect on yourself and your belief systems in the context of safeguarding adults from abuse (Knott and Scragg, 2007). We will explore the concept of difference, and seek to define this, so that we can work through ideas and concepts that will help us to gain a better understanding of our values, beliefs and attitudes. This will be contextualised in terms of life chances and experiences of different people within society through an examination of research. We will consider how this places some groups of people in situations that increase their potential risk of abuse. This will assist us to increase our capacity to practise in an anti-oppressive way.

The difference between anti-discriminatory and anti-oppressive practice will be debated with reference to legislation and policy. We will examine critical and radical social care theories so that we can better understand ourselves and people who use services and carers. Finally we will look at approaches that we can adopt that will support our ongoing development as reflective and competent social workers with a clear understanding of our role in safeguarding adults.

What do we mean by difference?

Britain is a diverse society that is differentiated by social and cultural divisions between people. Thompson (2006) explains that these divisions form social groupings and institutions that determine economic power and social status. Some groups are more influential and powerful than others.

When we talk about institutions we are generally referring to the processes within society that ensure its continuance such as those that national government is responsible for. This includes managing the economy, national security, public services, legislation and policy. There are other institutions too that are influential even if their power is more discreet such as religious organisations.

Another aspect of a diverse society is cultural. This can be defined as the dominant norms and values of a society and its institutions. These will be expressed through government legislation and policy as well as by the impact historically of the dominant religion, employment patterns, education system, and more subtly by the arts and media. Social care services are defined and shaped by culture too.

How we respond to these structural and cultural divisions will impact on our personal values, beliefs and behaviour. Payne (2005) cites Norton (1978) as first developing the concept of the personal, cultural and structural (PCS) analysis, which Thompson (2006) uses. If we use a case example we can see how this allows us to quickly map out how these concepts interface.

CASE STUDY

Dennis is 70 years old and lives alone. He has mobility difficulties, and experiences depression. Following stormy weather a number of slates came off the roof and some guttering needed to be replaced. Jon and Dave knocked on his door following the storm and said they were builders, who were very competitive in their costs. They advised Dennis that his entire roof and guttering should be replaced.

Dennis enjoyed their company as they were friendly and cheerful, often bringing Dennis a bottle of beer, and the three men would have lunch together. Dennis felt that he had found two new friends. He was surprised at how much the work cost, but Jon offered to drive him into town to get cash out of the ATM to pay for the work.

Dennis had handed over a significant amount of money for materials one afternoon, and had been expecting Jon and Dave back the next day, but they never returned. One room in the house was still not habitable due to a leak in the roof and the guttering had not been replaced even though the builders had been there for several weeks. Dennis was unable to contact the men on the mobile phone number that they had given him. It was six months later when Dennis saw Jon and Dave on the local news programme where they had been imprisoned for defrauding other older people by taking money for building work that they did not complete that he realised that he should have reported the incident to the police.

- *How might Dennis's experience and his response be understood using a PCS analysis?*
- *Do you think this incident is a safeguarding issue?*
- *What could you do as a social worker to support Dennis?*

COMMENT

Dennis told the social worker: 'I am an old fool to have allowed myself to be conned by rogues half my age.' At a personal level Dennis has internalised ageist feelings about himself, which is evidenced by him referring to himself as an 'old fool', and blames himself for being defrauded. He goes on to say 'we old ones are seen as easy pickings, and to be honest I felt too embarrassed to go to the police, they have better things to do, but now I realise I should have followed it up to prevent other old people being cheated'. These comments show that Dennis believes that at a cultural level in terms of society's attitudes and norms that older people are seen as legitimate targets for crime, and that an institution such as the police has more important things to do than investigate a crime against him even though at a structural level the police and criminal justice system are there to prevent crime and protect the public. Dennis is emotionally distressed as he liked and trusted Jon and Dave and they used their friendliness as a method to deceive him and steal from him. As this case illustrates this is not a random act of abuse towards Dennis: rather he has been targeted as have other older people by Jon and Dave (see Chapter 1).

This is a safeguarding incident. Dennis fulfils the criteria as a vulnerable adult as defined by the Lord Chancellor's Department, 1997 (Chapter 1), due to his age, limited mobility and experience of depression. He has experienced financial and emotional abuse. Dennis may require community support services, and is entitled to an assessment under the NHS and Community Care Act 1990 to assess his needs. He should be advised about Trading Standards in his local authority who investigate rogue traders, as well as the police. Dennis may like to become involved with Neighbourhood Watch and Victim Support as well as other local groups, clubs and befriending schemes. This would increase his social network, and enable him to become better informed, so if other traders come knocking at his door he will not be so trusting in future. Another task is to assist Dennis to re-evaluate himself more positively so that he can view himself as an older person who has learnt many things through his life, which are valuable to younger people, so that his increasing age is equated with experience and wisdom. Dennis can use this abusive incident as a way to educate other people that there are criminals who target particular areas because of the perceived vulnerability of the people living there (Pritchard, 2007). We will now consider in more detail the idea of vulnerability.

Making the connections – What makes some adults more vulnerable than others?

Martin (2007) contends that we need to define our understanding of the term 'vulnerability', and consider what causes people to be vulnerable. She differentiates between vulnerability that is created by the environments and services that people receive, and the characteristics or needs of people. How we understand this concept will impact on how we respond to adult abuse. If we view vulnerability as created by how people are looked after, we then need to ensure that social policy and practice are underpinned by respect, equality and social justice. If we see vulnerability as located in the individual due to their needs, we run the risk of locating the cause of the abuse within them, rather than how society views and supports people.

ACTIVITY **7.2**

Can you think of an occasion where you have felt oppressed? Maybe when other people have assumed that you are unable to do something such as a particular subject at school, being blamed for something that was not your fault, or being bullied. Oppressive behaviour involves being labelled and stereotyped which can be based on our social class, gender, ethnic origin, disability or sexual orientation. How did it make you feel? What helped you to deal with the situation?

COMMENT

You may have felt sad, angry, defeated or determined to fight back. Feelings of powerlessness are common, which persist if we find ourselves defined by others, our differences exaggerated, and other people's traditions, beliefs and views imposed on us. This can be experienced at an individual level as well as in a group (Gaine and Gaylard, 2010). What helped you to deal with the situation that you found oppressive? It may have been that someone supported you by listening to you, validating your feelings and providing reassurance. You might have been helped to work out a way of dealing with the difficulty, so that things changed for the better. It is important to reflect on our own experience and what is helpful to us. We can then learn to empathise with other people, and develop supportive approaches (Rogers, 1980). Now let us turn to thinking more about power, as a theory.

The concept of power

An understanding of power and its manifestations in how society organises itself and within personal relationships will have helped you to complete the above activity. Power is a problematic concept to define. Dalrymple and Burke (2006) cite Sawicki's (1991) critique of the philosopher Foucault's (1980) ideas. Power is not an object or thing that is held. People create power and use it. It is not something that oppresses people; rather it enables activity to take place. This is why we accept institutions that order civil life such as the criminal justice system. Power is not something that descends from societal structures; rather it operates from the 'grass roots' and permeates society, although there are structural inequalities created by economic systems, social class and so on. These are best challenged through 'grass roots' action. This explains why inequality continues to exist between the roles of men and women in the family, and within the workplace too, although the Sex Discrimination Act became law in 1975.

This challenges the idea that power is a bad thing. In fact it is powerlessness which impacts negatively on people. People's self-esteem and confidence are affected by poverty and lack of educational opportunity.

RESEARCH SUMMARY

Jacqui Pritchard's (1999) research with older people who have experienced abuse high-lighted the following good practice points. The consistent themes are the need to listen to the person, go at their pace and provide information, otherwise they feel out of control of the situation and things are done to them rather than with them.

The user perspective – Adult protection investigations

- *When social workers are investigating suspected abuse they should explain to the older person who they are and show an identity card.*
- *They should explain the purpose of their visit, speak clearly and not use jargon.*
- *They should be honest, explain about confidentiality, and with whom information will be shared.*
- *Social workers should ask the person what they want to happen, and listen to them.*
- *The social worker should allow the person time to consider the options and make decisions. The person should not be rushed to make long-term plans.*
- *People require support following an abusive incident which can be provided by a number of people, and it should be accepted that it takes time to get over abuse.*
- *People's gender and ethnic origin should not be ignored, and consideration should be given as to which social worker might best meet the person's needs.*

Pritchard, J (ed.) (1999) Elder abuse work. *London: Jessica Kingsley.*

Audit of power

Braye and Preston-Shoot (1995) suggest that an audit of power in social care provision highlights inequalities and where practice needs to change. If we were to develop an audit tool to assist us, we could start to change our practice. Set out in Figure 7.1 is a tool that could be used to audit power either for the individual or in terms of a service. If these characteristics are in place, power is shared and the service is person-centred where the user is central to the delivery of the service. This means that people's unique needs are recognised and diversity is viewed as positive and enriching rather than a difficulty or problem.

The tool provides examples of behaviours that ensure that social workers treat people who use services on the basis of equality. Even when social workers are required to intervene to safeguard someone, and this is at variance with the wishes of the person, it is still possible to be honest and provide advice and information. So people know how they can access legal advice, make a complaint to the organisation, and their local government councillor or Member of Parliament. People can be supported to do this through a referral to an organisation that provides advocacy services.

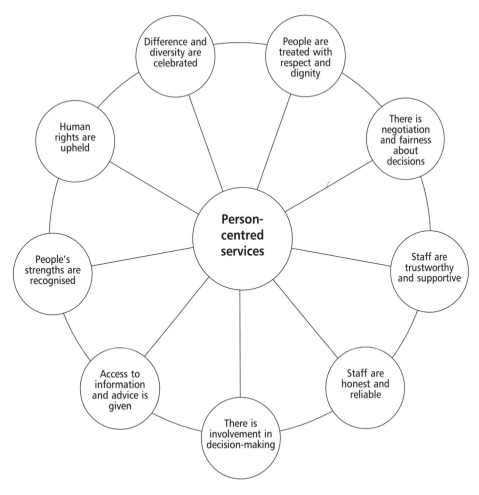

Figure 7.1 Tool to audit power

CASE STUDY

Rosy Segal, a 71-year-old woman, was admitted to Hollyhocks, an elderly mentally infirm (EMI) residential care home for older people, for one week's respite care. Ms Segal lived with her sister, who was the main carer. On the first night of Ms Segal's admission a male resident, Mr Williams, entered her bedroom and locked the door. The night duty staff became aware that he was not in his bedroom at 12.30am. They finally located him in Ms Segal's room, but he refused to open the door. They were unable to obtain any response from Ms Segal.

An hour later they used a duplicate key and gained entry to the room. They found Mr Williams partially dressed and Ms Segal in bed in an agitated and distressed state. Mr Williams was taken to his bedroom, and settled down by staff. Ms Segal was given a cup of tea.

> ### CASE STUDY continued
>
> The following afternoon the manager of the home contacted Ms Segal's social worker to alert her that a complaint was likely to be made by Ms Segal's sister, who was very upset and angry on visiting Ms Segal to find her withdrawn and tearful. The manager said that no real harm had been done to their knowledge, and anyway, Rosy would have forgotten all about it by tomorrow due to her dementia. *The manager went on to say that Mr Williams has dementia too, and probably thought Ms Segal was his wife. The manager said it had been* a bit of a shock for Rosy being a spinster.

ACTIVITY 7.3

1. What are your thoughts about how the care home managed this incident?
2. How would you describe the attitude of the manager towards Ms Segal?
3. How do you think this situation would have been dealt with if Ms Segal had been a young woman forcibly imprisoned and sexually assaulted in her hotel room?

COMMENT

If we consider this case in relation to the tool to audit power we can observe that a series of assumptions have been made regarding both Ms Segal and Mr Williams. There are clear gaps of knowledge, understanding and skills.

The following is a list of points regarding the above case.

- The home failed to raise an adult protection alert with the out-of-hours social work team. The lack of any social work and police involvement has meant that no investigation has taken place and the loss of any forensic evidence if a sexual assault has taken place. Collaborative working has not taken place; all the decisions have been made by the home.
- Ms Segal's sister should have been informed at the earliest opportunity, so she could provide support. Mr Williams's wife ought to have been advised about the incident too.
- The home had not sought a healthcare assessment for Ms Segal by asking the GP to visit, and assess her needs. Information and advice had not been sought.
- The home had not advised the CQC of a serious incident, and only referred to adults' services because it suspected a complaint would be made.
- The assumption was made that due to Ms Segal's dementia she would not be adversely affected by a possible sexual assault, and forced imprisonment. The gravity of the situation has been denied and the impact minimised. The abuse has not been named as sexual abuse, physical abuse (restraint) and emotional abuse. The staff have been neglectful in failing to realise that Mr Williams was not in his bedroom, and allowing him to remain with Ms Segal for an hour prior to entering the room.
- The belief that as Mr Williams has dementia he cannot be held accountable for his actions. This is without any assessment of his mental capacity, or the nature of his condition. Again this is an example of minimising and denying what has taken place. Additionally there has been no assessment of the possible risk that Mr Williams poses to other women.

COMMENT continued

- *The assumption that Ms Segal would have been shocked by Mr Williams's beha-viour because of her marital status, when in fact any woman would have found this behaviour frightening and distressing. The general tone that the manager is adopting is to trivialise the incident.*

It is the responsibility of social workers to develop an understanding of ageism. In Western societies youthfulness is valued rather than age, and older people are invari-ably assumed to be without any sexuality. There is a common acceptance of the disengagement theory of ageing, where old age is seen as a time of decline, loss and a withdrawing from purposeful activities and societal involvement (Cumming and Henry, cited by Fenge, 2006).

Anti-discriminatory and anti-oppressive practice

We need to define what we mean by anti-discriminatory and anti-oppressive practice. You may hear these terms being used as if they are interchangeable, but Braye and Preston-Shoot (1995) distinguish them.

- Anti-discriminatory practice challenges inequalities within a legal framework. This means that the recruitment and selection of staff, assessment, delivery and provi-sion of services meet statutory legal requirements, that is, they conform to the letter of the law.

- Anti-oppressive practice seeks to change the power structures that create social injustice at a personal, cultural and structural level. It operates from a value base that is politically informed, and questions taken-for-granted cultural assumptions about people. It therefore questions negative stereotypes of groups of people in society that are marginalised due to ethnic origin, gender, age, sexuality, disabil-ity and health status. Anti-oppressive practice is radical, proactive and dynamic in seeking to enhance the quality of people's lives.

Set out below is the background to the Stephen Lawrence case, which led to the Race Relations (Amendment) Act 2000, which requires public-sector organisations to have in place equalities schemes and to monitor the provision of services against criteria. Staff are required to behave in a non-discriminatory manner; in contrast to anti-oppressive practice that involves not just how we behave, but how we think, feel and act about issues of social justice, and our value base. It requires us not just to comply with the law but to challenge unfairness and inequality even when the prac-tice is within the boundaries of the law.

RESEARCH SUMMARY

Stephen Lawrence was murdered in Eltham, South London, in 1993 while waiting for a bus. The Metropolitan Police's investigation of the crime was shown to have been in-competent and there was a racist bias against Stephen. The alleged perpetrators escaped

---

RESEARCH SUMMARY *continued*

prosecution. This led to a public inquiry that reported in 1999 (Macpherson, 1999), which resulted in the Race Relations (Amendment) Act 2000.

The legislation requires all public authorities, not just the police force, to:

- *eliminate unlawful racial discrimination;*
- *promote equal opportunities;*
- *encourage good race relations.*

The Act identified the concept of institutional racism:

> The collective failure of an organisation to provide an appropriate and professional service to people because of their colour, culture or ethnic origin. It can be seen or detected in processes, attitudes or behaviour which amount to discrimination through unwitting prejudice, ignorance, thoughtlessness and racist stereotyping which disadvantages ethnic minority people. *(Macpherson, 1999)*

The legislation applies to race but it is useful to think about its application to other areas such as gender, sexual orientation, age and disability. Begum (2006) stresses the importance of engaging with black and ethnic minority service users in the design, delivery and evaluation of services. She speaks of interlocking discrimination that includes both institutional racism and disablism. When social workers lack cultural knowledge misunderstandings can occur (Moriarty, 2008). The impact of this in safeguarding is that people feel that their needs are poorly understood, and if there are cultural and language differences this creates a barrier to being able to access support. The use of advocacy services should be considered by social workers. The role of the advocate is to represent the person's views to ensure that their voice is heard (Brandon and Brandon, 2001).

ACTIVITY **7.4**

How would you assess your organisation against the concept of institutional racism, sexism, homophobia, ageism and disablism in terms of its policies and working practices? You may find it helpful to focus on the following criteria.

1. *Your organisation's workforce is representative of the population it serves. (The staff group are diverse in terms of race, gender, sexual orientation, age, including people with sensory and physical impairments.)*

2. *You are aware of the cultural needs of the local communities and how to meet those needs.*

The development of research skills will support your practice as a social worker. The Office for National Statistics (www.statistics.gov.uk) has community profiles of every area in Britain. You can access information by region, neighbourhood, and by putting your post code into the search engine. This provides information about the local population's ethnic origin, age, health, religion, businesses, work, education, housing, crime and environment. It is possible to assess whether local services are meeting local needs, for example numbers of referrals including Adult Protection Alerts should reflect the diversity of the local population.

Brief information about different ethnic groups can be accessed through the BBC's web site (www.bbc.co.uk/news/world); this enables you to access facts about different countries and be given basic information about the languages spoken and religion with a brief history. There are additional links to other sources of information. This enables you to prepare prior to meeting with service users and carers, so you can anticipate the nature of cultural differences and put plans in place to meet them, such as taking an interpreter. Social workers should access information about the nature and impact of different health conditions. The Department of Health's (www.doh.gov.uk) web site provides information about different policies and services for the full range of health conditions. NHS Choices (www.nhs.uk) provides a medical encyclopaedia of health conditions. There are a number of national voluntary sector organisations that specialise in particular disabilities such as MENCAP, MIND, Alzheimer's Society and so on which provide extensive information, while the Social Care Institute for Excellence (www.scie.org.uk) provides a wide range of research documents and learning resources. The point is that to safeguard people effectively you need to be able to build a relationship with them, so you can make an assessment. This can prove challenging if the person does not speak English or has no verbal communication. So you need to understand their cultural needs and the impact of their disability. We will now consider empowerment as a theory and its application to safeguarding work.

Empowering practice

Empowerment is seen as both a theory and method of intervention. Its aim is to support people to increase their personal, interpersonal and political power so they can take control of their situation and their response to it (Teater, 2010). This involves supporting people to develop a more positive sense of themselves, developing knowledge and understanding about their difficulty, so they are able to implement plans and access resources to achieve change. The skills that the social worker requires when working in an empowering manner when undertaking a safeguarding role are to:

- support people to recognise that the abuse is not their fault;

- appreciate their strengths;

- support their motivation and problem solving skills;

- provide reassurance and validate the person's feelings;

- be an ally and support the person to make their own choices.

Empowerment theory focuses on the importance of hopeful and affirming language so that the social worker is working collaboratively with the person and looking for solutions together by giving the service user the time to reflect back on how difficulties were managed in the past, so these coping strategies can be used now. We earlier looked at Pritchard's (1999) research that identified the views of older people that had been abused. They were very clear what mattered to them in terms of how the abuse was investigated and the support required. We will look at a case study to see how we can implement social work practice that is informed and empowering in its outcomes.

CASE STUDY

Abdullahi is 30 years old and came to Britain 10 years ago as an asylum seeker from Somalia. He acquired a traumatic brain injury (TBI) following an accident at work three years ago. This resulted in extensive hospitalisation and rehabilitation. Abdullahi has mobility difficulties and is cognitively impaired. His main source of support is a Personal Assistant (PA) that the Somalia Community Centre has arranged which is funded by Adults' Services. The Community Centre has contacted Adults' Services as they are concerned that Abdullahi has made two new 'friends', who seem to be interested in Abdullahi's personal injury compensation money. They have discussed this with Abdullahi, but he seems ambivalent about the situation. The Centre is requesting that Adults' Services investigates the situation.

ACTIVITY 7.5

What research would it be appropriate for you to do prior to arranging to meet with Abdullahi?

COMMENT

Prior to visiting Abdullahi it would be necessary to research the impact of TBI on people's personality and behaviour. People with TBI are particularly vulnerable to abuse due to poor memory and awareness, and can behave impulsively (Mantell, 2010). The views of the Community Centre should be sought about Abdullahi's health and cultural needs.

You need to know Abdullahi's preferred language and religion. The fact that he was an asylum seeker provides important information about his experiences in Somalia. Using a strengths' perspective Abdullahi has coped with being an asylum seeker and leaving Somalia during political unrest, as well as managing to live independently with the support of a PA (Teater, 2010; Moriarty, 2008). These strengths can be built on.

Mantell (2010) has developed a good practice list when working with people with TBI where there are safeguarding issues:

- gathering specific information about the cognitive and physical impact of the TBI on the person;

- using a multi-disciplinary approach so expertise is obtained from a range of professions such as occupational therapy and clinical neuropsychology;

- safeguarding concerns are taken seriously even if the person's memory is poor, and other information is sought to confirm their disclosure;

- completing recording so that triggers and patterns of abuse can emerge;

- involving the person with TBI in decision making as much as possible;

- communicating in a manner that meets the person's needs, for example using an alphabet board, avoiding jargon and long sentences;

- observing the person's behaviour will indicate if they are troubled or feeling stressed (see Chapter 8);

- where the person has mental capacity support them in making a will, advance directive to refuse treatment, and Lasting Power of Attorney for financial matters and welfare support (see Chapter 3).

Another important point is that competent and effective social workers ensure that they check the legislative framework in which they are operating – Bray, Preston-Shoots, Cull, Johns and Roche (2005 pxix) in their Knowledge Review of the teaching of law emphasise the importance of:

> *The law gives people rights, and it gives social workers discretion, and students need to learn to be accountable for how they use this. Sound use of law can be another step on the way to getting things right for people.*

Therefore knowledge of the law should involve its use not just in terms of compelling people to co-operate or in the allocation of resources, but in enabling people to receive the services and support to which they are entitled (see Chapters 2 and 3).

Good practice in the safeguarding of adults needs to be informed by anti-oppressive practice and the effective use of the law to protect people's human rights (Chapter 2). This will enable a societal shift in public attitudes where the abuse of adults becomes visible, and there is a personal and political commitment to rid society of this social oppression. Your role as a citizen and a social worker is crucial to achieve this out-come.

CHAPTER SUMMARY

In this chapter we started by thinking about our own values and beliefs. It is essential that reflection is a continuous process and that we are prepared to be challenged and that we challenge ourselves. It is only in this way that we are able to think critically about taken-for-granted assumptions which discriminate and oppress people.

We have sought to develop our understanding through the application of research and theory, which provides us with an opportunity to clarify issues. This has been developed further through looking at the tool to audit power. The importance of knowing and using the law and policy to ensure people receive social justice has been emphasised.

Anti-discriminatory and anti-oppressive practice have been defined and we have looked at theories of empowerment and types of advocacy. What is essential for us all is to take personal responsibility for our own learning and development, and never to cease to ask questions and confront practices that dis-criminate and oppress. Safeguarding adults is a balance between protection while working in an inclu-sive and empowering manner with people that use services. It is also about joining in debates with others that seek to move society forward, and as social workers we have a role to ally ourselves with people that use services and experience the impact of discrimination on a routine basis.

FURTHER READING

Braye, S and Preston-Shoot, M (1995) *Empowering practice in social work.* Buckingham: Open University Press.
This is a helpful book as it addresses the theoretical basis as well as our personal responsibility for our continuous professional development.

Dalrymple, J and Burke, B (2006) *Anti-oppressive practice: Social care and the law.* Maidenhead: Open University Press/Mcgraw-Hill.
This book links theoretical frameworks with good practice examples, which enable the concept of empowerment to be put into practice.

Gaine, C (ed) (2010) *Equality and diversity in social work practice*. Exeter: Learning Matters.
This book is accessible and comprehensive. It supports the development of best practice for social workers in terms of addressing equality and diversity issues.

Chapter 8

Developing user-focused communication skills
Colin Goble

ACHIEVING A SOCIAL WORK DEGREE

This chapter will help you to meet the following National Occupational Standards.

Key Role 1: Prepare for, and work with, individuals, families, carers, groups and communities to assess their needs and circumstances.

Inform individuals, families, carers, groups and communities about your own, and your organisation's duties and responsibilities.

Assess and recommend an appropriate course of action for individuals, families, carers, groups and communities.

Key Role 3: Support individuals to represent their needs, views and circumstances.

Assess whether you should act as an advocate for the individual, the family, carer, group and community;

Assist individuals, families, carers, groups and communities to access independent advocacy.

Advocate for, and with, individuals, families, carers, groups and communities.

Key Role 6: Demonstrate professional competence in social work practice.

Use professional assertiveness to justify decisions and uphold professional social work practice, values and ethics.

It will also introduce you to the following academic standards as set out in the social work subject benchmark statements.

5.6 Communication skills.

5.7 Skills in working with others.

Introduction

In this chapter we will examine the importance of user-focused communication skills in working to support adults in social work and social care contexts. Good communication skills are central to the provision of high-quality support in services for adults, and are a vital component of adult protection (Whittaker, 1995; Ferris-Taylor, 2003; Cogher, 2005). An important area to highlight from the start is the current government policy agenda which demands an increased level of involvement of service users at all levels of service design, from commissioning to delivery and evaluation (DoH, 2006). The rise of this agenda is partly a legacy of a history in social care in which service users have been excluded from positions of power and influence. It is also a history littered with instances where this powerlessness has spilled over into abusive and oppressive practice; and it is certainly the case that in the increasingly diverse and competitive service context of the future the ability to demonstrate a commitment to communicating with and listening to clients in a culture of respect will become a key quality indicator (see also Chapter 10).

The vulnerability of certain groups of people to abuse is often linked to an impairment in their ability to communicate effectively, whether because of 'intrinsic' biological or psychological impairment, or because of 'extrinsic' social and cultural factors which prevent them from communicating – or those with power from listening. It may also be an important factor in helping to establish 'capacity' in decision making as discussed in Chapter 3. The protection and empowerment of service users, then, is directly related to the creation of opportunities for their voice to be heard and carry influence. The emphasis of the current policy agenda on promoting this is a direct recognition from the highest political and leadership level of the need for user-focused communication to be placed at the centre of professional consciousness and practice.

We will define, clarify and describe 'user-focused communication', with particular reference to people with severe learning difficulties who we know to be especially vulnerable to various forms of abuse, including institutional abuse, and with whom the facilitation of good communication can provide important safeguards. The basic premise we are working to here is that if we can get it right for this client group, then we are likely to have knowledge and skills that will also be of equal value in working with other client groups, such as older people, people with mental health problems, and people with brain injury and neurological disorders. We will demonstrate that there is a direct relationship between communication issues and professional consciousness and practice, and that this relationship has important implications for the protection of adult at risk. We will begin by defining communication and attempting to identify some of the reasons why it is such a central issue in social care.

The importance of communication

Communication has been defined in its simplest form as:

> *a two-way process, involving the sending and receiving of a message.*

(Ferris-Taylor, 2003, p256)

The functions of communication in human beings are considerably more complex, however. Crystal (1992) reminds us that these functions include the exchange of ideas and information, the expression of emotion, social and cultural interaction, the control of reality, the ability to record facts and thoughts, and the expression of identity. Communication in humans is also 'multi-modal', involving gesture, facial expression, bodily posture and distancing, and eye contact, as well as the verbal and linguistic dimensions that we tend to focus on. Even the verbal dimension is a good deal more complex than we often recognise as we go about our day-to-day lives, involving the control and manipulation of tone and volume to add emphasis, for instance, to say nothing of the elaborate cognitive processing which constantly occurs to both produce and interpret spoken and written language.

It is difficult, therefore, to overestimate the importance of communication to human existence. Human beings have been designed by evolutionary processes to be 'social animals', and communication is a fundamental means by which we construct and manage our sense of self and our relationships with others, whether it be in family, work, leisure, or any other context. This importance is well captured by Crossley and MacDonald (1982, cited by Ferris-Taylor, 2003, p284) when they say:

> *Communication falls into the same category as food, drink and shelter. It is essential for life. Without it life is meaningless.*

ACTIVITY *8.1*

Think about yourself and the story of your life and identity. How it is that you have come to be known and identified as who you are. What are the most important aspects of 'you-ness'?

- *You might think, for example, about your names, how you acquired them, whom they connect you with, and how they define your sense of self.*

- *You might also think about your social, national, and ethnic identities, and how your story connects with others – the history and ongoing stories of your family, society, religion, and so on.*

- *You might also think about key ways in which you identify yourself – as a 'social worker' or 'social care worker' for instance – and what this means for your identity, sense of self-worth and self-esteem.*

- *Now think about how important to yourself it is to be able to communicate these ideas in the ongoing story of your life.*

COMMENT

Communication is tied up then with much more than merely getting our message across. It is central to our sense of who we are, how we feel about ourselves, and how we relate to the wider world. An impairment of communication is likely to have an impact on all of these things, exposing the affected individual to high risks of social exclusion, impaired psychological development and functioning, and damage to health and well-being. It is important to recognise, however, that impairments in communication may arise not just because of biological factors internal to individuals. Although human beings are from infancy biologically programmed to be communicative, the complexities of communication and language use have a major learned component, and for this learning to occur an individual needs exposure to, and involvement in, the rich communicative milieu of human society. Factors that prevent or impair this involvement can be equally, if not more, important in impairing communicative ability. So let us now consider why communication may come to be impaired in some individuals.

Causes of impaired communication

There are many factors that can work to impair an individual's ability to communicate effectively, and while there may be a single dominant factor, a mix of factors are usually at work in most instances. A useful distinction to make is between 'intrinsic' and 'extrinsic' factors. Intrinsic factors are those which are internal to the individual, and usually have a biological cause, while extrinsic factors are those which are external to the individual, and may have social, cultural and even economic and political causes. There is often an interaction between these factors too, with the beliefs and attitudes of social care workers and professionals relating to their understanding of intrinsic factors creating the context in which extrinsic factors become significant. We will return to this shortly, but first we will outline the most significant categories of intrinsic factors.

Intrinsic factors

The commonest intrinsic cause of communication impairment is impairment of intellectual functioning across a variety of disorders. These fall into the different categories, such as 'learning difficulties', 'brain injury', 'neurological disorders' and 'mental illness'. It is these that we shall look at first.

Intellectual impairment

Abnormal neurological functioning, and the intellectual impairment associated with it, is the most common cause underlying severe communication impairment. These impairments arise either from damage to, or abnormal development of, the structures of the brain itself and its functioning. This may arise from a wide variety of causes, such as brain injury resulting from a road traffic accident or stroke, or from genetic or metabolic abnormalities affecting foetal or childhood development; including many of the conditions associated with learning difficulties, such as Down's syndrome, autistic spectrum disorder and the so-called 'x-linked abnormalities' for example (Watson, 2003).

In some of these conditions there may be typical patterns of communicative impairment that can be identified. For instance, people with autistic spectrum disorders typically experience a significant degree of difficulty interpreting other people's non-verbal communication – so-called 'mind-reading' behaviours. As a result they have difficulty picking up or interpreting the emotive and non-verbal, expressive qualities of other people's communication, and are thus 'blinded' to the subtleties of communication and interaction that give it richness and meaning. The severity of this impairment can range from a total disconnection from the world (often associated with severe intellectual impairment – although perhaps with isolated areas of high ability in, say, art, music or arithmetic), to a relatively mild 'social awkwardness' (sometimes associated with a very high level of intellectual functioning and competence) in which the individual may come across as merely eccentric, or idiosyncratic in their manner (Anderson, 2003). The uniformities in the nature of the impairment experienced by people with autistic spectrum disorders strongly suggest that they arise because of a dysfunction in particular areas and structures of the brain – the amygdala for instance – although the severity of the impairment will vary dependent on the extent or degree of abnormality (O'Connell, 1998).

It is important to recognise that, whatever the underlying cause, the effect on an individual's communication of a condition affecting brain function will relate to the part of the brain that has been affected. The neurological basis of communication is highly complex, with some areas of the brain controlling the complex physiological processes involved in the production of speech, while other areas control grammatical organisation of speech production, and still others the interpretation of incoming speech. The result is that there are a wide variety of ways in which communication may be affected. For example, it is quite possible for there to be damage to brain structures which prevent an individual from being able to speak at all, while their ability to understand may be quite intact. Likewise, a person may appear to be able to produce speech of a highly lucid nature, but will produce it in a way that is random, repetitive, or unrelated to what is being said to them. Both Ferris-Taylor (2003) and Cogher (2005) give useful outlines of the nature and variety of communicative impairments which may arise in people with learning difficulties; and a similar principle underlies neurological damage impacting on individuals affected by brain injury, stroke, or degenerative conditions such as Alzheimer's disease – the nature of the communicative impairment will be determined by the area/s of the brain affected. The main difference between these 'groups' and people with learning difficulties in terms of communication is that, unless they are themselves affected by a learning difficulty, most of these individuals will usually have experienced normal development and functioning of communication before they sustained neurological damage. As a result there may be residual and learned abilities present which can be drawn upon, relearned, or rerouted via new neurological pathways via rehabilitation programmes.

The impact of an intellectual impairment on early and childhood language and communicative development cannot be overestimated. We have already identified that human beings are biologically programmed to communicate, and that this programming is the basis for the 'learned' elements of communication, including language itself, as well as 'non-verbal' cues, such as eye contact, posture, gesture and timing. Indeed, much of this non-verbal aspect of communication precedes, and is the backdrop to, the development of spoken language, instilling an elaborate socio-cultural framework of acceptable and unacceptable communicative behaviours – the 'social graces' – the learning and mastery of which are a major factor in enhancing communication and accessing social networks and the benefits that flow from them. Much of this learning takes place in the close and intimate interaction between carers (usually mothers) and infants. One impact of an intellectual impairment can be to disrupt this interaction. For example, it has been demonstrated that infants with Down's syndrome are typically less alert and slower at responding to communicative cues, such as smiling, or verbalisations from their mothers/carers, than non-intellectually impaired infants. This disruption of the natural pacing of interactive cues can lead to a reduction in communicative behaviours from mothers/carers, and thus a reduction in the learning opportunities for the infant, setting up an impoverished communicative cycle (Ferris-Taylor, 2003). The importance of knowing this is that, if mothers/carers are made aware and encouraged to increase, or exaggerate, communicative cues, and lengthen the time they wait for a response, then a positive and mutually rewarding communicative cycle can be created.

Similarly, we have already noted the difficulty that people with autistic spectrum disorders experience in understanding the communicative behaviours of others. One typical result of this difficulty is disruption of normal patterns of eye contact – a very powerful element in communicative behaviour. Too little eye contact makes a person feel they are not being listened or attended to, and will result in communication breaking down. Too much eye contact, on the other hand, can easily lead a person to feel intimidated or uncomfortable. Intense eye contact is strongly associated with aggression, or a desire to mate, and applying it wrongly can lead to very awkward consequences. Again, a knowledge of this can be used to create teaching and learning opportunities for people with autistic spectrum disorders that can help them to develop valued communication skills and behaviours, and thus improve their ability to interact socially.

Another group of impairments that could also be placed under this category would be those that relate to serious affective and/or psychotic illnesses, such as bipolar depressive illness or schizophrenia, although the impairment here might not be related to communicative faculties so much as perceptual and emotive processes. The end result, however, is a form of communication that, though it might be highly lucid, and even florid, is so detached from reality that the person is at very high risk of isolation and social exclusion. In psychotic illness treatments tend to focus on bringing abnormal perceptions – e.g. hallucinations – under control, primarily using medication. In affective disorders, such as depression, treatment may well focus more on communication, or 'talk-based' approaches, used in combination with drugs and behavioural techniques, such as cognitive behaviour therapy. These approaches aim to help the person to learn to recognise the things or situations that cause them to become anxious or depressed, and to develop ways to prevent them from initiating debilitating thoughts and behaviours.

Sensory impairment

What has been said earlier about the early learning of communication and language can also be applied to understanding the impact of sensory impairments. It has been shown, for example, that very young babies are visually attuned to the faces of carers, and, far from being passive in their communication, actually initiate communication from carers by imitating their behaviours, establishing a mutually reinforcing 'communicative loop' in the process (O'Connell, 1998). Mutual communicative eye contact is established and developed between mothers and babies during suckling, for instance, and the prompts and cues used by mothers to continue feeding are the earliest lessons an infant receives in the important communicative art of 'turn-taking'. If we understand this, then we can see that the presence of a visual impairment in the infant can potentially disrupt this eye-contact-driven communicative transaction. In fact, disruption of this communicative interaction can become as important a factor in the impairment of communication as any underlying neurological abnormalities, and where the two are combined, as they often are in individuals with severe and profound learning difficulties, then the effect, if mitigating measures are not put in place, can be one in which the child experiences severe communicative deprivation as they develop. In worst-case scenarios such deprivation can lead to the development of highly disturbed and distressing self-injurious behaviours that can be extremely difficult to address later in life. Not surprisingly, the presence of a visual impairment, combined with a learning difficulty, has been identified as a major risk factor in the development of severe challenging behaviours (Nind and Hewitt, 2001).

Similarly, hearing impairments can have a disruptive effect on the transactional aspect of learned communication. As with visual impairment, there is a high prevalence of hearing impairment among people with learning difficulties, increasing with more severe to profound levels of learning difficulty. And, as with visual impairment, the presence of a hearing impairment requires that carers need to take a major responsibility for ensuring that an affected individual is given maximal opportunities, both to learn to communicate and to be given continuing opportunities to communicate meaningfully throughout their lifespan. This may well include the opportunity to learn forms of communication, such as British Sign Language, or Makaton, other than spoken English. The deaf community have long made the point that sign language is more than just a substitute for speech for people with hearing impairments, but is a whole empowering and liberating linguistic milieu in itself! It is how we go about providing these opportunities that we will now go on to look at as we consider 'extrinsic' causes of communication problems.

Extrinsic factors

By extrinsic factors, we mean those factors in the external environment that may inhibit communication. Many of the intrinsic factors that we have identified are things about which, currently at least, it is possible to do very little. We cannot 'cure' autistic spectrum disorder or congenital deafness, for example. If that was where we left it, then the outlook would be very pessimistic indeed, with care involving little more than keeping people fed, entertained and comfortable; and, indeed, that is precisely what many services for these groups of people looked like for a long time. For much of the twentieth century many people with learning difficulties, for example, were warehoused in large isolated 'hospitals' on the basis of biomedical diagnoses. They were tended by nurses and overseen by doctors working to the rationale that they were suffering from incurable conditions, or pathologies, that required hospital-based care. A major effect of this was that attempts by people living in those institutions to communicate their needs, desires and wishes, were either ignored or belittled, coming as they did from a 'diseased mind' (Ryan with Thomas, 1987). Even worse, if this communication was 'behavioural' rather than verbal, and particularly if it involved actions perceived as aggressive or 'disturbed', then it frequently led to further 'pathologisation', under such terms as 'problem behaviour', or even 'psychosis', and was responded to with powerful psychoactive medications or behaviour-modification programmes – with little or no focus on attempting to improve people's quality of life (Goble, 2000). This in turn exposed people to the negative and isolating effects of prejudice and stigmatisation, and the experience of further exclusion and marginalisation from mainstream society (see Chapter 8). This institutional abuse exposed them to psychological harm, abuse and neglect and an increased risk of sexual and physical abuse, allowing abusers to work in the shadows – preying on people who either could not report the abuse, did not fully understand they were being abused, or were not believed or listened to when they could.

Arguably the most important extrinsic factor we can identify then is the perceptions and understanding of people with communication impairments held by professionals, staff and carers, and wider society. The practice of the caring professions has traditionally been 'expert led', based on a consciousness that placed people in the role of passive recipients of services. This often deprived service users of control and influence over what happened to them, at the same time holding their lives up for scrutiny as they were reduced to the status of 'cases'. One effect of this was to restrict the opportunity for service users to communicate about, and define, goals and outcomes meaningful to them. This approach still often persists where the location of the client's problem is the mind/brain, and is associated with communication impairment. The mind/brain is seen in Western culture as the seat of the autonomous self, personal individuality and rationality. To have an impairment of the mind/brain then is equated with losing all, or a critical part, of the self and the autonomy and independence that goes with it. Consequently people with learning difficulties and other forms of intellectual impairment are still often viewed as unable to accurately communicate about their own lives.

This kind of perception, when held by service staff and professionals, is the source of much 'institutional abuse'; a much more common form of abuse than random acts of criminality or violence. Institutional abuse can have a serious and negative effect on service users in a variety of ways. For example, on a day-to-day basis, the experience of not being listened to, or not being given the time or opportunity to communicate your needs, desires and wishes, can have seriously disabling effects. These can include long-term psychological harm as people's self-esteem is damaged, leading people to become vulnerable to depression and anxiety, and a variety of 'challenging behaviours' ranging from extreme withdrawal and passivity, or 'learned helplessness', to self-abusive and aggressive behaviours as they vent pent-up frustration and anger on themselves and others (Doyle, 2004). The negative effects on health can also be significant, as we can see below.

RESEARCH SUMMARY

The relationship between poor health and communication is extremely important for people who use social care services. People with learning difficulties continue to suffer from a much higher incidence of health problems than most other sections of the population. Some of the reasons for this include the impact of intrinsic factors such as those we looked at above. Research has shown, however, that health problems are often more general in nature, and unrelated to the cause of intellectual impairment itself, but frequently go unreported or undetected. For example, avoidable problems with teeth, feet,

RESEARCH SUMMARY *continued*

hair, diet, weight and continence have all been found to be widespread. Among the main reasons for this under-reporting and poor detection are problems with communication. Where an individual with intellectual impairment has poor, or even no, verbal communication they are reliant on care staff to pick up communicative behaviours that indicate health problems, or a change in health status. For this to happen care staff need to know the person well, and be sensitive to idiosyncratic modes of communication. All too often, it appears, this fails to happen, and a major factor underlying this failure tends to be a continuing tendency to 'pathologise' disability in general, and intellectual impairments, such as learning difficulties, in particular. Poor physical and mental health in service users is too often seen to be 'part of the condition' with the effect that actual health problems and issues faced by people go unrecognised and unmet (Greenhaulgh, 1994; Hart, 2003; and Gibson and O'Connor, 2010).

CASE STUDY

Dave is 51 years old and lives in a residential group home for five people with learning difficulties run by a voluntary sector agency. Until he was 35 he lived in a 30-bedded, all-male villa at a large mental hospital which had a high incidence of bullying and aggressive behaviour among the staff and residents. He had lived there since he was two years old.

Dave cannot speak, but can understand quite complex language very well. He is very able physically, and is quite fit and lean for a man of his age. However, he is very passive, standing around waiting until given instructions to do something by care staff – such as get dressed, have a shower, set the table for meals, most of which he can do very competently with minimal help. When not engaged in an activity such as this he spends his time in a favourite chair in the living room, gently rocking to and fro, repeatedly regurgitating, re-chewing and re-swallowing his last meal. The only time he will move without instruction is if there is loud noise, or shouting. Then he will stand up, retreat behind the chair and remain there until he is instructed to sit down again by a member of staff.

Dave is popular with the staff team as he is 'no trouble' and can be left for long periods while they can 'get on with other things that need doing', although there is also widespread distaste at his 'regurgitation' habit. The team leader is concerned that Dave is doing very little with his life despite being quite fit and able, and there are also concerns about his dental health as the constant regurgitation is having a bad effect on his teeth and gums.

ACTIVITY 8.2

What do you think Dave's behaviour is communicating in this situation?
Is he at risk from any form of abuse?
What communication strategies could help improve Dave's situation?

COMMENT

Given that Dave has no verbal communication we are largely reliant on interpreting Dave's behaviour and information as it has been recorded by staff in the past to understand his current situation. Dave's behaviour strongly suggests that he has learned to 'lie low' in order to avoid trouble, and to take evasive action if there is a hint of violence or aggression in the vicinity. Also, rocking and regurgitation are classic forms of self-stimulatory behaviour, often found in people who have lived for long periods in institutional environments with very little external stimulation. Despite Dave's lack of speech then, it is possible to glean quite a lot of important information from his current behaviour. If this is also backed up by detailed, accurate and respectfully written records then we have quite a lot of information to go on. Sadly this is not always the case. The files of many people who have spent long periods of their lives in large institutions tend to focus on largely negative information, and are effectively a record of disasters and problems.

In this case we can see that Dave has lived a life that has been, and is still, arguably, subject to institutional abuse. Dave's behaviour has been shaped by a mixture of neglect, self-preservation and self-stimulation. His passivity, which makes him popular with staff, is, in fact, learned helplessness. Despite his being physically able and demonstrating a good level of cognitive ability, the staff team are quite happy to let Dave stay within his very limited 'lifestyle' because it makes very few demands upon them and their time – he is 'a good client'.

Strategies to bring about positive change in Dave's life revolve around issues of communication. The team leader here will need first to communicate to the staff team that the current situation is no longer tolerable – Dave's life is effectively being wasted, and change will involve them becoming centred on Dave's needs, rather than their own. One strategy that can be used to good effect is to get key members of staff to map out Dave's life story up to this point, presenting it to the rest of the team, and using it as a basis for discussion and planning change. The use of life story work, of which 'lifemapping' is a form, can be a very powerful way of getting a staff team to understand the current behaviour of a person they work with in the context of their whole life story (rather than a depersonalised 'case history'). This helps to focus attention on the individual, personalising their situation, and developing a deepened sense of 'solidarity' with them – see for example Goble (2000) and Gray and Ridden (1999).

Building from this basis, the team's work could then focus on introducing Dave to various activities – given his physical ability, walking, cooking, shopping and even dancing are all possibilities – building up a profile of his likes and dislikes, and monitoring the impact on his behaviour, health and well-being. Although Dave may show some reluctance initially – remember this level of activity and interaction with other people will be a major life change for him – positive change is likely to occur quite quickly. This in turn is likely to reinforce the staff involved and communicate to Dave that contact with other people can be rewarding rather than a problem – creating what the American psychiatrist John McGee has described as 'a psychology of interdependence' (McGee, 1990).

Other important strategies will also involve the ongoing recording and handing over of important information about Dave, emphasising positive, rather than negative events and developments; and, last but not least, exploring the use of a sign language system – such as Makaton – to enable Dave to communicate his needs more effectively. This will necessarily involve training the staff team to use this system too, thus raising everyone's communicative competence.

Strategies for improving user-focused communication

This case study illustrates that one of the main differences when considering extrinsic factors affecting communication is that these are often things we can do something about. If many of the intrinsic factors related to communication impairment are beyond our ability to influence, then many of the extrinsic factors certainly are not. In particular, we can manipulate the environment within which care and support are delivered in order to ensure that user-focused communication is given maximum priority, and that our practice becomes empowering as a result.

ACTIVITY 8.3

Think about a service where you work or are on placement, and the factors that affect communication with service users there. What strategies could be used to improve that communication and make it more 'service-user focused'?

- You might also think about staff behaviour – particularly their communicative competence.

- You might also think about how the environment and environmental cues could be altered to improve communication.

- Finally, you might also think about the way the service itself is organised and functions – in particular, is there a strong commitment to include service users in all aspects of the organisation's functioning?

COMMENT

Let us look then at these three areas and how they can be used as strategies to improve communication. Firstly, we need to turn them from observations about a service into strategic statements that identify what action should follow. They would then become something like:

- train staff to understand the communicative needs of service users and develop communicative competence;

- assess and organise the physical environment to facilitate communication;

- create a 'collaborative culture' in the service's organisation and functioning.

Understanding service-user communication needs and developing competence

User-focused communication can only be facilitated by staff who are competent to do so. This means developing the knowledge and skills required to communicate effectively with service users and their carers or advocates, and it therefore means that understanding their communication needs is of paramount importance. The key to understanding the communicative needs of service users is to understand the impact of the impairment they experience and the way this relates to their communication. For an obvious example, if a person has a hearing impairment, then it is important that communication with them emphasises visual cues and signals. This means that it is important to ensure that a person can see and understand these cues. It may also mean that carers may have to prioritise learning sign-based forms of communication, such as British Sign Language (BSL) or Makaton; especially if a service user is, or may be taught to become, proficient in their use. Few things are more frustrating for a service user who is able to communicate perfectly well via a signing system only to have staff who lack the competence to use it. The same thing holds for people who use augmentative communication systems such as symbol-based systems like 'pic-syms', or computer-based voice systems.

Other forms of impairment are perhaps more difficult to understand, but it is no less important to try to do so. For example, people with autistic spectrum disorders often have a very literal understanding of language, combined with high levels of anxiety. One man that I worked with became very anxious if you told him that he needed to go out – unless you also added that he would be coming home again later. A service user affected by cerebral palsy may require longer to give a full and thorough answer to a question or request, and giving them time to do so is an important part, not just of communicating fully, but also of showing respect for them as an individual. This is a significant point. In understanding the impact of an impairment on communication it is important to recognise that, although there may be common features associated with certain 'conditions', it is good practice to focus on the individual rather than the condition. A 'person-centred approach' to communication will help to focus attention on ensuring that care and support are responsive to the needs of the individual, informed, but not driven, by 'expert knowledge' about 'conditions' and 'syndromes'.

As we saw above with Dave, the understanding and competence of staff are nowhere more important than in working with people who are unable to communicate verbally, or via some form of recognised language system. Working with service users in this situation requires particular attention to behavioural cues as forms of communication. For example, subtle changes in the behaviour of a person with a severe or profound learning difficulty, such as sleeping longer than usual, eating less than usual, showing signs of discomfort and agitation, or pleasure and enjoyment, can all be important communicative cues for carers. Particularly important here are the recording and accurate handover of information (both written and verbal) between carers and service agencies – say between a residential and a day service. The onus of communication falls more and more on carers the more the use of formal language is limited in the service user themselves. The knowledge and expertise of parents, relatives and others who know the individual well is a particularly important resource in this instance, and should be drawn upon as much as possible to inform care and support systems and practice. The use of 'likes/dislikes' profiles can be used to help create a means by which even people with the most profound communication impairments can express their preferences, make choices and be included in evaluating services.

Developing our understanding of service users and using that to develop our own communicative competence should be a top priority then. It is important, however, that we take every opportunity also to manipulate the physical environment to enhance communication as well.

Finally, it is vital that staff working with service users who have communication impairments are well trained and aware of adult protection issues, and that this is incorporated into the service's conception of professional communicative competence. For example, staff must be aware of behavioural changes and cues that may be associated with abuse. The sudden onset of depression, withdrawal from social contact, self-injury and distress at being touched are potential signs that abuse is, or has been, occurring. Though there may be other reasons for these things, a service context where workers are tuned into such cues will at least lead to them being considered, if only to be eliminated after further examination. It is also worth stating that such a time of crisis is not the time for staff to be struggling to develop their communication skills with service users! Rather, this competence needs to be in place and embedded in practice from the start.

Assessing and organising the physical environment to facilitate communication

The manipulation of the physical environment is often underestimated as a means of enhancing communication. Wherever care and support are delivered it should be considered, however. A useful starting point is to think about what could be done to the environment over which you have influence to 'enable' service users to communicate, or be communicated with, more effectively. Crossing a busy road alone for someone with a visual impairment would be almost suicidal, for example – until you build safe, well-marked places to cross, with lowered pavement edges, altered pavement surfaces to signal the edge of the pavement, and an audio signal to tell you when it is safe to cross. Add a visual, pictorial signal and you have also helped enhance communication for people with hearing and intellectual impairments. Pelican crossings are good examples of an enabling manipulation of the environment, incorporating communicative cues. They also provide clues as to what we might be looking to manipulate in other environments. For example, visual symbols, placed at strategic places on and around buildings where services are delivered, can be used to help people with hearing or intellectual impairments orientate their way independently. Similarly, textual cues, such as changes of wallpaper texture, and the installation of dado rails can be used to help people with visual impairments orientate.

Similar means can be used to communicate staff identities and roles to service users. Picture boards of staff can be used to help communicate to service users who is available and when, and to help service users to communicate who they wish to help or support them, for example. For people with visual impairments staff can use tactile signs, such as particular pendants, or textured badges to make themselves identifiable.

Use of 'multi-modal' forms of communication, such as audio, video/dvd and computer technology should also be developed. Many public and legal services provide information in various formats, and the widespread availability of communication technology means that there is very little excuse for not making maximum and imaginative use of it. The key is to think creatively, and to seek the views of the real 'experts' – service users themselves – by contacting local service user groups, for example, or independent living associations, to act as consultants on communication issues. This last point illustrates that the promotion of service user-focused communication will only happen if there is a commitment within a service to create a collaborative culture in which the necessary resources and skills are developed. We will now look further at what this involves.

RESEARCH SUMMARY

Creating a collaborative culture

Beresford and Trevillion (1995) conducted research that emphasised the importance of creating a 'collaborative culture' in care and support services, at the core of which lie communication skills that help to develop trust and good relationships between professionals, staff and different agencies, service users themselves, and their families, relatives and other carers. In particular, they place 'commitment to the involvement of service users' at the centre of their strategy for creating a collaborative culture and practice, and identify a number of key components to achieving this, such as:

- *allowing space and time for involvement, at whatever level the service user is able or willing to be involved;*

- *a commitment to including the service user, their advocate or representative in decision-making at all levels, including important life choices;*

- *avoidance of the use of professional jargon and keeping technical language in its appropriate context;*

- *a commitment to not sacrifice service user interests to inter-professional power play or disputes, and to be led by the needs of the service user.*

Among the most important communication skills required to promote a collaborative culture are the following.

- *Assertiveness skills The ability to be able to assert your own point of view or perspective in a way that is perceived by others as confident, rather than arrogant and/or aggressive. The key to an appropriate, assertive style of working is the development of self-awareness, focusing on awareness of body posture, use of appropriate language and the ability to listen actively, taking in the views and perspectives of others. It also involves knowing your limits – being confident enough to say 'I don't know', avoiding the use of jargon and technical/professional language wherever possible, using an explanatory communication style, and staying focused on finding solutions.*

- *Advocacy skills* Advocacy is a key part of the caring/support role, but needs to be approached with caution. It is important to recognise the potential for conflict between the role of 'advocate' and the role of 'professional'. A 'professional' is also, inevitably, a representative of the organisation they work for, and of the profession (social work, for instance) itself. These are 'interests' that can potentially conflict with the needs and desires of service users. The first stage of planning an advocacy intervention therefore is to ask the question 'am I the right person to do it?' A 'user-centred' focus may require us to accept that our client's interests are better served by an advocate who is independent of organisational and professional interests that may constrain us. As a rule, professional advocacy is probably best restricted to 'service level' advocacy – that is, advocating for access to the skills and expertise of other professionals within or across different services. This obviously requires knowledge about other professional roles, referral systems, finance issues, and of one's own position within the service context. This, combined with an informed and up-to-date knowledge of treatments, interventions and services which may help service users to meet their assessed needs, will form the basis of your 'case'. Key skills here will include preparation and presentation of this case to the appropriate forum. For a fuller discussion of advocacy see Chapter 3.

- *Negotiation skills* Work in social care tends to revolve around negotiating who will do what, how, by when, and who will pay for it. This involves the ability to recognise potential points of conflict, heading them off wherever possible, and resolving them effectively where conflict does arise. It is particularly important to avoid entering into negotiation with the idea that one party will 'win' and the other will 'lose'. Instead, a problem-solving approach needs to be used, with everyone focused on meeting the needs of the individual service user in the most satisfactory way possible. The skills relating to both assertiveness and advocacy referred to above may come into play here, but negotiation processes will be made a great deal easier if there is a good level of trust and mutual respect to begin with. Time spent establishing good lines of communication outside of the negotiation context, and building a good rapport – by visiting, introducing oneself, outlining your own role and perspective, and establishing a 'common cause' by emphasising your commitment to a user-focused approach – will be well spent.

- *Acting and working in a business-like manner* All of the above will be greatly helped if your own approach is grounded in behaviours associated with 'professionalism'. Behaviours which demonstrate reliability, punctuality and willing participation in operational processes of delegation and workload division will all contribute to demonstrating your commitment to making service user-focused collaboration work (see also Chapter 11).

- *Encouraging information sharing* Control of information and its dissemination is one of the ways in which professions have sometimes engaged in practices of 'isolationism' and 'tribalism'. The development of a collaborative culture requires a commitment to ensure that the correct information is shared at the right time and in the right format among the

RESEARCH SUMMARY *continued*

people who need to know in order that the best outcomes can be achieved for the service user. The need to protect sensitive information in line with legal and ethical requirements is vital, as also is the need to pass on and share information that may relate to protection of the service user. The importance of sharing information about injury, changes of behaviour and mental state (particularly when sudden) and/or signs of service user distress, cannot be overstated (see Chapter 12 where serious case reviews are discussed).

- **Constructive advice, supervision and mentoring** *Working in social care can be complex and demanding, and good support, supervision and governance systems are important to make it work successfully. The skills of advising, supervising and mentoring staff and other team members, sometimes from other professions and even from other organisations, are increasingly important. It is also important, however, to ensure that you receive good supervision and mentoring support – particularly if you are to remain reflective about your own practice. Joint and collaborative forums for inter-professional discussion and reflection are a useful way of sharing information and knowledge about each other's perspectives, skills and practice, and an opportunity to develop a sense of shared commitment to user-focused methods and approaches to meeting client needs (see also Chapter 10).*

CHAPTER SUMMARY

Service user-focused communication is central to the whole process of delivering user-led and person-centred care and support, and a key part of the adult protection and 'safeguarding adults' agenda. In particular it will:

- help to create environments in which service users' voices and behavioural communication are heard, respected and responded to;
- increase the likelihood that service users will be able to communicate about any forms of abuse they do experience;
- increase the confidence of everyone that service users' concerns will be taken seriously and remain at the centre of any investigations and care planning that arise from them.

It is also a vital part of the strategy to empower service users to take greater control over the care and support services they receive.

Summary of pointers for good practice

- Seek to understand the impact of an impairment – the intrinsic factors – that may affect the communication of a service user, always maintaining a 'person-centred' approach to the communication needs of individuals.
- Seek to understand the environmental issues – the extrinsic factors – that may affect the communication of a service user, always looking for ways in which the environment can be manipulated to improve communication.
- Develop your own communicative competencies, and those of your colleagues, in order to improve communication with service users, including developing skills in the use of augmentative and signing systems, and creative use of information technology and an awareness of the importance of behavioural cues as communication.
- Work towards a collaborative culture by creating commitment, time and space for service user involvement and communication, avoiding the use of jargon and technical language wherever possible, and keeping the interests of service users paramount in professional and organisational functioning.

Grant, G, Goward, P, Richardson, M and Ramcharan, P (eds) (2005) *Learning disability: A life cycle approach to valuing people*. Maidenhead: Open University Press/McGraw Hill.
The chapter by Cogher on communication is referred to in this chapter, but the whole book is itself an example of the promotion of a 'collaborative culture', with the voices of people with learning disabilities given emphasis.

Beresford, P and Trevillion, S (1995) *Developing skills for community care: A collaborative approach*. London: Arena.
Also referred to in this chapter, this is a very readable research-based overview of the entire area – and is written by service users.

PART 3
EFFECTIVE PRACTICE

Chapter 9

Organisational cultures and the management of change
Terry Scragg

A C H I E V I N G   A   S O C I A L   W O R K   D E G R E E

This chapter will help you to meet the following National Occupational Standards.

Key Role 2: Plan, carry out, review and evaluate social work practice with individuals, families, carers, groups, communities and other professionals.

- Unit 9: Address behaviour which presents a risk to individuals, families, carers, groups and communities.

Key Role 3: Support individuals to represent their needs, views and circumstances.

- Unit 10: Advocate with, and on behalf of, individuals, families, carers, groups and communities.
- Unit 11: Prepare for, and participate in, decision-making forums.

Key Role 4: Manage risk to individuals, families, carers, groups, communities and colleagues.

- Unit 12: Assess and manage risks to individuals, families, carers, groups and communities.

General Social Care Code of Practice

Code 1: Protect the rights and promote the interests of service users and carers.

- Respecting and where appropriate promoting individual views and wishes.
- Supporting service users' rights to control their lives and make informed choices about the services they receive.

Code 3: Promote independence of service users while protecting them as far as possible from harm.

- Bringing to the attention of your employer or the appropriate authority resource or operational difficulties that might get in the way of the delivery of safe care.

It will also introduce you to the following academic standards set out in the social work subject benchmark statements.

5.1.2 The service delivery context.

4.3 Defining principles.

5.1.4 Social work theory.

5.6 Communication skills.

5.7 Skills in working with others.

Introduction

It is not uncommon, following revelation of abuse in services, to hear a plea that there must be *an entire culture change in the way people are treated*. In spite of such pleas, often little appears to change. Understanding why culture change can be a complex and challenging process is the focus of this chapter. It will introduce you to the concept of culture in organisations and its impact on the way that services are provided, and the risks to service users and others when cultures develop which fail to ensure that people are protected from abuse. Organisational culture is a complex and contested area of organisational theory, but one which is important to understand if you are to work effectively in services where the potential for the abuse of vulnerable people is ever present. The first part of the chapter describes what is meant by organisational culture and how it impacts on organisations. The second part explores the influence of culture on organisations, drawing on some recent examples of institutional abuse that have been investigated and reported publicly. From this we can learn lessons from the poor management and practices in services that created the conditions where abuse occurred. The third part examines some of the processes of change when organisations need to ensure that practices safeguard service users and staff through the introduction of new working practices.

What are organisational cultures?

One of the problems in discussing organisational culture is that it can be difficult to define or explain precisely, and consequently difficult to change. Staff working in a service may not be consciously aware of the culture of their service, even though it has a pervasive influence over their behaviour and actions. Culture is formed from a collection of traditions, values, policies, beliefs and attitudes that prevail throughout an organisation (Pettinger, 2000). It is best described as the deeply set beliefs held by staff about the way they work, how work should be organised and how staff are controlled and rewarded within a particular organisation, which a number of people consistently share about the service, and is often described more simply as 'the way we do things around here'. It encompasses the climate and atmosphere surrounding an organisation and the prevailing attitudes within it, including standards, morale and general attitudes. Harrison and Stokes (1992) go further and describe culture as those aspects of an organisation that give it a particular climate or feel, and that it is to an organisation what personality is to an individual, and helps distinguish one organisation from another. From these descriptions we can see that cultures can be a powerful source of influence and control in organisations. This helps us to understand why poor quality services often fail to modernise their practices, even when new policy initiatives, research findings and models of good practice are helping reshape other services, and why they may be ignored in the face of overwhelming evidence.

A central issue in studies of organisational culture is whether it can be 'managed', and is therefore susceptible to change as a result of management intervention. Some researchers believe that organisations *are* cultures, and therefore less susceptible to change. Others believe that organisations *have* cultures, and that the manifestations of culture are socially constructed, and therefore amenable to change (Ogbonna, 1993). It is also suggested that organisations are made up of a number of subcultures, whereas other researchers see organisations having a dominant culture (Johnson and Scholes, 1992). Whichever viewpoint we adopt, it is clear from research that changing a culture can be a long and potentially difficult process. Much will depend on the strength of the culture, the degree to which the organisation is threatened by external forces (for example, a damning report on the standards of service-providing by external regulators), and the extent of change required if the organisation is to improve its practices significantly.

On the other hand, if problems are identified by managers, staff or other stakeholders, and the need for change is clearly apparent, and providing those attempting to change the organisation have sufficient power and influence (for example, a newly appointed director or chief executive, respected leaders, managers or practitioners), and they can convince sufficient staff of the value of making changes, it is likely to be successful. This means that a programme of change can be put in place before the organisation is forced to change as a result of external pressures, with managers and staff recognising that the service is no longer providing appropriate provision and proactively introducing changes to improve the service, based on an awareness of wider service developments nationally.

ACTIVITY 9.1

In order to help you begin to understand that all organisations have their own unique culture, reflect on your experience of two different organisations where you have worked or you know well. To help you make sense of the complex world of culture we will use a model of culture developed by Schein (2004) which identifies three layers of culture that you will find helpful when analysing different organisations.

- *Outer or surface layer which comprises artefacts and products, for example buildings, symbols, systems and structures that can be easily observed.*
- *Middle layer which encompasses the norms and values of the service that are demonstrated through attitudes and behaviours, statements made in documents, and by influential people, office layouts, dress codes and so on.*
- *Inner layer which comprises the basic assumptions commonly held by a workgroup which Schein refers to as the essence of culture, which are more difficult to access and only uncovered through in-depth studies of organisations.*

Using Schein's three layers as a starting point, are you able to identify different aspects of culture in the organisations you used for this exercise? What do the buildings and other physical symbols of the organisation say about its culture? Similarly, what do the attitudes and behaviours of staff tell you about the organisation? Finally, but more complex, are you able to suggest what are some of underlying assumptions and beliefs held by the staff about how they cope with the day-to-day demands on the organisation?

COMMENT

This activity has asked you to think analytically about services that you are aware are different, but have probably taken for granted. Using a cultural analysis is valuable in starting to understand why services have different atmospheres and ways of doing things and attitudes among the people who work in them. These are all the manifestations of different cultures – sets of values, norms and beliefs – which in turn are reflected in different structures and systems, and the kinds of people attracted to work in them and their relationships with each other and those they serve.

The influence of culture on an organisation

In this section we dig deeper into the concept of culture and examine how it can influence an organisation. Staff in social care services may hold a range of differing beliefs about various aspects of their service, but there is also likely to exist a set of core beliefs and assumptions that are held in common by the majority of staff. This set of beliefs that are held in common are described as a paradigm by Johnson and Scholes (2002), and are said to evolve over time and embrace a range of assumptions, including the nature of the service, its management and the routines which are important to its success. The paradigm of the service is cultural in that it is held commonly by staff, taken for granted and not seen as problematic. Because it is taken for granted it is more easily perceived by those outside a service than those that work within it to whom it is self-evident.

When ways of working are taken for granted, staff may recognise changes that are taking place around them, but this does not necessarily mean that they see such changes as directly relevant to their organisation. If we take the above explanation as a starting point for understanding how culture influences an organisation, we can begin to understand why some organisations continue to provide poor-quality service over a long period of time, even though they are receiving signals, both internal and external, that things are changing around them and that their standards are no longer appropriate. The need to change a service is not determined by external forces, but by power of the paradigm, with the information from outside the organisation filtered through the powerful assumptions which represent the 'reality' of the organisation. This also helps us understand how difficult it can be to change an organisation which fails to respond to signals that it needs to change.

CASE STUDY

In the joint reports of the Commission for Social Care Inspection and the Healthcare Commission (CSCI, 2006, 2007a) into the Cornwall and Merton and Sutton learning disability services, certain features were common to both services which provide an insight into the culture of these services. Both services were poorly led with a lack of strategic vision and inadequate management arrangements. Serious abuse had taken place, with inadequate use of adult protection procedures. Attitudes towards service users were paternalistic and failed to provide opportunities for them to develop greater independence, make choices and become part of their communities. Similarly, both services restricted the activities of service users, creating a model of care that promoted dependency. Alongside these shortcomings, the services had inadequate levels of staffing, with poor levels of staff support and training. The limitations of both services begin to reveal something of the power of cultures that are powerful determinants of practice and make the introduction of change so problematic.

COMMENT

We can see from the case study of these services that they had a number of similar features, which suggests that cultural beliefs and assumptions about people with learning disabilities were deeply rooted in these services. These beliefs may have acted as a form of internalised control that influenced how managers and staff responded to the needs of service users, and that past attempts to improve these services came up against these deeply held beliefs to the detriment of service users' needs.

The cultural web

One way of making sense of organisational culture is to use the concept of the 'cultural web' to represent the 'taken-for-granted' assumptions or paradigm of an organisation and the physical manifestations of organisational culture developed by Johnson and Scholes (2002). The cultural web can be used to understand an organisation's culture through its rituals, routines, stories, structures and systems. Observing these aspects of its culture will enable you to begin to understand the clues to the taken-for-granted assumptions or paradigm of the organisation and its influence on all its activities. It can help us understand why, even when new strategies are formulated to improve a service, achieving change can be difficult. The elements of culture that make up the web are as follows:

- Rituals are the special events through which the organisation emphasises what is important and reinforces 'the way we do things around here', and signal what is especially valued.

- Routines include the way members of the organisation behave towards each other, and towards those outside the organisation. They may lubricate the workings of a service and be beneficial, but because they represent a taken-for-granted approach to practice can be difficult to change.

- Stories told by members of the organisation to each other, to outsiders, to new recruits, that embed the organisational history and flag up important events and personalities, and highlight mavericks who deviate from the norm.

- Symbolic aspects such as logos, offices, titles and the language and terminology used, particularly in regard to service users.

- Control systems, which are used to measure and reward what is important and focus attention and activity, and can be used to shape the behaviour of staff and service users.

- Power structures associated with the most powerful people in the organisation and what is actually valued, and closely associated with a core set of assumptions and beliefs.

- Organisational structures, both formal hierarchical structures and informal ways which reflect the power structure, define important relationships and emphasise what is important in the organisation, and influence working practices, constraints and norms that exercise control over individuals.

All these ingredients of the culture web protect the paradigm which sits at the centre of the web and powerfully influences how people behave in organisations. Some of this can be recognised from the evidence of the CSCI inspections of the Cornwall and Sutton and Merton services where poor and abusive practices were deeply embedded in the organisations and taken for granted, and demonstrated how several elements of the cultural web reinforced the dysfunctional systems and processes, making the potential for change more difficult.

ACTIVITY **9.2**

Reflect on different organisations you are familiar with using the cultural web as the template to help you make sense of your chosen organisation and its culture. As you apply each of the elements of the cultural web, consider the following questions:

- *What do these tell you about the culture of the organisation?*
- *Are you able to identify how the different elements of its culture support the taken-for-granted assumptions that are held in common and form the paradigm of the service?*
- *How much could some of the elements of the cultural web be a barrier to introducing change?*

COMMENT

This activity, using the elements of the cultural web, can be helpful in clarifying what constitutes the culture of the service, and some of the aspects of the culture that could be barriers to change. It can also give you an insight into some of the challenges facing a service when ways of working are deeply embedded and rarely questioned, which can make change more difficult.

Culture and socialisation

One of the difficulties facing staff who join an organisation where there is a deeply embedded and dominant culture is that it strongly influences how they behave. When staff are newly appointed they observe how managers and staff conduct themselves and adjust their behaviour accordingly, and are encouraged to conform to ways that are acceptable to the workgroup. Through this process staff learn new ways of working as the culture is learned, shared and transmitted. This is particularly so in the informal and invisible organisation below the surface that has a powerful influence on how new staff respond to demands made on them, through the power of the grapevine, informal leadership, needs and relationships (Hafford-Letchfield, 2006).

Socialisation in this way results in compliance and conformity to the values, beliefs, attitudes, rules and patterns of the behaviour required, and the way a service works becomes embedded in their unconscious behaviour patterns (Pettinger, 2000). We have seen from the CSCI reports that both services investigated had a poor record on staffing, with shortages of staff, reliance on temporary staff, and importantly a low investment in training that could have transmitted positive attitudes with emphasis on anti-oppressive practice, promoted positive messages about individuals, and supported and empowered individuals to have a voice which is listened to, and acted upon (Williams, 2006). Training alone would not necessarily change an organisation's culture, but it could act as a countervailing force along with other more strategic initiatives.

Even in services where there is a history of more effective working practices, attempting to introduce new ways of working may challenge deeply embedded subcultures, with the view that *the way we've always done things works best*. Although staff may not make explicit statements to this effect, their practices may continue as before, in spite of management statements about improvements in the service. This is often described as the 'rhetoric and reality of change', where new initiatives and innovations come up against resistance informed by what is taken for granted in day-to-day practice.

Introducing change can be particularly difficult where the existing culture is strongly embedded as a result of years of practices that have reinforced particular forms of working, especially if they are supported by management decisions and powerful individuals whose actions and statements shape the behaviour of junior or newly appointed staff. The culture may be so powerful that staff who are unhappy with current practices are inhibited from raising matters about poor performance for fear of ostracism or bullying. Whistleblowing in such situations becomes extremely difficult because there is no confidence that senior managers will recognise, let alone respond to, exposure of abusive cultures. Similarly, complaints by service users and their carers can often be disregarded as they are in a weak position in terms of power in the organisational structure and their views can be ignored where they challenge the dominant belief system.

RESEARCH SUMMARY

A Commission for Health Improvement (CHI) investigated an older persons' service at Rowan Ward, in the Manchester Mental Health and Social Care Trust, in 2002, where there had been allegations of physical and emotional abuse of patients by care staff. This investigation led to the identification of a series of risk factors for abuse, including a poor and institutionalised environment, low staffing levels, with high use of bank and agency staff, little staff development and poor supervision, lack of knowledge of incident reporting, a closed and inward-looking culture, with weak management at ward and locality level and geographical isolation (CHI, 2002).

COMMENT

The research summary describes a service where a combination of structural and work processes exposed the service to poor practices. The culture was closed and inward looking and gives us some idea of the difficulties in changing this service, where there were long-established, outdated practices and where attempts to modernise the service had been thwarted by strong staff resistance, with weak leadership and management. What is particularly significant about this investigation was the concern expressed by CHI that the factors identified at Rowan Ward keep cropping up in other poor-quality services and that they constitute a series of factors that may suggest a high risk of abuse happening in a service (DoH, 2005).

Processes of change

In this section we will examine some of the important aspects of managing change processes with the intention of building a positive culture that supports the strategy and values of the service, and that places the needs of service users at the forefront. We have seen in the preceding section that organisational cultures are the result of deeply held beliefs about working practices which make it difficult to introduce change, and that in the examples of poor quality services change was often resisted and only revealed as a result of inspection by a powerful external organisation. This suggests that changing cultures in organisations can be a difficult and lengthy process which needs to take account of the all those factors that are likely to lead to resistance, particularly where we are asking staff to change their strongly held beliefs which may be subconscious and therefore less accessible to call for changed practices.

The importance of vision and values

The starting point for any attempt to change the culture of a service needs to be rooted in the underpinning values that constitute the basis for a high-quality service and that engages with service users and carers and explores how a service can be provided from their perspective. Without a strong and coherent vision of the sort of service they want to provide, those responsible for managing a service will find it more difficult to engage with staff, users and carers in developing a set of shared principles about good practice. It is in relation to a vision for services that the concept of social role valorisation is particularly important as it can help challenge negative perceptions of people at risk of social exclusion (Cocks, 2001). The associated service evaluation model PASSING (Williams, 2009) is valuable in requiring learners to experience services from the users' perspective that can change attitudes of staff even when their managers are unwilling to embrace change.

We have seen in the examples of services investigated that there was poor-quality management at different levels in the service. The poor quality of management was compounded by a lack of strategic vision about the future of the services. Services which were not guided by the *Valuing people* policy (Department of Health, 2001a). Nor was there an understanding and willingness to use adult protection policies and procedures to safeguard service users (Cambridge, 2007). Managers have a key role in change, both in terms of setting out a direction for the service and motivating staff to strive to reach new goals, but also in sponsoring and legitimising the change process on a day-to-day basis (Gilbert, 2005). This discussion of managing the change process raises issues about the way leaders create the conditions that enable others to change their practice. The view taken by Smale (1998) is that leaders are part of a complex set of interacting factors, that are all responding and contributing to the culture of the organisation, and that it is the quality of their behaviours and activities that is the key to effective implementation of change.

Managing the change process

Managers need to be skilled at managing the transition as a service moves from its present state to a desired future state, and recognise and accept a degree of turbulence or disorganisation and temporarily lowered effectiveness that can characterise this transitional stage. An important part of this initial stage is to identify and declare the purpose of change and why it is needed, so that staff understand why they are being asked to change and also recognise that the existing situation is no longer appropriate to meet the needs of service users. In any change process it is likely that not everyone will support the new ways of working, at least initially. In managing the change process it is necessary to identify early on those staff who are interested in change and who are willing to engage with the change process, and have the energy to overcome the inertia present in all systems. These will include the 'champions' of change who have the energy to promote change in service systems, and also those staff who are opinion leaders in services, who are seen as role models who other staff respect and follow. On the other hand, some staff will be resistant to change. They may have their own preferred solutions, and see problems in the changes being promoted. All these responses require those leading change to listen to staff who have to implement the changes, and work to create a convergence of thinking and action (Smale, 1998).

ACTIVITY 9.3

Reflecting on your experience of different organisations, can you think of a proposed significant change that resulted in some staff supporting the change and others opposing it, or at least questioning some aspects of it?

- *How was the proposed change introduced?*
- *How much were staff consulted and engaged in testing out its practicality?*
- *Was it a directive that staff were expected to comply with?*
- *How much was the change genuinely adopted? Was it just behavioural compliance or 'lip service' paid to the change?*
- *What does the example you chose tell you about the complexity of introducing change?*

COMMENT

This exercise should have made you think more deeply about some of the difficulties facing managers and others who are tasked with introducing change in services. The nature of the change, the rationale for introducing it, the timescale for its adoption and the level of engagement with staff who are responsible for implementing it, are all factors that need to be taken into account. These, and many other factors, have to be considered when introducing a significant change in an organisation.

Different levels of change

Change can take a range of forms and is related to the extent to which a service is able to modify its activities, for example, to enable it to develop up-to-date policies and procedures. If a service is managed proactively, is responsive to its external environment and anticipates the need for change, progress can be achieved through a proactive process of incremental change, where over time the service gradually adapts to new ways of working, drawing on models of best practice. This form of evolutionary change is rooted in continually analysing the need for change and using change models to improve the performance of the service. This has much in common with the concept of learning organisations (Gould and Baldwin, 2004), which continually adjust their strategies as the environment around them changes. Such incremental change was lacking in the examples of abusive regimes where closed, inward-looking, isolated services have failed to change incrementally until exposed through the media or external inspection.

Where managers fail to see the need for major changes, but adapt the current ways of operating within the existing paradigm, this can eventually result in a crisis when the organisation's future is at risk. Failing to change sufficiently to fundamentally improve the organisation can lead to strong external pressure that may result in transformational change which challenges the existing paradigm and means the imposition of change to the taken-for-granted assumptions and 'the way we do things around here' (Johnson and Scholes, 2002). Such change usually comes about as a result of both reactive and proactive processes. For example, if there is a significant deterioration in performance or strong external criticism which threatens the future of the service, then the management may find themselves in a forced transformational change situation where the existing paradigm and service routines can no longer meet the new requirements. As happened in Cornwall and Sutton and Merton, this is likely to be disruptive and painful, with significant consequences for those who manage and staff the service.

Long-standing managers are often trapped in the same paradigm as other staff and less aware of the signals that suggest radical change is needed. Radical change of transformational nature often follows the appointment of a new senior manager with a remit to introduce change, in the face of a crisis or rapidly deteriorating performance. In the reports of Cornwall and Sutton and Merton Trusts we saw that change had been attempted in the past, but these changes had not had a significant impact on these services, and were peripheral to the main problems and insufficient to deal with the poor conditions and practices that led to abuse. Any changes that were made appeared to be bounded within the existing paradigm in the services, when more radical levels of change were needed to transform these services. Ultimately the intervention of an external agency resulted in forced change that challenged the existing paradigm and began the transformation process.

Leadership and management behaviour

Successfully implementing change, particularly where there is need for transformational change, is a complex and demanding activity by those leading the change. Achieving ownership of a new strategic direction among all the stakeholders in a service requires skills of a high order. This involves those leading change to be particularly sensitive to the organisational context, working across boundaries with different staff groups, service users and external stakeholders. Gilbert (2005) discusses a number of reasons why change can fail, and provides a list of important actions that are necessary to improve the chances of success. These include the importance of determining the need for change at the outset, developing a vision and strategy and communicating that vision, establishing a sense of urgency, working with the human factors, including broad action on systems and resources to create visible improvements. Above all, rooting the new approach in the culture of the service, where staff and service users can make the connection between new behaviours and organisational success.

Although organisational cultures that are deeply embedded are seen as difficult to change, Schein (2004) argues that a culture can be influenced by what those who lead a service pay attention to. This perspective on change suggests that what leaders systematically work on and communicate to others sends out signals to the rest of the organisation about what is considered to be important. For example, if the leader is someone who engages with staff, communicates the importance of good practice and works to create a culture of openness and trust, this will send out signals about what is valued, which in time will begin to change the organisation. At the practice level, leadership on the part of front-line managers is also important, as they support, monitor and develop practice and are the bridge between senior management and frontline staff (Scragg, 2010). A part of their role is to interpret organisational strategies in terms of day-to-day practice, and at the same time act as an anchor and guide for staff at times of change. They also have a particularly important role in promoting and sustaining practice standards through support for individual practitioners and teams in their supervisory and consultative responsibilities (Kearney, 2004). It is also important to stress that first-line managers tend to be trusted more than senior managers, adding credibility when communicating and explaining the need for changes to practice (Larkin and Larkin, 1996).

Styles of managing change

Those leading the change process will need to consider the styles of management (Johnson and Scholes, 2002) necessary to adopt in order to achieve the aims of the change process, as this will differ according to the organisational context and the degree of pressure for change. The following styles describe a range of approaches, with different combinations of style adopted according to organisational context and the degree and urgency of the change required.

- Education and communication are used when staff need to learn new skills which are crucial for working in new ways. Communicating the vision through meeting with those working at the front line, testing out the vision and reinforcing it are an essential role for change managers.

- Collaboration and participation are used as a means of engaging with those affected by the change, asking them to help design the process and thereby increasing ownership and commitment to the change.

- Intervention is used when a change agent or others are given delegated responsibility to work with staff on particular aspects of the change process, including, ideas generation, detailed planning or the development of rationales for change. Again involvement is likely to lead to greater commitment to change.

- Direction is used when those leading the service use their authority to set the direction, means and speed of change. Closely associated with this style is coercion, where change is imposed through the use of managerial power. These styles may be used when an organisation is facing a crisis and survival is heavily dependent on rapid change.

Whichever methods are used, and most change processes use a combination of methods, there are advantages and disadvantages. A management style based on education and communication, and collaboration and participation, can be time consuming, although they are likely to increase ownership and commitment to change. Intervention, direction and coercion have advantages of speed, but risk perceptions of manipulation or at worst non-acceptance by staff. Again the context, scale and urgency of change will to some extent dictate the style adopted by those leading change.

Supporting staff through change

Changing a service will encompass a range of factors, including the 'hard' strategic, structural and systems changes and the 'soft' human issues, concerned with staff, their skills and the style of management that enables staff to respond constructively to change. A critical part of change is the understanding that staff affected by change will have to work in new ways, developing new skills and attitudes and fundamentally question practices that the old culture reinforced on a daily basis. Working in a social care environment is recognised as emotionally demanding where staff need high levels of energy to provide a quality service, with a lack of resources and support by the management of a service a frequent reason why change can falter. Change can also bring with it a range of emotions, including shock, denial and guilt as staff come to terms with the need to change. These reactions are similar in many other significant life transitions and require sensitivity and trust on the part of those leading change based on relationships of transparency and honesty (Gilbert, 2005). In most large-scale change situations it is recognised that levels of performance may drop as staff grapple with new ways of working and develop new skills. Targeting the barriers that make it difficult for staff to work in new ways is a key part of managing change, alongside developing systems of emotional support for staff who can be particularly tested at times of major change.

CHAPTER SUMMARY

This chapter has introduced you to the concept of organisational culture and its influence on how a service is provided. The first section has revealed the range and complexity of factors that support an organisation's culture and why it can be resistant to change. We have seen how deeply held basic assumptions make change and innovation difficult in services and why successive change initiatives can fail. In the second section, the pervasive influence of culture on organisations is discussed, highlighted by the case study which demonstrates the power of cultural factors, and where staff, with lack of appropriate leadership, training and support, carry attitudes into their work that can reinforce patterns of abuse. Finally the chapter has described the management processes that are involved in changing a service, and the complex and challenging agenda involved in transforming services where powerful cultures have developed over many years and can be resistant to change.

FURTHER READING

It would be helpful to download the summaries of the CSCI joint reports (2006/2007) and the Healthcare Commission report (2003) so that you understand the range of issues identified in these services and the factors that were identified as contributing to institutional abuse. These reports can be found at **www.cqc.org.uk**

Gilbert, P (2005) *Leadership: Being effective and remaining human*. Lyme Regis: Russell House. Provides a valuable insight into the demands of leadership in services, particularly the qualities leaders need when managing change.

Scragg, T (2010) *Managing change in health and social care services*. Brighton: Pavilion Publishing. Examines change from a range of perspectives, emphasising the complexity of change in health and social care organisations.

Williams, P (2009) *Social work with people with learning difficulties*. 2nd edition. Exeter: Learning Matters.
Explores issues of work with people with learning difficulties from a range of perspectives with particular emphasis on positive approaches to work with people who are at risk of abuse.

Chapter 10

Effective collaborative working
Teri Cranmer

A C H I E V I N G   A   S O C I A L   W O R K   D E G R E E

This chapter will help you to meet the following National Occupational Standards.

Key Role 2: Plan, carry out, review and evaluate social work practice with individuals, families, carers, groups, communities and other professionals.

• Interact to achieve change and development and to improve life opportunities.

Key Role 5: Manage and be accountable, with supervision and support, for your own social work practice within your organisation.

• Work within multi-disciplinary and multi-organisational teams, networks and systems.

• Contribute to evaluating the effectiveness of the team, network or system.

• Deal constructively with disagreements and conflict within relationships.

Key Role 6: Demonstrate professional competence in social work practice.

• Work within agreed standards of social work practice and ensure own professional development.

• Manage complex ethical issues, dilemmas and conflicts.

• Contribute to the promotion of best social work practice.

It will also introduce you to the following academic standards set out in the social work subject benchmark statement.

3.7 Nature and extent of social work.

5.1.2 The service delivery context.

5.1.3 Values and ethics.

5.1.5 The nature of social work practice.

5.1.6 Skills in working with others.

Introduction

This chapter explores the strengths and weaknesses of working with other disciplines. It will consider ways of working within multidisciplinary teams and with colleagues based within disparate settings. Particular attention will be given to developing an understanding of the differing focus and value base of different professionals within statutory organisations. The chapter will conclude with positive approaches to respecting, accommodating and developing cohesive practice.

What do we mean by collaborative working?

Collaborative working is about working with people who use services and their carers as well as with other professionals and agencies. Collaboration, when used within the context of adult safeguarding, means to work with others to achieve effective outcomes to safeguard and protect vulnerable people. Central to effective collaboration is good communication with all those concerned, particularly people who use services and their carers.

The first issue to consider is what is meant by 'collaborative working'. We use a variety of terms to describe the way in which we work with people and agencies such as multi-agency, multidisciplinary, trans-disciplinary, integrated, inter-agency and inter-professional working. Quinney (2006) refers to this as *the lexicon of terms* (see Figure 10.1).

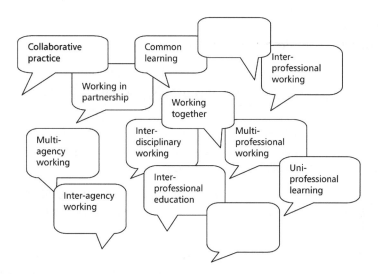

Figure 10.1 The lexicon of terms (Quinney, 2006)

*ACTIVITY **10.1***

What do you think each of these terms means?

Many people use these terms interchangeably. However, they don't all mean the same thing. Did you consider for example the difference between 'multidisciplinary' and 'multi-agency'? A multidisciplinary team refers to one with members from different disciplines such as social work, occupational therapy and psychology. However, all of these staff could be employed by one agency, so the team would be multidisciplinary but single agency. If the different disciplines were employed by different agencies (local authority, primary care trust, voluntary organisation, etc.) the team would be both multidisciplinary and multi-agency.

Do each of these terms equate to collaboration? I would suggest that there is more to collaborative working than being based in a team of people from different disciplines or developing joint-funded posts or policies and procedures. It is possible to work within a multi-agency or multidisciplinary setting without developing collaborative practice.

If we use the word 'partnership' there is an implication of equality within the relationship, a mutual trust and respect and a shared agreement of visionary direction. It is this notion of equality that enables us to work in collaboration. A team consisting of community nurses, social workers and occupational therapists clearly has a mix of disciplines but they need to work together to develop a shared understanding of how they each contribute to the team in order to achieve effective outcomes for the people supported by the team. Joined-up working requires joined-up thinking.

Whittington (2003) helps us to see how partnership working supports collaboration by describing partnership as being the formal relationship and collaboration as the knowledge and value base utilised in putting the formal processes into practice. Whittington (2003, p16) defines partnership and collaboration as:

> *Partnership is a state of relationships at organisational, group, professional or inter-professional level, to be achieved, maintained and reviewed;* and *collaboration is an active process of partnership in action.*

Effective partnership has to be worked at; it requires commitment and investment from all the contributing parties. There are a number of elements that need to be in place to achieve effective collaborative working.

- *Knowledge of professional roles* it is important to be aware of the roles and responsibilities of other professionals as well as having a clear understanding of your own role.

- *Willing participation* motivation for and commitment to collaborative practice are important if collaborative practice is to be achieved, along with expectations that are realistic and a positive belief in the potential effectiveness.

- *Confidence* refers to both personal confidence and professional confidence.

- *Open and honest communication* includes active listening and constructive feedback that seeks to clarify and develop understanding.

- *Trust and mutual respect* takes time to develop and is essential for people to feel 'safe' to deal with areas that are challenging or may lead to conflict.

- *Power* a non-hierarchical structure where power is shared is a preferred model but responsibility and accountability need to be clear. It can be difficult to maintain some of these elements such as open and honest communication when you feel subordinate to the other party you are collaborating with.

- *Conflict* clear ground rules along with a reflective and open approach can help prevent and resolve conflict. Conflict can also produce creativity and energy.

- *Support and commitment at a senior level* without this, effective implementation of decisions and actions and can be difficult to achieve.

- *Professional culture* the culture of different professional groups may hinder collaborative working but also provide the opportunity to consider another perspective.
(adapted from Quinney, 2006)

Partnership working is explained by Pratt et al. (1999) through a behavioural model that consists of a relationship between competition, co-operation, co-ordination and co-evolution (Figure 10.2).

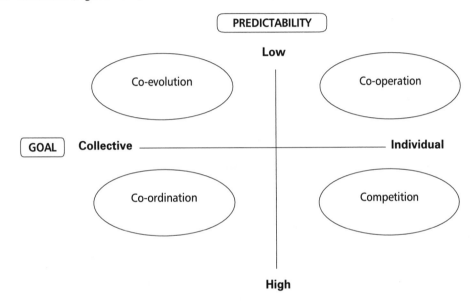

Figure 10.2 Partnership behaviour (Pratt et al., 1999)

Competition can be either individual or organisational and can be a powerful catalyst for change, e.g. league tables and star systems; aspiring to achieve a higher star rating can influence organisations to improve operational practices to the benefit of their customers.

Co-operation is achieved when participants may have different goals but see their future as linked, e.g. the local social service authority works to increase the safety of vulnerable adults, the local police need to reduce crime. These goals can be achieved more effectively if the two organisations co-operate.

Co-ordination requires each participant to understand their individual contribution to achieving an agreed, combined goal, e.g. a safety plan for an adult at risk is likely to include different tasks and responsibilities for the individuals and organisations involved to enable the overall goal of a safer environment.

Co-evolution is a more dynamic partnership in which participants work together to develop the means of achieving a shared goal within a new environment, e.g. building a pathway that leads to a shared aim of increased empowerment for service users through self-directed support.

Although all four of these approaches can elicit change and engender positive working relationships, it is co-evolution that is most likely to create a strong collaborative framework:

> we use the term co-evolving partnership to describe behaviour in which the partners are committed to co-design something together for a shared purpose. This is about lifting the game to a new level of operation. It is not about past patterns that are known to work or about coordinating known good practice. It is about working together into the future, which is not yet knowable. (Pratt et al., 1999, p104)

CASE STUDY

A multidisciplinary/multi-agency community team have been alerted about Susan, a young woman with a learning difficulty. Day centre staff had noticed that she had become withdrawn and uncommunicative since her mother's partner moved into the family home. Susan has now arrived at the centre with bruising to her face and arms. It was inferred that mother's partner was implicated. Because there were adult safeguarding implications the referral was passed to the social work manager, who initiated an adult protection investigation. The investigation process involved a social worker from the community team, staff from the day centre and the police. On investigation it was found that, while Susan had become withdrawn at the centre, at home she had become aggressive, particularly towards herself. Susan had been hitting her head on the wall and slapping her face; her mother had to restrain her to prevent injury. It was recommended that Susan be referred to the psychologist for a behavioural assessment. Susan was closed to social work and her name added to the psychologist's six-month waiting list.

ACTIVITY 10.2

- Which of Pratt's environments do you think most fits the way this team is currently working?

- Consider ways they could change their working practices to develop a more equal and collaborative approach.

- Think about a multi-agency/multidisciplinary team that you are familiar with. Where would it be located on Pratt's partnership behaviour grid?

COMMENT

This community team appears to be working in quite a disjointed way with referrals deemed to be for individual disciplines rather than for the team as an holistic entity. Although a multi-agency, multidisciplinary team, they are not working inter-disciplinary, i.e. across the disciplines. This isolationist approach appears to have led to a 'this is yours not ours' attitude between the disciplines which has resulted in the service user, carer and day centre being left unsupported.

Collaboration in the context of safeguarding

Having considered the term 'collaboration' we now need to place it into the context of adult safeguarding. In Chapter 1 Gaylard explains the policy framework that supports adult safeguarding and introduces us to *No secrets* (DoH, 2000). This document has a clear expectation that agencies will work together to develop a coherent policy to protect vulnerable adults and prevent abuse. A particular emphasis is placed on the responsibility for the statutory agencies that provide health and social care, regulators of those agencies and criminal justice agencies to work together in partnership to develop and implement policies and procedures. The guidance stated that they should do this in collaboration with all agencies involved in the public, voluntary and private sectors and in consultation with service users, carers and representative groups. The aim was to co-design something for a shared purpose that will take them into a joint future, i.e. to co-evolve.

A national review of *No secrets* was held in 2008–09 resulting in an outcomes report, *Safeguarding adults: Report on the consultation on the review of 'No Secrets'* (DH 2009). This document stated an intention to develop a cross-government response to consider how to implement the outcomes of the review. Due to the change of government in May 2010 this proposal has yet to be actioned. However, the themes from the review have continued to inform practice and the development of national policy for example, the emphasis on inclusion and that safeguarding should be built on empowerment (see Chapters 3 and 8), is reflected in the coalition government's White Paper *A vision for adult social care: Capable communities and active citizens* (DH, 2010) and the Care Quality Commission's guidance about compliance: *Essential standards of quality and safety* (CQC, 2010).

No secrets clearly lays out an expectation of collaboration across and between agencies at all levels, that is:

- operational;

- supervisory line management;

- senior management staff;

- corporate/cross authority;

- chief officers/chief executives;

- local authority members.
(DoH, p16)

Given this directive from the Department of Health and assuming an understanding that all the agencies involved see themselves as acting in the best interests of the people who use their services, you might expect that developing a cohesive joint policy would be reasonably straightforward. However, think back to the above case study – a team of staff all working in the best interests of the same service user group but working separately, not together. This could be seen as a microcosm of the inter-agency strategic group. Each of the statutory services will have their own core objectives, performance indicators, access criteria, budgetary constraints, etc. They will each be constrained by different legislative frameworks that dictate what they can and can't provide. On a more operational level, such issues as account-ability, role and responsibility, information sharing, communication and resource availability can create barriers. Additionally, some agencies may take a defensive stance, concerned to protect their own professional identity.

RESEARCH SUMMARY

Williamson (2007, p120) breaks these factors down into five specific issues.
Factors inhibiting partnership working: Concern with organisational self preservation

Structural issues:	*Geographical boundaries, management hierarchies*
Procedural issues:	*Different lines of accountability, different degrees of discretion*
Professional issues:	*Different values/cultures*
Financial issues:	*Budgetary constraints*
Policy issues:	*Different priorities, overlaps and gaps in service*

Williamson notes that organisational change at a strategic level is difficult to achieve. Organisations have a strong incentive in maintaining the status quo, are reluctant to devolve or share power and consequently often prefer to work within closed systems. It is often not until there are strong external factors in place to influence change, such as performance indicators measuring partnership working, that real change can begin to be achieved.

ACTIVITY **10.3**

No secrets suggests that each local authority should develop a multi-agency manage-ment committee or safeguarding board to oversee the strategic direction of the adult safeguarding agenda. The purpose of the group is to facilitate partnership working across the continuum between operational practice and strategic direction. The group should have agreed objectives and priorities for its work.

For this activity it would be helpful if you downloaded the latest Adult Safeguarding Board and Adult Protection Committee (Wales) annual report on the local authority website.

- *What key priorities have the Adult Safeguarding Board identified as areas for improve-ment?*
- *What is the impact of these priorities on the place where you are working?*

COMMENT

What sort of impact would you expect the key priorities of the Adult Safeguarding Board to be making in your organisation? Where would you see the impact? Do the Board's key priorities match the priorities identified in your organisation's business plan? Are they discussed in team meetings and supervision? Are there any visible shifts in practice, attitude and culture?

The drivers for collaborative working

One of the key drivers for making change is pressure from regulatory bodies. Within adult social care this comes in the shape of the Department of Health's Performance Assessment Framework for Social Services. The Department of Health has been slow to introduce performance indicators related to adult safeguarding, collecting only minimal information through the local authority self-assessment process. A more holistic framework, the Comprehensive Area Assessment, was introduced in April 2008 but abolished by the coalition government in November 2010. It is currently unclear what will take its place but recently published consultation documents indicate that we are moving towards sector-led improvement in which councils are key players, for example taking on public health responsibilities from the Primary Care Trusts. It is proposed that the Care Quality Commission will continue to register care providers and undertake risk triggered inspections of councils in relationship to safeguarding (see *Transparency in outcomes*, DH, 2010 and *DH Business plan 2011–15*, DH, 2010).

The Association of Directors of Adult Social Services (2005), recognising the need for consistent good practice across the country, published *Safeguarding adults – a National Framework of Standards for good practice and outcomes in adult protection-work*. Although written from the perspective of local government being the lead agency, the framework gives a strong focus to the need for multi-agency partnership working. The 11 measurable standards cover all aspects of safeguarding from strategic planning to operational practice both within and across organisations. The need to work in partnership with people who use services and their carers permeates the document.

On a strategic level, *Safeguarding adults* encourages organisations to look at the relationship between the multi-agency safeguarding committee and other multi-agency partnerships that form the local strategic partnership (see Figure 10.3). This diagram of the relationship between key local partners is a good illustration of the need for co-ordinated working.

ACTIVITY 10.4

Although Safeguarding adults *is fundamentally a strategic document looking at how organisations are working together on a macro level, elements of each of the standards can be transposed down to joint and individual working at an operational level.*

Consider standard 3:

Each partner agency has a clear, well-publicised policy of zero tolerance of abuse within the organisation.

- *How does your practice measure up against this standard?*
- *What actions can you take to improve your personal practice?*

Figure 10.3 The safeguarding adults partnership (ADSS, 2005)

COMMENT

I am sure that we all like to think that we take a zero-tolerance approach to abuse, but how easy is this in reality? In its broadest sense 'zero tolerance' means challenging many of the norms of our society. Within the workplace it could be colleagues, managers, the systems and processes of the organisation, service users and their carers. There are a lot of pressures to turn a blind eye and maintain the status quo. How easy is it to challenge those who hold the power, to disrupt the comfort of the workplace, to see a friend and colleague investigated and dismissed? Do you have the energy to take on oppressive systems that you may feel powerless to change? If it is difficult for you, how easy is it for the people who use services to feel empowered to make a difference?

Working collaboratively across statutory organisations

Cross-agency barriers

As we have already seen, different organisations, agencies and disciplines may all be working in the best interests of the people who use their services but this will not necessarily be through a collaborative relationship.

RESEARCH SUMMARY

In their research into the effectiveness of multi-agency working in adult protection, Perkins et al. (2007) found that lack of commitment, variable priorities, lack of clarity of roles and responsibilities, and time and resource pressures were the most frequently mentioned barriers.

The different statutory organisations each have their own core business, performance framework and budgetary constraints. Sometimes these will cause tension between organisations, making an effective collaborative relationship difficult to achieve. For example, one of the performance measures for acute trusts is the length of time a patient remains in hospital. Staff are therefore under pressure to discharge patients as soon as they are medically fit. The length of time it can take to assess a patient's social care needs and arrange an appropriate care package can cause tension between the trust and the local authority.

Similar tension can occur between the police and the mental health trust following the detention of a person under section 136 of the Mental Health Act 2007. This section authorises the police to detain a person and remove them to a place of safety if they are found in a place to which the public have access and appear to be suffering from a mental disorder causing them to need immediate care or control. Gathering information, co-ordinating an assessment and arranging any required services can take a considerable number of hours. Police officers may have to remain with the detainee throughout the process, taking them away from their primary role of maintaining law and order.

The body that currently regulates and inspects local social service authorities and NHS Trusts in England and Wales is the Care Quality Commission (CQC), which also regulates registered social care providers from both the statutory and independent (private and voluntary) sectors. The CQC publication *Our safeguarding protocol: The Care Quality Commission's commitment to safeguarding* (CQC, 2010) reinforces the expectation that organisations and agencies will work in partnership with each other and with people who use services, and their carers.

The Commission's protocol lays out the main areas and the process by which it will work in partnership with other agencies to ensure that people who use services live a life free from abuse, neglect and discrimination. This is a relationship that is difficult to balance as CQC is endeavouring to work in partnership with agencies that it is mandated to inspect and sanction. I would suggest there are inherent difficulties for CQC in developing good collaborative working with providers and across the local authority and other social care commissioners. Considering the elements required for effective collaborative working and Whittington's (2003) definition of partnership and collaboration discussed at the start of this chapter: how easy is it for there to be professional confidence, open and honest communication, trust and shared power when one organisation has a role to 'police' some of the others?

Positive approaches to joint working

Having looked at the some of the difficulties of working collaboratively across statutory agencies, let us now consider some examples of how agencies can work well together to safeguard vulnerable adults. Perkins et al. (2007) found the key strengths to be:

- shared expertise;
- more effective approach;
- shared responsibility;
- strategically effective approach.

In 1991 the Secretary of State for Health, William Waldegrave, wrote: *Community Care is inseparable from local health care and our policies require much closer coordination of health and social services* (DoH, 1991). There have been many papers, circulars and guidance documents published since then, reiterating this sentiment. A similar statement was made nearly 15 years later in the Care Services Improvement Partnership (CSIP) publication *Everybody's business.* This document informs us that *the complex nature of older people's mental health requires a whole systems response that cuts across health and social care, physical and mental health, mainstream and specialist services* (CSIP, 2005b, p8).

The Youth Justice and Criminal Evidence Act 1999 set out a range of special measures to assist vulnerable or intimidated witnesses to give their best evidence in criminal proceedings. The guidance for implementing this Act is set out in *Achieving best evidence in criminal proceedings* (Home Office, 2002), commonly referred to as ABE. In respect of child witnesses ABE is clear that there is a joint responsibility between the local authority and the police. There is no such guidance for the interviewing of vulnerable adult witnesses. There is no duty to work jointly with the local authority other than to gather information to enable them to work effectively with the witness. However, in many authorities there are local agreements to enable joint working in the best interest of vulnerable witnesses. These include:

- joint interview training to ensure that the best possible evidence can be gathered whether it is a criminal offence or not, ensuring that health and local authority staff are aware of good interview practice such as open questions and recorded interviews;

- joint police/social work ABE interviews when appropriate;
- local authority involvement in the Home Office-led multi-agency public protection arrangements (MAPPAs).

Norfolk's Police Adult Protection Unit

Norfolk established a jointly staffed Adult Protection Unit towards the end of 2001, leading from the White Paper No secrets around recognising partnership working as a way to safeguard vulnerable people in the county. The police had already established an adult protection unit within the family protection unit, and an opportunity arose to develop this further with the addition of specialist social workers trained in adult protection and embedded into the unit. While the unit is predominantly police staffed, the social workers share the same office space and computer system access is provided to both on each other's systems.

The specialist social workers in the unit accept all referrals concerning abuse to a person unknown to the department, where no prior active social work intervention has been identified. Those referrals that involve a person active to the department become the responsibility of the active social worker within a locality or specialist service. In all cases both the police and social workers of the unit remain as a resource for advice and information to all concerned parties. In some cases they will jointly work with local personnel in serious/complex matters.

One of the greatest strengths has been the gain of knowledge about the separate and quite distinct role that police and social workers perform. This has led to a better understanding around process and especially in being able to take issues forward for resolution and ensures that the capture of evidence and the welfare of the individual are dealt with seamlessly.

(Honnor, 2008, personal communication)

Developing your own collaborative practice

Much of what we have considered so far has been about organisational collaboration. How does that translate into individual practice? What do you need to bring to the collaborative table? The members of a partnership – service user, carer, friends, relatives, volunteers and other professionals – are a team in the broad sense of the word. Payne (2000) calls this an *open team*. Payne (2000) looks at the elements of team working and how each individual impacts on a team; this relates to open teams as well as traditional (closed) teams.

It is important to recognise that within collaborative working (an open team) there are likely to be similar dynamics to those found within more traditional teams such as Belbin's list of personality types and traits.

RESEARCH SUMMARY *continued*

- *Company worker: methodical, practical, reliable, conscientious; can be seen as inflexible.*

- *Chairperson: calm, enthusiastic, self confident; might be perceived as bossy and intimidating.*

- *Shaper: dynamic, outgoing, challenging; may be over-reactive, challenging and abrasive.*

- *Plant: individualistic, loner, serious, unorthodox; can be perceived as unrealistic and oversensitive, might be isolated or scapegoated within the team.*

- *Resource investigator: extrovert, versatile, communicative; tends to lose interest in the long-term aspects and issues.*

- *Monitor–evaluator: hard-headed, analytical, dispassionate; may appear overcritical and pessimistic.*

- *Teamworker: sympathetic, sociable, avoids conflict; likely to be indecisive as takes on everyone's views.*

- *Completer–finisher: hardworking, orderly, conscientious, consistent; might be overly perfectionist, preventing things from moving forward until every 'i' has been dotted and every 't' has been crossed.*

(adapted from Belbin, 1981)

When you start to think about your own role within collaborative networks you will quickly realise that you belong to numerous open teams and may take different roles within each one.

ACTIVITY 10.5

- *Consider which of Belbin's roles you take in your different networks and think about the impact you have on those networks.*

- *What steps can you take to improve your own collaborative practice?*

COMMENT

You are likely to have found that you take different roles in different networks. Did you think about why you take those particular roles? What causes you to act and respond differently in different settings or with different people and personalities?

Another useful tool for developing your own collaborative practice is Northmore's (2007) checklist for partnership working.

- *Follow through requests and give colleagues feedback.*
- *Be honest: if you can't help, say so, or direct them to someone who can.*
- *Stick to time commitments.*
- *Don't create artificial barriers – turn off the answering machine.*
- *Make an effort to see colleagues you do not normally see face to face.*

(adapted from Northmore, 2007, p108)

CHAPTER SUMMARY

In this chapter we have considered what is meant by the term 'collaborative working' and how this fits into the context of adult safeguarding. You have been introduced to some of the theoretical and legislative frameworks and thought about how these impact on local practice. Consideration has been given to the strengths and barriers to effective joint working. Finally you have been given some tools and ideas for developing your own good collaborative practice. Reflective practice is a key tool that you can use to improve your working relationships, considering why you work well with some people and what the barriers are to good collaborative working with others. Remember, successful collaborative working requires agencies to break down real and imagined barriers.

FURTHER READING

McCray, J (2007) Reflective practice for collaborative working. In Knott, C and Scragg, T (eds) *Reflective practice in social work.* Exeter: Learning Matters.
This chapter on collaborative working leadership presents a practical tool to aid reflective practice.

Perkins, N, Penhale, B, Reid, D, Pinkney, L, Hussein, S and Manthorpe, J (2007) Partnership means protection? Perceptions of the effectiveness of multi-agency working and the regulatory framework within adult protection in England and Wales, *Journal of Adult Protection,* 9 (3), 9–23.
This article examines the effectiveness of the multi-agency approach in adult safeguarding. It draws on research into partnership working and the perceptions of the regulatory framework to protect vulnerable adults across local authorities in England and Wales.

Whittington, C (2003) A model of collaboration. In Weinstein, J, Whittington, C, and Leiba, T (eds) *Collaboration in social work practice.* London: Jessica Kingsley.
This chapter develops a model of collaboration that describes and links key participants, the people who use services, their carers and professionals, and the teams and organisations to which they relate.

Chapter 11

Working with risk
Chris Smethurst

A C H I E V I N G   A   S O C I A L   W O R K   D E G R E E

This chapter will help you to meet the following National Occupational Standards.

Key Role 2: Plan, carry out, review and evaluate social work practice with individuals, families, carers, groups, communities and other professionals.

- Interact with individuals, families, carers, groups and communities to achieve change and development and to improve life opportunities.

Key Role 4: Manage risk to individuals, families, carers, groups, communities, self and colleagues.

- Assess, minimise and manage risk to self and colleagues.

Key Role 6: Demonstrate professional competence in social work practice.

- Work within agreed standards of social work practice and ensure own professional development.
- Manage complex ethical issues, dilemmas and conflicts.
- Contribute to the promotion of best social work practice.

Introduction

An understanding of the concept of risk is integral to understanding the theory and practice of safeguarding adults. However, research has indicated that social workers still struggle with the notion of risk, risk assessment and risk management. For many practitioners, working with risk is central to their everyday practice; yet this work can be characterised by uncertainty and anxiety. As we shall explore in this chapter, the fear of 'getting it wrong' is the shadow that can haunt decision-making. Consequently, a procedural, tick-box approach to risk assessment and decision-making can appear to offer a degree of security and certainty. However, this approach can produce unthinking, defensive and potentially oppressive practice (Thompson, 2000). At the other end of the spectrum, some practitioners may prefer to rely on 'gut instinct'. This too can potentially result in dangerous practice: idiosyncratic, unsafe decisions which are lacking in evidence of a systematic attempt to consider relevant factors. This chapter will explore notions of risk in relation to anti-oppressive practice (also see Chapter 8). You will be encouraged to explore your own perceptions in relation to risk and be introduced to the key elements in risk assessment.

ACTIVITY 11.1

Identify a time in your life when you took a risk.
On reflection, how objectively did you weigh up the potential positives and negatives of the action you took? Is there anything you know now that might have influenced your decision either way?

Possibly you reached a decision by dispassionately balancing the potential positive and negative consequences of taking a risk. However, it is possible that your feelings about what you were proposing to do, your desire to take the risk or anxiety about doing so, might have led you to downplay some of the potential consequences and exaggerate others. It is important to recognise that it can be difficult to separate out the emotional context of decision-making when it comes to risk (Joffe,1999). This might be a useful theme to reflect upon in your practice and while reading the rest of this chapter.

Concerning hindsight, you might realise that you were unaware of some of the factors that could have influenced your decision: you were not in possession of all the information that would have helped you. Similarly, at the time you made your decision, you could not be certain exactly how it would turn out. Hindsight offers 20:20 vision; yet, in social work decision-making is often fraught with uncertainty. Decision-makers are not in possession of a crystal ball nor may they be in possession of all the facts; they may not be able to predict, with certainty, how different factors may combine to influence events. Decision-making can be particularly difficult when situations are chaotic, at times of crisis, or when working under pressure of time: these are conditions that will be readily familiar to social work practitioners. Consequently, it is perhaps not surprising that there is some evidence that, when it comes to working with situations of risk, social workers often feel hostages to fortune: unable to accurately predict either good or bad outcomes in a given situation (Shaw and Shaw, 2001). This, of course, poses a risk for the worker: they may feel overwhelmed, anxious and fearful of making mistakes. These are themes that we will be addressing in this chapter.

What do we mean by 'risk'?

There is currently a wealth of literature that discusses the evolution of our understanding of the concept of risk. However, Shaw and Shaw (2001) argue that the idea of risk was rather taken for granted in social work until as recently as the mid-1990s. Risk assessment and management were not necessarily seen as activities that were potentially contentious and problematic. In addition, risk and risk-taking were associated with positive outcomes as well as preventing negative ones. The assertion of the right to take risks was, and remains, a key feature of the underpinning philosophies of practice with, for example, people with learning difficulties (Wolfensberger, 1972; O'Brien, 1992). However, it is arguable that the term 'risk' has become increasingly associated with risk of harm to self and others; and, as such, has become intrinsically linked with notions of 'protection', 'safeguarding' and 'risk avoidance' (Alaszewski, 1998; Titterton, 2005). In addition, Alaszewski (1998) suggests that the word 'risk' is associated with concepts such as 'vulnerability', 'dangerousness', 'accountability' and 'blame'.

Consider the following definition of risk: *the possibility of beneficial and harmful outcomes and the likelihood of their occurrence in a stated timescale* (Alberg et al., 1996, p9). This definition is elegantly simple, and neatly addresses the notion of positive risk-taking as well as the possibility of harm. It suggests that probability, the likelihood of a beneficial or harmful outcome occurring, is important in our under-standing of risk. This of course makes sense: just because it is possible that something will occur does not make it probable that it will happen. You will have perhaps recognised the importance of timescale in understanding risk. To understand prob-ability we need to consider the possibility that the likelihood of something occurring may increase, or decrease, over time. In addition to considering probability, it is necessary to consider the significance of the potential outcome. For example, although it may not be very probable that an intended course of action will result in serious harm or death, the significance of that outcome is obviously considerable.

Predicting the probability or significance of an outcome, be it beneficial or harmful, can be problematic and it is this activity, the assessment of risk, that is a dominant feature in the policy and practice of social work. Morgan (2007, p3) provides a useful definition of risk assessment:

> *the gathering of information through processes of communication, investigation, observation and persistence; and analysis of the potential outcome of identified behaviours. The process requires linking the context of historical information to current circumstances, to anticipate possible future change.*

You may note the emphasis on using what has occurred in the past to predict what may occur in the future. However, this is not an exact science. For example, a driving career, free from accidents, does not guarantee that I will not reverse into a lamp post at some stage in the future, nor that the actions of someone else might result in me having a car accident. The actions of others are variables over which I may have little control, or be unable to accurately predict. Assessing risk in social work is frequently subject to many variables, which may interact in subtle ways to affect the predicted outcome of a decision. Similarly, an assessment of risk may represent a snapshot in time, a frozen picture of a situation that is vibrant, fluid and possibly confused. There-fore, it is essential to accommodate this in flexible and responsive plans and actions that emerge from the assessment. What is being referred to here is a robust process of risk management, which Morgan (2007, p3) defines as: *the statement of plans and the allocation of responsibilities for translating collective decisions into real actions.* According to Morgan, the activities of risk management involve: *preventative, respon-sive and supportive measures to diminish the potential negative consequences of risk and to promote the potential benefits of taking appropriate risks* (2007, p3).

CASE STUDY

Mr Roberts is 28 years old and lives on his own in a flat that has been adapted to take his wheelchair. Mr Roberts currently pays for personal assistance via the individual budget scheme that has been piloted in his city. He is very satisfied with the current arrange-ments and appears to have more money available to fund his social life. He particularly enjoys going to pubs and clubs and quite likes to get drunk on a Saturday night. On some weeks, following a particularly 'heavy' weekend, Mr Roberts runs short of money; consequently, he sometimes runs low on food.

Mr Roberts's ex-girlfriend has contacted the social services team. She states that Mr Roberts has made friends with a group of men with whom he goes drinking. She is concerned that they are exploiting him by subtly pressurising him into lending them money on their nights out. She has spoken to Mr Roberts about this, but she says that he refuses to listen to her.

*ACTIVITY **11.2***

What risks can be identified from the case study?
What role, if any, should a social worker have in this situation?

COMMENT

You might have speculated that Mr Roberts may indeed be at risk of exploitation. You might have considered that the word of Mr Roberts's ex-girlfriend would need corroboration. It is likely that you would have considered concepts such as duty of care and the legal mandate for any potential intervention. However, you might have considered that any discussion about whether there is a social work role in this situation would hinge upon consideration of notions of vulnerability: specifically, does the fact that Mr Roberts uses a wheelchair, and qualifies for community care services, automatically make him 'vulnerable'? Therefore, it is possible that there are further risks to Mr Roberts from intrusive, or heavy-handed, intervention. The extent to which notions of risk and vulnerability are socially constructed, and the implications for practice, will be considered in the next section.

The social construction of risk: Implications for practice

Kemshall (2002) argues that the increasing preoccupation with risk in social care has been largely influenced by the rationing of resources. Kemshall suggests that, across the political spectrum, a consensus has emerged which has challenged the notion of universal access and provision of welfare services in favour of the targeting of resources upon those in greatest need. She contends that targeting and gate-keeping have largely defined the scope and focus of the activity of welfare agencies in recent years. Notions of risk and vulnerability have increasingly defined eligibility for service provision and the assessment of risk and of vulnerability have become the key factors in resource allocation. Arguably, risk has supplanted need as the key focus of assessment activity. We can question whether the increasing attention to risk in social care has been determined primarily by the financial pressure to ration resources. Social work practice does not exist in a vacuum, detached from the concerns and cultural obsessions of wider society. It can be argued that risk is socially constructed and is influenced by cultural norms and attitudes. In essence, what this means is that society devotes greater attention to some potential hazards than others: our risk awareness is either heightened or, culturally, we are more accepting of some risks and not others. For example, despite the greater risks to children posed by abusers who are known to them, society is perhaps more alert to the risks posed by strangers. Similarly, the considerable risks presented by alcohol appear to elicit less social concern than the statistically smaller problems presented by illegal drugs.

The social construction of risk is illustrated by the question of how we define 'vulnerability'. McLaughlin (2007) notes that, in recent years, the definition of 'vulnerable adult' appears to have expanded to include all individuals in receipt of community care services. Although eligibility criteria for social care services are still largely determined by risk, one can argue that this is no clear reason, other than the political desire to ration expenditure, why risk has supplanted social definitions of need. Therefore, it is potentially oppressive to assume that a person is 'vulnerable' merely because they appear to be in need of social care services. In fact, such a notion appears to be in contradiction with the principles of the social model of disability.

The increasing societal preoccupation with risk has been noted by a number of authors and has been identified as one of the characteristic features of western cultures. Beck (1992) identifies the notion of the *risk society*, characterised by anxiety about the perceived and potential hazards of contemporary existence. According to Beck, the possibility that something may go wrong in the future amplifies the perceived risk in the present. Consequently, society becomes characterised by a *precautionary principle* where the mantra 'better safe than sorry' informs our reaction to potential risks (Furedi, 1997).

These principles can perhaps be identified in social work policy and practice as a defensive approach to risk. Risk minimisation or risk avoidance can be characteristic of attempts to ensure that 'nothing goes wrong'. However, social work is practised in real-life situations and real life can never be risk free. Uncertainty, ambiguity and contradiction are the staples of social work practice (Parton, 1998); yet, evidence exists that social work agencies have increasingly adopted ever more complex policies, procedures and bureaucratic forms of assessment to attempt to ensure that practitioners 'do not make mistakes'. This approach has been particularly evident in child protection (see Chapter 5), where it has been noted that child death inquiries invariably produce responses that are bureaucratic and procedural (Ayre, 2001; Ferguson, 2005).

Ayre (2001) suggests that the defensive and bureaucratic approach to risk has been driven by the criticisms and scrutiny that social work has been subjected to in recent times. Alaszewski (1998) argues that notions of risk are indivisible from issues of accountability and blame, and blame avoidance would indeed appear to be a characteristic of much social work policy and practice. Fear of blame is, of course, not restricted to social work practitioners and agencies: arguably, many organisational and societal attitudes to risk are informed by what is known as 'blame culture'. Douglas (1992, pp15–16) provides an interesting summary of societal attitudes to risk when she states:

The (system) we are in now is almost ready to treat every death as chargeable to someone's account, every accident as caused by someone's criminal negligence, every sickness a threatened prosecution. Whose fault? is the first question.

ACTIVITY **11.3**

The quote from Douglas (1992) is a comment on societal attitudes to risk. These attitudes are frequently mirrored in the media coverage of events where 'something has gone wrong'. You may wish to consider the current treatment of stories concerning health and social care issues to consider whether or not media coverage reflects the pattern identified by Douglas (1992).

COMMENT

It is arguable that, in order for blame to be attributed to an individual or organisation, it is reasonable to assume that they should have been able to predict the negative outcome of their actions: in essence, they should have 'seen it coming'. However, Titterton (2005) argues that, following a tragedy, many investigations into social work practice have been blighted by 'hindsight fallacy': an assumption that what is obvious to investigators, in hindsight, should have been obvious to practitioners at the time, even if they were not in possession of facts which subsequently came to light. Titterton suggests that it is wrong to assume that a negative outcome automatically means that the decision-making preceding it was flawed. This might appear to be a strange assertion, but Gorman (2003), drawing on Beck's work, argues that in social care it is often the case that there are many potential courses of action in relation to a particular problem. Any one of several courses of action may be appropriate, but it may be difficult to predict exactly how circumstances may alter, or interact, to affect the outcome. Consequently, it is virtually impossible to remove an element of uncertainty from decision-making.

RESEARCH SUMMARY

Mitchell and Glendinning (2007) provide an interesting and accessible review of the research concerning risk perception and risk management in relation to different service user groups in adult social care. Their summary concerning people with learning disabilities gives a useful insight into notions of vulnerability and the perceptions and social construction of risk. Although the principles of positive risk-taking are well established in the practices of social work and nursing staff, there is evidence that carers tend to be more risk-averse, adopting a view that people with learning disabilities are in need of protection through risk avoidance.

The issue of sexuality appears to be perceived as particularly problematic by carers and this seems to reflect the concerns of wider society. Shakespeare et al. (1997) note that people with learning disabilities are assumed to be asexual. Similarly, they are viewed as being vulnerable and naïve (Banim et al., 1999) and at particular risk of exploitation. Paradoxically, people with learning disabilities can also be perceived as sexually threatening or as potential abusers (Stanley, 1999).

RESEARCH SUMMARY *continued*

The consequence of the societal perceptions of risk to people with learning disabilities, and the perceived threats posed by them, is that the opportunities to enjoy personal relationships are often severely restricted. It would seem that the 'better safe than sorry' principle acts to ensure that relationships between people with learning disabilities are viewed as inherently 'risky' and something to be avoided or prevented.

Working with risk: Principles of good practice

We have explored the argument that risk is socially constructed and that policy and practice may be informed by the notion of 'better safe than sorry'. This approach can result in defensive practice, where practitioners operate the precautionary principle of safety first in an attempt to ensure that service users, and practitioners themselves, are not exposed to risk (Thompson, 2000). Defensive practice may be well meaning but the consequences may be oppressive: the principles of service user autonomy and self-determination may be compromised. The research summary demonstrates that people with learning disabilities may be denied the opportunities for relationships through defensive and oppressive approaches to the issue of sexuality.

The research summary reveals that the professional values and principles held by practitioners may be at odds with those of parents/carers, or with those that are common in society as a whole. It is worth considering the extent to which social workers assume that their professional and personal values are self-evidently correct. This does not necessarily protect practitioners from criticism that their practice is lacking in 'common sense'. In fact, practitioners may find that their practice should be at odds with common sense, if those societal attitudes labelled as common sense are characterised by ignorance or prejudice. Consequently, it has been argued that risk assessments and risk-management strategies should state the value base that has informed decision-making (Lawson, 1996). This has two benefits: it ensures that the principles of service user autonomy and self-determination are prominently stated and that the principles that inform the decision-making process are more transparent.

It is important to recognise that decision-making can be complicated if it involves a difficult choice between two alternatives, when neither appears to be particularly attractive. Practitioners may be unclear about what the right choice is, and struggle with unravelling the ethical arguments that support one course of action over another. Banks and Williams (2005) identify these situations as *ethical dilemmas*, distinct from *ethical problems*, where the ethical course of action is clear.

ACTIVITY **11.4**

From your own practice experience, identify an ethical dilemma that you have encountered. Upon reflection, were the advantages and disadvantages of each potential course of action thoroughly evaluated? How did you feel working with this ethical dilemma?

With complex and challenging dilemmas, it is important to adopt a methodical and structured approach to achieve a resolution. Simply relying upon 'gut instinct', or adopting a mechanical/procedural approach, may prove to be insufficient to address the complexities of the situation. In this chapter, we will explore a model of working which may be helpful in complex and ethically challenging situations. Working with risk often involves effective engagement with professional dilemmas that may be stressful, challenging and unpleasant for the practitioner. Banks (2005) argues that ethical practitioners require professional confidence, commitment and competence in recognising ethical dilemmas as well as the courage to act upon their convictions.

If risk assessment and management strategies need to make explicit the values and ethical principles that inform them, there is a good case for ensuring that the legal framework, underpinning decision-making, is prominently featured. Perhaps, social workers are perceived to possess powers that exceed their legal mandate. However, there is evidence to suggest that, in relation to risk and safeguarding, social workers in adult social care are sometimes unclear about their legal responsibilities, powers and constraints (Preston-Shoot and Wrigley, 2002). The statutory framework underpinning adult social care is, arguably, rather fragmented and subject to conflicting interpretation. Therefore, in the area of safeguarding, it is essential that social workers have a clear understanding of the legislative framework in which they operate. Chapters in this book provide a thorough overview of current policy and legislation.

In the last section we noted that, when working with risk, there may be no obvious correct course of action. Decision-making can be further complicated when all options appear to be less than ideal, when the situation poses professional dilemmas, when a trade-off needs to occur between potential benefits and potential harms. In these situations, it is possible that decision-making can become muddled. However, Titterton (2005) provides a useful and simple model which allows complex issues to be unpacked in a way that enables potential choices to be presented in a transparent way.

Central to Titterton's approach is the notion of shared responsibility for decision-making. Lawson (1996) highlights that, in order for risk-management strategies to work, 'stakeholders' in decision-making need to be identified and involved. Titterton (2005) stresses the importance of a clear understanding of the difference between 'acceptable' and 'unacceptable' risks. It is important to acknowledge that the clear line between such risks can become blurred in complex situations where service user autonomy and self-determination are balanced against duties to 'protect'. Preston-Shoot and Wrigley (2002) reveal that, in relation to safeguarding adults, social workers were often unclear whether the principles of service user self-determination could override the social worker's duty to intervene.

The model proposed by Titterton (2005) gives clarity to complex situations by providing a simple but systematic framework for decision-making. In essence, Titterton's model requires that:

- the potential choices or courses of action be systematically identified;

- the potential dangers for each option are identified for each of the stakeholders;

- the potential advantages of each course of action are similarly identified.

The model is deceptively simple, but Titterton (2005) demonstrates how important it is to weigh up advantages/disadvantages of each option and to make these transparent. Risk may be constantly evolving; it is not static and can change as circumstances alter. Arguably, the Titterton model allows additional or changed factors to be incorporated and management strategies to be revised accordingly.

CASE STUDY

Frank is 19 years old and has cerebral palsy and learning difficulties. He can stand and transfer, but requires a seating system for mobility. He is incontinent of urine and occasionally incontinent of faeces. In the past, he has had epileptic fits and these are now well managed with medication. He has not had a seizure in two years.

On leaving school, Frank decided that he wanted more independence and was placed in a residential home. Two months after entering the care home, he met and started a relationship with Sharon, a 24-year-old woman. Sharon lives in a one-bedroom ground-floor flat in the estate. Four months after meeting Sharon, the care home manager informs you that Frank has told them that he is moving in with her and that she will be his carer. The manager is concerned about how he will manage, but considers that he does have the capacity to make the decision.

Sharon and Frank confirm that this is what they want to happen and that Frank has told her about his care needs and she will be able to manage. You speak to the GP, who shares the care home's concerns, but confirms that he believes Frank has the capacity to choose.

The district nurse visits on a weekly basis. Initially she considers that they are managing well, but over the next month she contacts you to say that she is concerned that Frank's level of physical hygiene and the general state of cleanliness in the house are deteriorating. When you visit, Frank is unshaven, his hair is lank and unwashed and his clothes are dishevelled; Frank has always presented as well-groomed and in clean clothes. He also smells of urine. Frank says that Sharon is managing well and that he has never been happier. He has also decided to stop taking the epilepsy drugs as they make him feel sick. He has not discussed this with his GP. Frank and Sharon state that they do not want any interference in their lives and do not want any help from social services. They do agree, however, to talk to you about your concerns and the suggestions that you have.

ACTIVITY 11.5

What would your concerns be about this situation?
What are the legal and ethical principles that would inform what you do next?
Use the model outlined by Titterton (2005) to identify potential options and the advantages and disadvantages of each potential course of action.

Ensuring safe practice

Although it is possible to explore various models and principles of working with risk, it is important not to overlook one of the major factors in ensuring good practice: confident and well-supported practitioners. Poor support, poor supervision and organisational practices that do not support reflection have been shown to be contributory factors to the poor practice revealed in a number of child death inquiries. Ferguson (2004) reveals the extent to which repeated exposure to the anxiety and stress of child protection can sometimes numb practitioners' abilities to step back and reflect upon what they are seeing. Similarly, stress and overwork can contribute to poor decision-making and chaotic, dangerous practice (Wallis, 2007). However, these issues are underexplored in relation to the practice of safeguarding adults.

CASE STUDY

Simon works in a team with a number of vacancies; consequently he is covering the work of absent colleagues. Simon's manager is required to manage a number of teams, which means that he has little contact with her and has not received supervision for a number of months. Simon is allocated a new piece of work with Mr and Mrs Jones. Mrs Jones has been providing care and support for her husband, who has dementia.

On his first visit, Simon notes that Mr Jones is rather uncommunicative so he directs all his communication via Mrs Jones. Simon is impressed by the selflessness of Mrs Jones; he is also rather appalled and embarrassed that the couple have received no support from any agency, despite the obvious difficulty in providing support for Mr Jones. However, Mrs Jones is adamant that she does not trust anyone to help support Mr Jones, citing a bad experience of cruel treatment when Mr Jones was last admitted to hospital. Simon is concerned about Mrs Jones's ability to cope: she seems to be struggling and is very stressed. He is impressed by her evident love for Mr Jones. Simon is determined to help the couple and win their trust and is gratified when Mrs Jones says that he is not a bit like the social workers she has read about in the papers.

Simon arranges to visit again and leaves with good intentions but the pressure of his other work means that Simon's visits to the Joneses become irregular and lack any planned purpose or outcome. However, he feels that continuing to visit the Joneses will enable him to monitor risk to Mr and Mrs Jones to see if the situation gets any worse. He hopes to engage Mrs Jones by exploring benefit entitlement, as financial worries seem to be a major source of stress. Although his visits seem to focus mainly on listening to Mrs Jones's problems, Simon thinks that at least he is able to provide Mrs Jones with someone to talk to. He secretly admits that his visits provide a pleasant interlude from the bureaucracy and stress of his other work. Returning from a two-week holiday, Simon is horrified to learn that Mr Jones has been admitted to hospital, apparently after being hit by Mrs Jones, and that a medical examination revealed a number of injuries that were consistent with Mr Jones being struck.

The case study illustrates what can happen when work with risk lacks focus. If Simon had had the opportunity in supervision to discuss his work, perhaps the situation would not have been allowed to drift. He would appear to have placed too great an emphasis on building a relationship with Mrs Jones, perhaps to the extent that he lost some of his ability to reflect objectively on the Joneses' situation and upon his professional role. Arguably, the problems of Mrs Jones masked the needs of Mr Jones. Simon seemed to put too great a store in Mrs Jones's apparent love for her husband, to the extent that he may have assumed that Mrs Jones's love and willingness to care could compensate for the difficulties she and Mr Jones were encountering.

Some of the issues highlighted in the case study are reflected in the literature on safeguarding children. Barber (2005) argues that social workers, trained to focus on service user strengths, may find it difficult to retain objectivity when confronted by risks. Similarly, Cousins (2005) highlights the possibility that social workers may over-estimate the abilities of parents who have good intentions. This literature draws on early work concerning the *rule of optimism* (Dingwall et al., 1983); where social workers rationalise inaction in the face of safeguarding concerns because of their belief in the good intentions of carers. Having engaged with this mind-set, social workers or other practitioners may be reluctant to view emerging concerns object- ively; and may even be willing to accept implausible explanations for things that should give cause for concern.

Working with risk, particularly in the area of safeguarding, can be stressful and uncomfortable. In the case study, Simon thought that assisting with financial issues and providing someone for Mrs Jones to talk to would help reduce some of the stresses. Dale et al. (1986) suggest that workers may focus on less contentious issues, such as the solution of material problems, in the hope that reducing stress in the family will remove causes for concern. Similarly, workers may be reticent in identifying and raising concerns for fear of damaging relationships with carers. Arguably, such approaches can be potentially dangerous.

CHAPTER SUMMARY

To work effectively in situations of risk the following issues and principles need to be considered or acknowledged.

1. Risk may be minimised, but it is often unrealistic to expect risk to be eliminated entirely.
2. Attempts to eliminate risk can result in defensive practice which is oppressive to service users.
3. Interventions need to be explicit concerning their legal mandate.
4. Similarly, assessments and plans may need to emphasise the principles and values that inform them.
5. However, respect for service user self-determination should not be used as an excuse for inaction.
6. Risk assessments may be improved by comprehensive information-gathering but decision-making will often be dependent on incomplete knowledge of all the factors.
7. Involvement of service users, carers and other stakeholders is integral to good practice.
8. Contingency plans should be made for potential crises that can reasonably be foreseen.

CHAPTER SUMMARY *continued*

9. To discourage defensive and oppressive practice, agencies need to take a corporate responsibility to risk: the primary concern of individual practitioners should not be the fear of blame for a decision that later proves to be incorrect.

10. Working with risk involves stress, anxiety and uncertainty. Supervision and support for workers, from their manager, agency and other colleagues, are essential. Working in isolation, with little support and recognition, increases the risk to workers' well-being and decreases their effectiveness.

(adapted from O'Rourke and Bird, 2000; Smith, 2005; Morgan, 2007)

FURTHER READING

Titterton, M (2005) *Risk and risk taking in health and social welfare.* London: Jessica Kingsley. This interesting and accessible book provides a useful overview of approaches to risk assessment and risk management.

Chapter 12

Inquiries and Serious Case Reviews: Listening and learning
Jill Manthorpe and *Stephen Martineau*

Introduction

This chapter investigates the potential for learning from some of the rare but important publications called serious case reviews (SCRs). While the names of similar serious case reviews investigating the deaths or serious harm of children have almost become household names (Victoria Climbié, Baby Peter (Baby P)), there are few reviews concerning adults that have become public knowledge. Despite this, there are concerns among practitioners that their own practice might be subject to investigation. Some local authorities and their partner agencies have circulated leaflets to their staff to advise them of their duties and the processes that they will need to be aware of in the event of an SCR being underway. Here, for example, is an extract from one Adult Safeguarding Board's leaflet:

What SCRs mean for practitioners
As soon as each organisation becomes aware that a case is being considered for an SCR all relevant records and any archived records will be collated. Every partner member of the KSAB is asked to review their records to check if there

has been any agency involvement with the adult or family. Each agency involved is asked to identify a senior member of staff, without direct involvement or line management of the staff involved in the case, to coordinate and produce the Internal management reviews (IMRs). The author of the IMR will then put together a diary of events and actions, identifying each time the person was seen, spoken to or listened to. They will review and evaluate the practice of all professionals.

(Adult Safeguarding Board, 2010)

While such publications are designed for frontline practitioners their contents are also potentially relevant to managers and indeed students. Their actions and inactions may be under scrutiny – with all the fear and apprehension that this may bring.

In this chapter we outline the importance of learning from the messages of SCRs but also offer a critical perspective on them. As sources of evidence about practice they have considerable advantages compared with many other accounts or summaries because they often reflect the complexities, pressures and dilemmas of social work and other professional practice. However, there is always the risk of making judgments with the benefit of hindsight.

The importance of Inquiries and Serious Case Reviews

SCRs in respect of an adult at risk are inquiries conducted by Adult Safeguarding Boards at local level when harm or death to an adult at risk has occurred. They have not been scrutinised much until recently, partly because they are not always publicly available. Despite the interest in local adult SCRs among the adult safeguarding community, few people have explored their content, process, methods of analysis, or recommendations. There are some exceptions. Hilary Brown (2009) has recently reported on her observations as an independent chair of eight adult SCRs across a small number of local authority areas, particularly in Kent where procedures have long been in place. Deborah Kitson (2009) has also identified lessons arising from publicly available national reports (not all of them SCRs) into deficiencies in the care and treatment of vulnerable adults in institutional or long-term care settings (see also Fryson and Kitson, 2010). Margaret Flynn (2008) has been prominent in publicising the lessons to be learned from the SCR into the murder of Steven Hoskin which she chaired (for more detail of this SCR and its lessons for practice see Social Care TV (2009) and Cornwall Adult Social Care Adult Protection Committee (2007)).

Our own analysis of 22 SCR reports (Manthorpe and Martineau, 2010a; 2010b) explored:

- Where and why a SCR is taking place; detail of victim(s), alleged abuser(s) and setting(s).

- The form of abuse (covering also neglect) using the categories outlined in *No secrets* (DH, 2000).

- Threshold of SCR (if this was expressly considered) – the reason why a SCR was felt to be appropriate.

- Review personnel – whether the review was conducted by internal or external people, and who else gives evidence or takes an active role.

- Stated purpose(s).

- Methodology or processes – was this a review mainly of documents and summaries of different organisations' views and records? Were there formal hearings or visits?

- Cost (rarely reported).

- Timescale – and why the report started when it did, for example, did it have to wait for the results of criminal or disciplinary proceedings?

- Lessons/recommendations – to whom are these directed and what do they recommend in specifics and in general points?

- Follow up/action plan – is there one? Who is responsible for monitoring what happens and how?

- Reflections on the SCR – does the process seem to have been 'worth it'?

In its Review of *No secrets* (Department of Health, 2008; 2009) the English government received many requests that SCRs should be more consistent and that lessons learned should be more widely circulated among social workers, other professionals, regulators and policy makers. In contrast to SCRs that must take place by law following the deaths of, or serious harm to, children, and to the mandatory system of mental health inquiries where reports are publicly available, because adult safeguarding SCRs are not public documents there are few opportunities to consider them collectively or even to get hold of them.

So why do organisations hold a SCR if they are not required to do so? They do so because there are strong suggestions in *No secrets* (Department of Health and Home Office, 2000) that they should do so and because most Adult Safeguarding Boards have included them as part of their business and presumably find them valuable. With small variations in wording, most local authorities and their local partners in adult safeguarding in England have a policy that says something along the following lines.

The purpose of a Serious Case Review is neither to reinvestigate nor to apportion blame. The purpose is to:

- *establish whether there are lessons to be learnt from the circumstances of the case about the way in which local professionals and agencies work together to safeguard vulnerable adults;*

- *review the effectiveness of procedures (both multi-agency and those of individual organisations);*

- *inform and improve local inter-agency practice;*

- *improve practice by acting on learning (developing best practice);*

- *prepare or commission an overview report which brings together and analyses the findings of the various reports from agencies in order to make recommendations for future action.*

Many of these policies and procedures are based on voluntary consensus among local authorities at national level (Association of Directors of Adult Social Services, 2006) although there are local variations. Indeed, SCRs are not the only form of inquiry in adult safeguarding. Such inquiries may take place within NHS organisations under different remits (see Manthorpe et al., 2011). One recent example concerns the murder of four older women in hospital. In March 2008, staff nurse Colin Norris received a prison sentence of a minimum term of 30 years following his conviction for the murder of four patients and the attempted murder of a fifth in 2002 at Leeds Teaching Hospitals NHS Trust (LTHT). Over six months from May to November 2002, Norris injected insulin into five non-diabetic patients, who had surgical repairs of hip fractures. The patients suddenly became severely hypoglycaemic, resulting in brain damage, which was either the cause of or a significant contributor to their deaths. The Strategic Health Authority inquiry (Yorkshire and the Humber Strategic Health Authority (YHSHA), 2010a) found that adult safeguarding systems were not in place in the hospital at the time. The NHS treated such events as Serious Untoward Incidents:

> *LTHT has taken steps to address the requirements of the* No secrets *guidance on adult safeguarding. Significant progress was made with the establishment of Trust procedures and a steering group in 2006 and at this time the procedures were reflective of the 2000 guidance. The procedures were further updated in 2007. There has also been the appointment of a Nurse Consultant and Lead Nurse with the responsibility to lead on safeguarding for the Trust.*

> (YHSHA, 2010a, p21)

From the same Strategic Health Authority, another independent inquiry report commissioned by NHS Yorkshire and the Humber, declared that it was unlikely that Sister Anne Grigg-Booth, a senior night nurse practitioner (NNP) at Airedale NHS Trust, *deliberately set out to harm patients*. The report into incidents that took place between 2000 and 2002 declares that she *was not a Beverley Allitt or Colin Norris in that her actions were almost entirely open*. Notwithstanding this, Sister Grigg-Booth had been charged with three offences of murder, one offence of attempted murder and 13 offences of administering noxious substances with the intention of causing harm. She died before her trial in 2005. Despite the inquiry's views of a lack of intent, it was scathing in its criticism of the hospital culture, clinical governance systems and management. It noted, for example:

> *The night staff in particular appeared to operate in a vacuum, separated from the world of day staff, save for brief handover arrangements for continuity of patient care. The normal arrangements for ensuring their involvement in management meetings and professional briefings appeared to be deficient and the supervision, challenge and professional support offered to Sister Grigg-Booth and the NNPs (night nurse practitioners) was woefully*

inadequate. Of great concern is the fact that they were effectively left to their own devices.

(YHSHA, 2010b, p130)

We present these examples to show that many organisations undertake reviews when they judge that things have gone wrong. There may be much to learn from them, as well as cases that directly investigate social work practice.

For example, in the following case, the coroner required the local authority's chief executive to produce a report to respond to the coroner's concerns. While this is not termed a SCR we suggest it very much reflects referrals to local authorities. It might be easy for a student social worker to place him or herself in some parts of this scenario:

CASE STUDY

Frontline practice
Death of 88-year old woman: report to social services requiring a response.
An 88-year old woman lived alone following the death of her husband. She was not always compliant with her medication, and was always very reluctant to accept medical care. Neighbours offered to help support her but became concerned when they had not seen her for some time.

The police and ambulance service were called... They did not find her in need of medical attention, she seemed clean and well cared for as did the property. Her blood sugar levels were low, but restored with sugared drinks and glucose. She was judged mentally competent to look after herself and the property. (two days later), the ambulance service faxed the details through to social services.

The referral was taken by a non-qualified, temporary member of staff, and passed to the duty manager, who considered it non-urgent. That same day a neighbour rang social services with her concerns. She rang twice more, the third call being four days later... A social worker visit was then scheduled for five days later... (two days later), the woman had been found dead.

The inquest recorded an open verdict but the coroner sent a report under Rule 43 to the chief executive of the council. The coroner drew attention to the need for further training on eligibility criteria, better communication about how decisions were reached, better investigation where information is lacking, clear investigation and responses to external concerns, clearer distinction between social work and medical responses (Report to Council, 2009).

ACTIVITY 12.1

This activity asks you to think about what you would need if you were to be setting up an Inquiry or Serious Case Review (SCR) (perhaps in a case similar to the above). As an Inquiry may be high profile locally and influenced by people outside your organisation, we suggest you focus on the initial stages of a SCR. The following five points should help you group your thoughts together.

ACTIVITY **12.1** *continued*

1. *When thinking about resources, we mean human resources as well as money to hire rooms and obtain refreshments, so think how much time you will be asking of people. Where could the SCR meetings be held? What sort of budget should be in mind?*
2. *Establishing a set of terms of references could be helpful. This is usually placed at the start of the report. Whose job should it be to set these up? What might they contain, e.g. mentions of confidentiality, what sorts of evidence will be acceptable?*
3. *A chronology of events is generally seen as very helpful but whose responsibility should that be? If you leave it to the Review Panel or a chairperson this could take a very long time and be expensive. Who else could take on this role?*
4. *How will you enlist the co-operation of other agencies? Force or persuasion? Will you invite family members or the vulnerable person who has been harmed or placed at risk of serious harm? How might this be best handled?*
5. *Lastly, how will any lessons be assembled and then learned or adapted into a system change?*

COMMENT

Most local authorities and their partners in Adult Safeguarding Boards will have set up a policy and procedure around these practical matters. These will be available on the Board's website. Together staff in safeguarding services and local managers will share these responsibilities, perhaps aided by colleagues in legal or chief executive departments. If the local authority and its partners have decided to join together its membership and administration of Children's and Adult Safeguarding Boards then these tasks will be shared.

We are all limited in our understanding of SCRs because many of them are reported in summary form and so we have scant detail of most of them. For example, in a reflection on the executive summary of a SCR that was undertaken by the Cornwall and Isles of Scilly Safeguarding Adults Board (2009) into the death of JK, a 76-year-old woman found dead in her own home, Peter Scourfield (2010) outlined three question areas arising from this report but noted that they remain unanswerable because the report format is a brief summary. This can make the reading and analysis of SCRs rather frustrating. In this instance the following questions arose from his reading of the summary but other readers may have followed different questions. 1) were the needs of the woman in this case seen as related to her being a victim of crime? 2) did her needs arise from her disabilities? or 3) were her 'lifestyle choices' bundled together so that neither these views nor her disabilities were dealt with effectively? Despite his request to see the full report, he was only able to have sight of the public document – the executive summary – and so like us he finds it hard to make anything more than guesstimates of what might have been better or worse courses of action or practice.

A further complication that arises around inquiries in adult safeguarding is that when professional and agency involvement is scrutinised then many agencies might be involved. There are often interfaces with other services and organisations. Here is an extract from an inquiry published in 2010 about a case of domestic violence where the victim was also a 'vulnerable adult':

> *... (the vulnerable adult) refused involvement of adult services with his case but a MARAC (multi-agency) risk assessment could have enabled agencies to share and bring together the information about the risk in the household...* the report from the local Adults Safeguarding Board about one SCR to the local authority overview and scrutiny committee (OSC) stated, The multi-agency safeguarding adult procedures will be re-written to clarify the link between the safeguarding adults and domestic violence services. In particular the revised document will clarify when agencies can share information about an adult who is able to make their own decisions and who is refusing support to address domestic abuse.

Such documents get to the heart of many practice dilemmas in adult safeguarding; that is the rights of adults to refuse interventions have to be set in the context of concern about people in vulnerable situations who may be subject to undue influence (see Chapter 3 on situational incapacity). SCRs can be learning documents in this respect – highlighting areas of practice where there are no easy answers and where frontline practitioners will need to seek out supervision and managerial support. There are not always clear messages from SCRs and, rightly, many report authors seem to try to avoid an over-simplifying approach.

Learning the lessons at organisational level

Some SCRs or inquiries present firm conclusions and recommendations and some do not step back from shaming and blaming practitioners and organisations. In cases involving vulnerable adults, hospital care has dominated the headlines. Powerful patient groups also take up and publicise the findings of such reports and inquiries. One example of this is the description of the neglect experienced by one older woman which could have been seen as an isolated example of bad practice. This is how the hospital concerned initially responded to the complaint made by the daughter of the woman in question, Elin Styles, whose complaints its managers initially met with bland, formulaic reassurances about 'regret' and 'learning lessons', as are similarly portrayed in the other 16 stories featured in the Patients' Association (2010) report. Unfortunately as the Parliamentary Ombudsman (2011) has recently observed, these are not single mishaps. The problem of poor quality care for older people in the NHS is a system failure, not a localised one, and it could bring the service down. Adult safeguarding has been at the margins of many such incidences and inquiries but there may be much greater role for it to combine forces with agents of change.

There is ample evidence of this system-wide problem of poor practice in the NHS and although stories are valuable in attracting the attention of policy makers they need also to be seen as not just one off events if things are to improve. In this sector we are now seeing that individual cases are being backed up by general data confirming that the problems are system wide. This evidence has recently come from the National Confidential Enquiry into Patient Outcome and Death (NCEPOD) (2010). The NCEPOD reviewed the care of frail older people who had died after surgery, in 2008. It found that only just over a third of those who died had received good care. The big failings for the other two thirds were in not giving enough pain relief, in inadequate hydration of post-operative patients, and in providing adequate nutrition. In over a quarter of cases the operation was not performed in a timely way. Almost half of those who needed emergency hip replacement were not seen by a consultant surgeon at any time between their admission to hospital and their death. What does this have to do with social work? On the face of it not too much but we would argue that the NHS has systems of accountability and transparency that are not commonly found in local authority commissioned or provided services. We need to be alert to the possibility that endemic poor practice and system failure are happening in social care, specifically in areas (care homes and home care including personal budget funded care and self-funded support) where social workers may be responsible for reviews and monitoring. Investigations, such as SCRs, can help see beyond individual encounters and practice.

ACTIVITY 12.2

Please consider the following case study:

You are the social worker who is visiting an older man, Mr Archer, with suspected memory loss who has been referred by his GP. You are in a hurry as you have several other visits and it has been hard to find a place to park. You press the doorbell and shout through the letterbox as there is no reply. You ring the telephone number you have been given and hear the ringing in the house. There is no sign of anyone and you wonder if he has remembered that you are calling today. You wait a bit and then post a note through the letter box. Three days later you read that a person has been found dead in suspicious circumstances at this address.

What are your initial fears? What are your first actions? Whom do you tell – at work and in your personal life?

COMMENT

We expect that anyone whose activities are going to be investigated when there is a chance of blame and criticism are going to be worried. For professionals there are risks of being called to account by an employer but also by a professional registration body. There are risks of losing one's employment, reputation, and status. Sources of support lie with colleagues (difficult to sustain if a person is suspended), with friends and families, and with professional organisations or unions. A set of interviews with people who had been suspended from residential services following allegations or incidents (Rees and Manthorpe, 2010) provides an illustration of the personal costs of feeling under suspicion and the practical consequences that might follow suspension.

COMMENT *continued*

Our second point relates to keeping records. In the summary of this visit we have set out the events but which of them are in the records of your visit? How long did you wait? Are there any ways in which you can begin to substantiate your account, for example, find the number you called on your phone and make a note of the time and duration of this call? Find the notebook where you tore out the page for your message? Find your parking receipt? Draw a map of where you parked and your route? This may sound defensive but your memory is likely to be fresher the nearer the time you write things down. These are small points but they will help the investigator build up the chronology of events if there is a SCR or similar. Jacki Pritchard (2011) and Gill Constable (2009) have drawn up an extensive guide to recording in adult safeguarding – looking at best practice and evidential requirements. She maintains that social workers should develop the habit of writing summaries regularly and provides substantial guidance on the practicalities of this. We agree with her that social workers need to have skills in constructing chronologies and our view is that students on practice should be extended the opportunity to do such tasks, and that practice assessors could facilitate this but also offer constructive feedback on this work. Gill Constable (2009) also focuses on the importance of case recording and report writing.

ACTIVITY 12.3

We now suggest that you read a SCR, in summary form. This is likely to be all that is obtainable because these often do not pertain to the most high profile and therefore atypical events or circumstances. To access one of these we suggest you use an internet search engine and enter 'serious case review adult' or similar. You might like to see if there is one from your local authority or you might like to choose one that focuses on the area of practice or user groups which are of particular interest to you. It may take some time to find out such information.

COMMENT

When you have located a SCR summary to read, we suggest you turn back to pages 181–2, the set of bullet points we think are helpful in reading an SCR. Make notes on these, recording what is there and what is missing. Are family members referred to or the views of the vulnerable adult? A note of caution, however, because this is a summary it is likely that there is much that you won't be able to answer. But there will be much food for thought in the recommendations. We have noticed, for example, that there are sometimes recommendations from the authors of SCRs for greater monitoring but this seems at odds with the 'light touch' monitoring of personalisation. Are there any recommendations that seem to you to create tensions in practice?

CHAPTER SUMMARY

From our examination, consultation and reflection on the largest sample of SCR reports we could find, we have concluded that although the purpose of such reviews is well understood, the reports themselves often lack transparency about their purpose and activities. We have recommended that a greater degree of standardisation of approach would raise the quality and usefulness of these reports and the degree to which their findings and messages could be centrally collated (Manthorpe and Martineau, 2010a; 2010b). There are risks of establishing a further 'inquiry industry' but we believe that there is potential to improve our learning from practice by distilling their recommendations and considering the potential for risk minimisation. However, we need to consider the longer term impacts of SCRs on safeguarding work, social work practice and organisational cultures. They can take up great time and energy; and of course focus on what went wrong (apparently). Currently SCRs relate mainly to social care; and other systems of inquiry and investigation, such as those we have mentioned in the NHS, are relatively under-explored. The potential for thinking about and learning from a systems review process as is currently being developed for children's reviews (SCIE, 2010) also seems persuasive. It may be that if adult and children's safeguarding activities work closer together then there will be greater sharing of such developments.

Summary of good practice

Being aware of how to set up and conduct a SCR is important. The following tasks are important and many practitioners will be involved along the course of the review:

- identify and locate resources;
- agree purpose and terms of reference;
- construct chronology;
- ascertain co-operation and carry out an investigation;
- establish ways to monitor and learn and put them into the system.

Practitioners will need to develop skills in this area but many of these are transferable. Students may learn much in practice about activities of recording and case summary work; as well as risk assessment and risk management. This can be integrated with learning about the work of other agencies, the legal framework and systems of personal and professional accountability in other parts of their programmes.

FURTHER READING

Pritchard, J with Leslie, S (2011) *Recording skills in safeguarding adults*. London: Jessica Kingsley.

Warner, J (2006) Inquiry reports as active texts and their function in relation to professional practice in mental health. *Health, Risk and Society*, 8 (3), 223–37.

Acknowledgements and disclaimer

This chapter draws on work commissioned by the Department of Health and the Department of Health & Comic Relief on the subjects of Serious Case Reviews and on Secondary Data in Elder Abuse. We are grateful to them for funding and to participants in the studies. The views expressed in this article are the authors' alone and should not necessarily be seen as reflecting those of the Department of Health or Comic Relief.

Conclusion

This book has covered a range of topics in the evolving field of safeguarding adults. It has introduced you to the concepts and practice dilemmas that have informed our understanding of adult abuse and explored suggestions to promote best practice. By developing your understanding of the complex issues involved in safeguarding adults we hope to influence how you undertake all your work, encouraging practice that promotes the rights and welfare of people who use services.

Safeguarding adults should not be seen as a procedure, but as a mind-set, a way of approaching your work that never loses sight of the individual at the centre of your practice. It is not sufficient to only focus on our own practice for this can become tacit collusion with the poor practice of others. This requires an active rather than passive engagement with people, whether professionals, carers (family members or friends) or people who use services. It is through questioning our own and other people's actions that we improve practice and change situations. At the heart of this interaction is sensitive, but assertive, practice driven by reflection rather than routine.

In the first part of this book (Chapters 1, 2, 3 and 4) we have provided you with some of the key concepts and the legal framework that inform the safeguarding of adults. We explored how safeguarding adults policy and practice have evolved (Chapter 1) and highlighted that the reliance on a raft of legislation in England, Wales and Northern Ireland can be inadequate to address the challenges of complex abusive situations. Chapters 2 and 3 focused on the two laws which will have the most significant impact on safeguarding the rights of people. Chapter 4 highlighted the differences in the Scottish legislature and how they have developed the Adult Support and Protection (Scotland) Act 2007 to significantly increase their ability to intervene to protect adults from abuse. The positive impact of this legislation would appear to point the way forward for the rest of the UK. However, in these chapters we have cautioned you about the risks associated with overreliance on legislation to provide the answers in situations which are often messy and uncertain.

The second part of the book developed the empowering themes advocated in the first part. It started by reminding us that adult abuse is not a unique phenomenon but exists alongside and has many similarities with child abuse and domestic violence. Indeed, these different forms of abuse frequently occur in the same household. Chapter 5 demonstrated how safeguarding adults has shared a similar evolution to safeguarding children and highlighted the transferability of many of the lessons that have been learnt to empower the person who has been abused. Chapter 6 challenged arbitrary or resource-led distinctions between domestic violence and adult abuse and cautioned against procedural, pathologising approaches in favour of empowering partnerships.

We explored the centrality of anti-oppressive practice to ensuring that we safeguard the rights, needs, wishes and beliefs of carers and people who use services (Chapter

7). Communication (Chapter 8) is essential to ensuring that people who use services are heard, that we understand their wishes and needs to prevent situations becoming abusive and to give them the confidence and trust to disclose to us if they are abused.

The third and final section explored how we can develop more effective practice. Poor communication and organisational cultures (Chapter 9) are frequently highlighted in inquiries into institutional abuse. Organisations need to promote cultures which are not only open and responsive to the needs of their clients, carers and the wider society, but also to engaging and co-operating with other agencies (Chapter 10). Essentially, reflection is required at an organisational as well as individual level. The nature of risk (Chapter 11) and its assessment has always been a central issue in safeguarding, perhaps even more so, now that it is reflected in the new term 'adult at risk'. Whilst its significance has been reaffirmed, it remains an imprecise science and we must be wary of personal or managerial tendencies towards defensive practice in favour of person-centred defendable practice. Critical, reflective and defendable practices were all points underlined at the end of this book where we considered the lessons that can be learned from Serious Case Reviews (Chapter 12). We are now reaching a point where there have been a sufficient number of these investigations to enable considerable learning not just in the area in which they have occurred but also across the UK. However, the reluctance to publish more than summaries of these reviews and the lack of standardisation impacts on their potential quality and wider utility. Yet we must be committed to draw on every opportunity to learn from mistakes and be proactive at the individual, cultural and institutional levels.

We hope you have found this book on safeguarding adults helpful in providing an insight into how you can develop your practice and stimulated you to explore the issues raised with your practice learning supervisor. We also hope that once you are qualified you will retain a commitment to the principles highlighted here as part of your continuing professional development. Safeguarding adults is everyone's business and necessitates ongoing vigilance.

Appendix

Subject benchmark for social work

3 Nature and extent of social work

3.7 Contemporary social work increasingly takes place in an inter-agency context, and social workers work collaboratively with others towards interdisciplinary and cross-professional objectives. Honours degree programmes as qualifying awards are required to help equip students with accurate knowledge about the respective responsibilities of social welfare agencies, including those in the public, voluntary/independent and private sectors, and acquire skills in effective collaborative practice.

4 Defining principles

4.1 As an applied academic subject, social work is characterised by a distinctive focus on practice in complex social situations to promote and protect individual and collective well-being.

4.2 At honours level, the study of social work involves the integrated study of subject-specific knowledge, skills and values and the critical application of research knowledge from the social and human sciences, and from social work (and closely related domains) to inform understanding and to underpin action, reflection and evaluation. Honours degree programmes should be designed to help foster this integration of contextual, analytic, critical, explanatory and practical understanding.

4.3 Contemporary definitions of social work as a degree subject reflect its origins in a range of different academic and practice traditions. The precise nature and scope of the subject is itself a matter for legitimate study and critical debate. Three main issues are relevant to this.

- Social work is located within different social welfare contexts. Within the UK there are different traditions of social welfare (influenced by legislation, historical development and social attitudes) and these have shaped both social work education and practice in community-based settings including residential, day care and substitute care. In an international context, distinctive national approaches to social welfare policy, provision and practice have greatly influenced the focus and content of social work degree programmes.

- There are competing views in society at large on the nature of social work and on its place and purpose. Social work practice and education inevitably reflect these differing perspectives on the role of social work in relation to social justice, social care and social order.

- Social work, both as occupational practice and as an academic subject, evolves, adapts and changes in response to the social, political and economic challenges and demands of contemporary social welfare policy, practice and legislation.

4.6 Social work is a moral activity that requires practitioners to recognise the dignity of the individual, but also to make and implement difficult decisions (including restriction of liberty) in human situations that involve the potential for benefit or harm. Honours degree programmes in social work therefore involve the study, application of, and critical reflection upon, ethical principles and dilemmas. As reflected by the four care councils' codes of practice, this involves showing respect for persons, honouring the diverse and distinctive organisations and communities that make up contemporary society, promoting social justice and combating processes that lead to discrimination, marginalisation and social exclusion. This means that honours undergraduates must learn to:

- understand the impact of injustice, social inequalities and oppressive social relations.

Subject knowledge, understanding and skills

Subject knowledge and understanding

During their degree studies in social work, honours graduates should acquire, critically evaluate, apply and integrate knowledge and understanding in the following five core areas of study.

5.1.1 Social work services, service users and carers, which include:

- the relationship between agency policies, legal requirements and professional boundaries in shaping the nature of services provided in interdisciplinary contexts and the issues associated with working across professional boundaries and within different disciplinary groups.

5.1.2 The service delivery context, which includes:

- the significance of legislative and legal frameworks and service delivery standards (including the nature of legal authority, the application of legislation in practice, statutory accountability and tensions between statute, policy and practice);

- the contribution of different approaches to management, leadership and quality in public and independent human services.

5.1.3 Values and ethics, which include:

- the conceptual links between codes defining ethical practice, the regulation of professional conduct and the management of potential conflicts generated by the codes held by different professional groups.

5.1.4 Social work theory, which includes:

- social science theories explaining group and organisational behaviour, adaptation and change;

- models and methods of assessment, including factors underpinning the selection and testing of relevant information, the nature of professional judgement and the processes of risk assessment and decision-making.

5.1.5 The nature of social work practice, which includes:

- the nature and characteristics of skills associated with effective practice, both direct and indirect, with a range of service-users and in a variety of settings.

Subject-specific skills and other skills

5.3 All social work honours graduates should show the ability to reflect on and learn from the exercise of their skills. They should understand the significance of the concepts of continuing professional development and lifelong learning, and accept responsibility for their own continuing development.

Communication skills

5.6 Honours graduates in social work should be able to communicate clearly, accurately and precisely (in an appropriate medium) with individuals and groups in a range of formal and informal situations, i.e. to:

- make effective contact with individuals and organisations for a range of objectives, by verbal, paper-based and electronic means;

- listen actively to others, engage appropriately with the life experiences of service users, understand accurately their viewpoint and overcome personal prejudices to respond appropriately to a range of complex personal and interpersonal situations; identify and use opportunities for purposeful and supportive communication with service users within their everyday living situations.

Skills in working with others

5.7 Honours graduates in social work should be able to work effectively with others, i.e. to:

- involve users of social work services in ways that increase their resources, capacity and power to influence factors affecting their lives;

- consult actively with others, including service users and carers, who hold relevant information or expertise.

Skills in personal and professional development

5.8 Honours graduates in social work should be able to:

- advance their own learning and understanding with a degree of independence;

- reflect on and modify their behaviour in the light of experience;

- identify and keep under review their own personal and professional boundaries;

- manage uncertainty, change and stress in work situations;

- handle inter and intrapersonal conflict constructively;

- understand and manage changing situations and respond in a flexible manner;

- challenge unacceptable practices in a responsible manner;

- take responsibility for their own further and continuing acquisition and use of knowledge and skills;

- use research critically and effectively to sustain and develop their practice.

References

Abrahams, H (2007) *Supporting women after domestic violence.* London: Jessica Kingsley.

Action on Elder Abuse (2007) 30 January News Release.

Adams, R (2003) *Social work and empowerment.* Basingstoke: Palgrave.

Ahmed, M (2009) Failure to commit to adult protection legislation lambasted. *Community Care*, 20 July.

Alaszewski, A (1998) Risk in a modern society. In Alaszewski, A, Harrison, L and Manthorpe, J (eds) *Risk, health and welfare.* Buckingham: Open University Press.

Alberg, C, Bingley, W, Bowers, L, Ferguson, G, Hatfield, B, Hoban, A and Maden, A (1996) *Learning materials on mental health: Risk assessment.* Manchester: University of Manchester/Department of Health.

Anderson, M (2003) *Autistic spectrum disorders.* In Gates, B (ed.) *Learning disabilities: Towards integration.* London: Churchill Livingstone, pp183–204.

Annandale, E (1998) *The sociology of health and illness: A critical introduction.* Oxford: Polity.

Association of Directors of Adult Social Services (ADSS) (2006) *Vulnerable adult serious case review guidance – Developing a local protocol.* London: ADSS.

Association of Directors of Social Services (ADSS) (2005) *Safeguarding adults – A national framework of standards for good practice in adult protection work.* London: ADSS.

Ayre, P (2001) Child protection and the media: Lessons from the last three decades. *British Journal of Social Work*, 31 (6), 887–901.

Baker, A (1975) Granny battering. *Modern Geriatrics*, 5(8), 20–4.

Banim, M, Guy, A and Tasker, P (1999) Trapped in risky behaviour: Empowerment, disabled people and sexual health. *Health, Risk and Society*, 1, 209–21.

Banks, S (2005) The ethical practitioner in formation: Issues of courage, competence and commitment. *Social Work Education*, 24 (7), October, 737–53.

Banks, S and Williams, R (2005) Accounting for ethical difficulties in social welfare work: Issues, problems and dilemmas. *British Journal of Social Work*, 35, 1005–22.

Barber, N (2005) Risking optimism: Practitioner adaptations of strengths-based practice in statutory child protection work. *Child Abuse Prevention Newsletter*, 13 (2), Winter. Melbourne: Australian Institute of Family Studies.

Barnes, C (1999) *Exploring disability: A sociological introduction.* Cambridge: Polity.

BBC www.bbc.co.uk/news/world

BBC News (2011) Scrapping vetting scheme 'puts children at risk', 11 February.

Beck, U (1992) *Risk society.* London: Sage.

Begum, N (2006) *Doing it for themselves: Participation and Black and Ethnic Minority services users.* UK: SCIE and Race Equality Unit.

Belbin, RM (1981) *Team roles and work.* Oxford: Butterworth-Heinemann.

Bennett, J (2010) Assessing mental capacity. In *Social Care and Neurodisability*, 1 (3).

Beresford, P (2007) *The changing roles and tasks of social work from service users' perspectives.* Shaping Our Lives Network. London: General Social Care Council.

Beresford, P and Trevillion, S (1995) *Developing skills for community care: A collaborative approach.* Aldershot: Arena.

Brandon, D and Brandon, T (2001) *Advocacy in social work.* Birmingham: British Association of Social Workers.

Braye, S and Preston-Shoot, M (1995) *Empowering practice in social work.* Buckingham: Open University Press.

Braye, S, Preston-Shoot, M, Cull, L-A, Johns, R and Roche, J (2005) *Teaching, learning and assessment of partnership work in social work education.* Bristol: Social Care Institute for Excellence.

The Bridge Child Care Consultancy (1995) *Paul. Death through neglect.* London: Islington Area Child Protection Committee.

British Bankers Association (2005) *The Banking Code – Setting standards for banks, building societies and other banking service providers.* London: BBA Enterprises Ltd.

Brockbank, A and McGill, I (1998) *Facilitating reflective learning in higher education.* 2nd edition. Buckingham: Society for Research into Higher Education and Open University Press.

Brown, H (2009) The process and function of serious case review. *Journal of Adult Protection,* 11: 38–50.

Brown, H and Turk, V (1993) Defining sexual abuse as it affects adults with learning disabilities. *Mental Handicap,* 20, 44–55.

Brown, K (ed.) (2006) *Vulnerable adults and community care.* Exeter: Learning Matters.

Brown, R and Barber, P (2008) *The social worker's guide to the Mental Capacity Act 2005.* Exeter: Learning Matters.

Butler, G and Hope, T (2007) *Manage your mind. The mental fitness guide.* Oxford: Oxford University Press.

Butler-Sloss, Lord Justice (1987) *Report of the Inquiry into child abuse in Cleveland.* London: HMSO.

Calder, M (2004) *Children living with domestic violence: Towards a framework for assessment.* Lyme Regis: Russell House.

Cambridge, P (2007) In safe hands, protecting people with learning disabilities from abuse. In Carnaby, S (ed.) *Learning disability today.* Brighton: Pavilion Publishing.

Care Quality Commission (2010) *Guidance about compliance: Essential standards of quality and safety.* London: CQC. **www.cqc.org.uk/publications**

Care Quality Commission (2010) *Our safeguarding protocol: The Care Quality Commission's commitment to safeguarding.* Newcastle upon Tyne: CQC. **www.cqc.org.uk/publications**

Care Services Improvement Partnership (2005a) *Moving on: Key learning from Rowan Ward.* London: Department of Health.

Care Services Improvement Partnership (2005b) *Everybody's business, integrated mental health services for older adults: A service development guide.* London: DoH. **www.olderpeoplesmental health.csip.org.uk**

Cockram, J (2003) *Silent voices: Women with disabilities and family and domestic violence.* Centre for Social Research, Edith Cowan University, Western Australia. **www.wwda.org.au/**

Cocks, E (2001) Normalisation and social role valorisation: guidance for human services development. *Hong Kong Journal of Psychiatry*, 1 (1), 12–16.

Cogher, L (2005) Communication and people with learning disabilities. In Grant, G, Goward, P, Richardson, M and Ramcharan, P (eds) *Learning disability: A life cycle approach to valuing people.* Maidenhead: Open University Press/McGraw-Hill, pp260–84.

Collins, S (2007) Social workers, resilience, positive emotions and optimism. *Practice*, 19 (4), 259–69.

Comic Relief (2007) *UK study of abuse and neglect of older people: Prevalence survey report.* London: Comic Relief and the Department of Health.

Commission for Health Improvement (2002) *Investigation into matters arising from care on Rowan Ward, Manchester Mental Health and Social Care Trust.* London: CHI. **www.chi.nhs.uk.**

Commission for Social Care Inspection (2008) *Putting people first: Equality and diversity matters.* London: Commission for Social Care Inspection.

Commission for Social Care Inspection (2007a) *Joint investigation into the service for people with learning disabilities provided by Sutton and Merton Primary Care Trust.* London: CSCI. **www.csci. org.uk.**

Commission for Social Care Inspection (2007b) *Safeguarding adults protocol and guidance.* CSCI. **www.csci.org.uk**

Commission for Social Care Inspection and Health Care Commission (2006) *Joint investigation into the provision of services for people with learning disabilities at Cornwall Partnership NHS Trust.* London: Commission for Health Care Audit and Inspection.

Constable, G (2009) Case recording and report-writing skills. In Mantell, A (ed) *Social work skills with adults.* Exeter: Learning Matters.

Corby, B (2006) *Child abuse. Towards a knowledge base.* Maidenhead: Open University Press/ McGraw-Hill.

Cornwall Adult Social Care Protection Committee (2007) *The murder of Steven Hoskin: Serious case review: Multi-agency and single-agency recommendations and action plans.* Truro: Cornwall Adult Social Care Adult Protection Committee.

Cornwall and Isles of Scilly Safeguarding Adults Board (2009) *Serious Case Review: Executive summary report of a female adult (JK), final version.* Truro: Cornwall Council.

Cousins, C (2005) 'But the parent is trying...' The dilemmas workers face. *Child Abuse Prevention Newsletter*, 13 (1) Winter. Melbourne: Australian Institute of Family Studies.

Crawford, K and Walker, J (2004) *Social work with older people.* Exeter: Learning Matters.

Crystal, D (1992) *The Cambridge encyclopedia of language.* Cambridge: Cambridge University Press.

Daily Mail (2007) Killer of teacher still poses 'a genuine and present threat'. *Daily Mail*, 21 August. **www.dailymail.co.uk**

Dale, P, Davies, M, Morrison, T and Waters, J (1986) *Dangerous families: Assessment and treatment of child abuse.* London: Tavistock.

Dalrymple, J and Burke, B (2006) *Anti-oppressive practice: Social care and the law.* Maidenhead: Open University Press/McGraw-Hill.

Daniel, P and Ivatts, J (1998) *Children and social policy.* Basingstoke: Macmillan.

Davidson, J and Gottschalk, P (eds) (2011) Chapter 5 in *Internet child abuse, current research and policy.* Milton Park: Routledge.

Department for Constitutional Affairs (2007) The Mental Capacity Act Code of Practice. London: The Stationery Office.

Department for Constitutional Affairs (1997) *Who decides?* London: The Stationery Office.

Department for Education and Skills (2006) *Working together to safeguard children: A guide to interagency working to safeguard and promote the welfare of children.* London: DfES.

Department for Education and Skills (2003) *Every child matters.* London: The Stationery Office.

Department of Health (2010) *A vision for adult social care: Capable communities and active citizens.* London: DH. **www.dh.gov.uk/en/Publicationsandstatistics**

Department of Health (2010) *DH Business plan 2011–15.* London: DH. **www.dh.gov/uk/en/Consultations**

Department of Health (2010) *Transparency in outcomes.* London: DH. **www.dh.gov/uk/en/Consultations**

Department of Health (2009) *Report on the consultation: The review of No Secrets guidance.* London: Department of Health.

Department of Health (2009) *Safeguarding Adults: Report on the consultation on the review of 'No Secrets'.* London: DH. **webarchive.nationalarchives.gov.uk**

Department of Health (2008) *Safeguarding adults: A consultation on the review of the 'No secrets' guidance.* London: Department of Health.

Department of Health (2007a) *Independence choice and risk: A guide to best practice in supported decision making.* London: The Stationery Office.

Department of Health (2007b) *Being the gay one: Experiences of lesbian, gay and bisexual people working in the health and social care sector.* London: The Stationery Office. **www.dh.gov.uk/en/Publicationsandstatistics**

Department of Health (2007c) *UK study of abuse and neglect of older people. Prevalence survey report.* London: The Stationery Office and Comic Relief.

Department of Health (2007d) *Mental Health Act.* London: The Stationery Office. **www.publications.parliament.uk/**

Department of Health (2006) *Our health, our care, our say: A new direction for community services.* London: The Stationery Office.

Department of Health (2005) *Independence, well-being and choice: Our vision for the future of social care for adults in England.* London: The Stationery Office.

Department of Health (2003) *Fair access to care services: Eligibility criteria for adult social care.* London: Department of Health.

Department of Health (2001a) *Valuing people: A new strategy for learning disability for the 21st century.* London: The Stationery Office.

Department of Health (2001b) *National Service Framework for Older People.* London: The Stationery Office.

Department of Health (2000) *No secrets: Guidance on developing and implementing multi-agency protection of vulnerable adults.* London: The Stationery Office. **www.dh.gov.uk/en/Publications andstatistics**

Department of Health (1995) *Child protection: Messages from research.* London: HMSO.

Department of Health (1991) *Achieving change. Progress review.* London: DoH.

Department of Health and Home Office (2000) *No secrets: Guidance on developing and imple-menting multi-agency policies and procedures to protect vulnerable adults from abuse.* London: Department of Health.

Department of Health and Social Security (1974) *Report of the committee of inquiry into the care and supervision provided in relation to Maria Colwell.* London: HMSO.

Dimond, B (2008) *Legal aspects of mental capacity.* Oxford: Blackwell.

Dingwall, R, Eekelaar, J and Murray, Y (1983) *The protection of children: State intervention and family life.* Oxford: Blackwell.

Director of Public Prosecutions (2010) Policy for prosecutors in respect of cases of encouraging or assisting suicide. Available from: **www.cps.gov.uk/publications/prosecution**

Douglas, M (1992) *Risk and blame: Essays in cultural theory.* Abingdon: Routledge.

Doyle, C (2004) Getting the message across: Exploring the functions of challenging behaviour. In Turnball, J (ed.) *Learning disability nursing.* Oxford: Blackwell.

Drake, R (1999) *Understanding disability politics.* Basingstoke: Macmillan.

Dunning, J (2010) Personalisation: Cuts threaten transformation agenda. *Community Care*, 19 May. Available from **www.communitycare.co.uk**

Edinburgh, Lothian and Borders Chief Executive Group (2009) *Adult support and protection: Ensuring rights preventing harm.* **www.nhsborders.org.uk**

Edinburgh, Lothian and Borders Chief Executive Group (2003) *Protecting vulnerable adults: Ensuring rights and preventing abuse.* **www.edinburgh.gov.uk**

Equality and Human Rights Committee (2010) Bill of Rights. Available from **www.equalityhuman rights.com**

Fenge, LA (2006) Promoting inclusiveness: Developing empowering practice with minority groups of older people – the example of older lesbian and gay men. In Brown, K (ed.) *Vulnerable adults and community care.* Exeter: Learning Matters.

Ferguson, H (2005) Working with violence, the emotions and the psycho-social dynamics of child protection: Reflections on the Victoria Climbié case. *Social Work Education*, 24 (7), 781–95.

Ferguson, H (2004) *Protecting children in time: Child abuse, child protection and the consequences of modernity.* Basingstoke: Palgrave Macmillan.

Ferris-Taylor, R (2003) *Communication.* In Gates, B (ed.) *Learning disability: Towards integration.* London: Churchill Livingstone, pp255–85.

Flynn, M (2008) How the NHS is failing vulnerable adults. *Health Services Journal*, 8 April. **www.hsj.co.uk**

Ford, R, Webster, P and Tendler, S (2007) We may declare an emergency to quit rights act, says Reid. *Times*, 25 May.

Fryson, R and Kitson, D (2010) Human rights and social wrongs: Issues in safeguarding adults with learning disabilities. *Practice*, 22(5): 309–20.

Furedi, F (1997) *Culture of fear: Risk-taking and the morality of low expectation.* London: Cassell.

Gaine, C and Gaylard, D (2010) Equality, difference and diversity. In Gaine, C (ed) *Equality and diversity in social work practice.* Exeter: Learning Matters.

Giarchi, G (1996) *Caring for older Europeans.* Aldershot: Arena.

Gilbert, P (2005) *Leadership, being effective and remaining human.* Lyme Regis: Russell House.

Gillman, M, Swain, J and Heyman, B (1997) Life history or 'case' history: The objectification of people with learning difficulties through the tyranny of professional discourse. *Disability and Society*, 12, 675–94.

Glasser, S (2002) Psychiatry's painful past resurfaces in Russian case. *Washington Post*, 15 December, p37. **www.bio.net/bionet**

Goble, C (2000) Partnership in residential settings. In Astor, R and Jeffries, K (eds) *Positive initiatives for people with learning difficulties: Promoting healthy lifestyles.* Basingstoke: Macmillan, pp69–78.

Goffman, E (1968) *Stigma: Management of spoilt identity.* London: Penguin.

Gould, N and Baldwin, M (2004) *Social work and critical reflection and the learning organization.* Aldershot: Ashgate.

Gray, B and Ridden, G (1999) *Lifemaps of people with learning difficulties.* London: Jessica Kingsley.

Greenhaulgh, L (1994) *Well aware: Improving access to health information for people with learning difficulties.* Anglia and Oxford Regional Health Authority/NHS Executive.

Hafford-Letchfield, T (2009) *Management and organisation in social work.* 2nd edition. Exeter: Learning Matters.

Hague, G, Thiara, R and Magowan, P (2007) *Disabled women and domestic violence: Making the links. Interim report for the Women's Aid Federation of England.* **www.womensaid.org.uk**

Hale, B (2010) *Mental health law.* 5th edition. London: Sweet and Maxwell.

Hanmer, J and Itzin, C (eds) (2000) *Home truths about domestic violence: Feminist influences on policy and practice.* Abingdon: Routledge.

Harris, J (2000) *An evaluation of the use and effectiveness of the Protection from Harassment Act 1997.* London: Home Office.

Harrison, R and Stokes, H (1992) *Diagnosing organizational culture.* London: Pfieffer and Company.

Hart, S (2003) Health and health promotion. In Gates, B (ed.) *Learning disabilities: Towards inclusion.* London. Churchill Livingstone, pp289–309.

Havant Women's Aid (2006) *Annual report.* Havant: Havant Women's Aid.

Healthcare Commission (2007) *Investigation into the service for people with learning disabilities provided by Sutton and Merton Primary Care Trust.* London: The Stationery Office.

Healthcare Commission (2003) *Investigation into matters arising from care on Rowan Ward, Manchester Mental Health and Social Care Trust.* London: Healthcare Commission.

Home Office (2002) *Achieving best evidence in criminal proceedings: Guidance for vulnerable or intimidated witnesses including children.* London: Home Office Communication Directorate.

www.homeoffice.gov.uk/documents

Home Office (1945) *Report by Sir Walter Monckton on the circumstances which led to the boarding-out of Dennis and Terence O'Neil at Bank Farm, Minsterley and the steps taken to supervise their welfare.* London: HMSO.

Howe, D (1987) *An introduction to social work theory.* Aldershot: Wildwood House.

Hughes, J (2006) *Chairing multiagency adult protection meetings.* Making Connections, Training and Consultancy.

Humphreys, C and Stanley, N (eds) (2006) *Domestic violence and child protection: Directions for good practice.* London: Jessica Kingsley.

Humphreys, C and Thiara, R (2003) Mental health and domestic violence: 'I call it symptoms of abuse'. *British Journal of Social Work*, 33, 209–26.

Hurndall, J (2007) *Defy the stars: The life and death of Tom Hurndall.* London: Bloomsbury.

Jay, N (2007) Peer mentorship: Promoting advocacy and friendship between young people. *Learning Disability Today*, 7 (3), 18–21.

Joffe, H (1999) *Risk and the other.* Cambridge: Cambridge University Press.

Johns, R (2007) Who decides now? *The British Journal of Social Work*, 37 (3), 557–64.

Johnson, G and Scholes, K (2002) *Exploring corporate strategy.* 6th edition. Harlow: Pearson.

Johnson, ML (ed.) (2005) *The Cambridge handbook of age and ageing.* Cambridge: Cambridge University Press.

The Joint Committee on Human Rights (2010) *The Equality and Human Rights Commission: The 13th report of the session 2009–10.* London: The Stationery Office.

The Joint Committee on Human Rights (2004) *The meaning of public authority under the Human Rights Act 1988: The seventh report of the session 2003–4.* London: The Stationery Office.

Jordan, B (1990) *Social work in an unjust society.* Hemel Hempstead: Harvester Wheatsheaf.

Kalaga, H, Kingston, P, Penhale, B and Andrews, J (2007) *A review of literature on effective interventions that prevent and respond to harm against adults.* Scottish Government Social Research. **www.scotland.gov.uk/socialresearch**

Kearney, P (2004) First line managers: The mediators of standards and quality of practice. In Statham, D (ed.) *Managing front line practice in social care.* London: Jessica Kingsley.

Kempe, C, Silverman, F, Steele, B, Droegemuller, W and Silver, H (1962) The battered child syndrome. *Journal of the American Medical Association*, 181, 17–24.

Kemshall, H (2002) *Risk, social policy and welfare.* Buckingham: Open University Press.

Kitson, D (2009) The abuse in institutions and the resulting inquiries. In Pritchard, J (ed) **Good practice in safeguarding adults: Working effectively in adult protection**. London: Jessica Kingsley, pp. 120–37.

Knott, C and Scragg, T (eds) (2010) *Reflective practice in social work.* 2nd edition. Exeter: Learning Matters.

Kurrle (2001) quoted in Crawford, K and Walker, J (2004) *Social work with older people.* Exeter: Learning Matters.

Laming, Lord (2003) *The Victoria Climbié Inquiry.* London: The Stationery Office.

Larkin, TJ and Larkin, S (1996) Reaching and changing frontline employees. *Harvard Business Review*, June, 95–104.

Lawson, J (1996) A framework of risk assessment and management for older people. In Kemshall, H and Pritchard, J (eds) *Good practice in risk assessment and risk management 1*. London: Jessica Kingsley.

Lee, S (2007) Speaking up. *Action Points*, 33, February.

Leslie, S (2008) Using the Mental Capacity Act to protect vulnerable adults. In J Pritchard, (ed) *Good practice in safeguarding adults: Working effectively in adult protection*. London: Jessica Kingsley.

London Borough of Brent (1985) *A child in trust: Report of the panel of Inquiry investigating the circumstances surrounding the death of Jasmine Beckford*. London: Borough of Brent.

London Borough of Greenwich (1987) *A child in mind: The protection of children in a responsible society – Report of the commission of inquiry into the circumstances surrounding the death of Kimberley Carlisle*. London: Borough of Greenwich.

London Borough of Lambeth (1987) *Whose child? The report of the public inquiry into the death of Tyra Henry*. London: Borough of Lambeth.

Lord Chancellor's Department (1997) *Who decides? Making decisions on behalf of mentally incapacitated adults*. Department for Constitutional Affairs. London: HMSO.

Macdonald, AJD, Roberts, A and Carpenter, I (2004) De facto imprisonment and covert medication use in general nursing homes for older people in South East England. *Aging Clinical and Experimental Research*, 16 (4), 326–30.

Macpherson, Sir W (1999) *The Stephen Lawrence Inquiry*. CM 2462-I. London: The Stationery Office.

McCreadie, C (1994) From granny battering to elder abuse: A critique of UK writing, 1972–1992. *Journal of Elder Abuse and Neglect*, 5 (2), 7–25.

McDonald, J (2005) Neo-liberalism and the pathologising of public issues: The displacement of feminist service models in domestic violence support services. *Australian Social Work*, 58 (3), 275–84.

McGee, J (1990) *Being with others: Toward a psychology of interdependence*. 2nd edition. Omaha, NE: Creighton University.

McGee, J, Menolascino, FJ, Hobbs, DC and Menousek, PE (1987) *Gentle teaching: A non-aversive approach to helping persons with mental retardation*. New York: Human Sciences Press.

McKenzie, P (2000) *A community response to abuse*. Abingdon: Routledge.

McLaughlin, K (2007) Regulation and risk in social work: The General Social Care Council and the Social Care Register in context. *British Journal of Social Work*, 37, 1263–77.

Mantell, A (2010) Traumatic brain injury and potential safeguarding concerns. *The Journal of Adult Protection*, 12(4), November.

Manthorpe, J and Martineau, S (2010a, online) 'In our experience': Chairing and commissioning serious case reviews in adult safeguarding in England. *Journal of Social Work*. **dx/doi.org/**

Manthorpe, J and Martineau, S (2010b, online) Serious case reviews in adult safeguarding in England: An analysis of a sample of reports. *British Journal of Social Work*. **dx/doi.org**

Manthorpe, J and Martineau, S (2009) *Serious case reviews in adult safeguarding*. London: Social Care Workforce Research Unit, King's College London. **www.kcl.ac.uk**

Manthorpe, J, Stevens, M, Hussein, S, Heath, H and Lievesley, N (2011) *The abuse, neglect and mistreatment of older people in care homes and hospitals in England: Observations on the potential for secondary data analysis*. London: Social Care Workforce Research Unit.

Marks, D (1999) *Disability: Controversial debates and psychosocial perspectives*. Abingdon: Routledge.

Martin, J (2007) *Safeguarding adults*. Lyme Regis: Russell House.

Means, R and Smith, R (1998) *Community care policy and practice*. 2nd edition. Basingstoke: Macmillan.

Mental Capacity Act 2005. **www.legislation.gov.uk/acts/**

Messman-Moore, TL and Long, PJ (2000) Child sexual abuse and re-victimisation I: The form of adult sexual abuse, adult physical abuse and adult psychological maltreatment. *Journal of Interpersonal Violence*, 15 (5), 489–502.

Milner, J (2001) *Women and social work: Narrative approaches*. Basingstoke: Palgrave.

Milner, J and Myers, S (2007) *Working with violence: Policies and practices in risk assessment and management*. Basingstoke: Palgrave.

MIND/Norah Fry Research Centre (2009) *Personalisation in mental health: What do we know?* Available from: **www.bristol.ac.uk.norahfry**

Mitchell, W and Glendinning, C (2007) *A review of the research evidence surrounding risk perceptions, risk management strategies and their consequences in adult social care for different groups of service users*. Social Policy Research Unit, University of York.

Morgan, B (2007) *Sussex Safeguarding Adults Road Show*.

Morgan, S (2007) *Working with risk*. Brighton: Pavilion Publishing.

Moriarty, J (2008) *The health and social care experiences of black and minority ethnic old people* [on line]. Available from: **http://www.raceequalityfoundation.org.uk** (Accessed on 10 December 2010.)

Morris, J (1993) *Independent lives: Community care and disabled people*. Basingstoke: Macmillan.

Mullender, A (1996) *Rethinking domestic violence: The social work and probation response*. Abingdon: Routledge.

National Confidential Enquiry into Patient Outcomes (2010) *An age old problem*. London: National Confidential Enquiry into Patient Outcomes.

NHS Choices www.nhs.uk

Nind, M and Hewitt, D (2001) *A practical guide to intensive interaction*. Kidderminster: BILD Publications.

Norfolk County Council (2004) *Taywood Review*. Norfolk County Council.

Northmore, S (2007) Improving partnership working in housing and mental health. In Balloch, S and Taylor, M (eds) *Partnership working, policy and practice*. Bristol: Policy Press.

O'Connell, S (1998) *Mind reading: An investigation into how we learn to love and lie*. London: Arrow Books.

Office for National Statistics http://www.statistics.gov.uk

Ogbonna, E (1993) Managing organisational culture: fantasy or reality? *Human Resources Management Journal*, 3 (2), 42–55.

O'Hagan, K (1993) *Emotional and psychological abuse of children.* Buckingham: Open University Press.

O'Keefe, M, Hills, A, Doyle, M, McCreadie, C, Scholes, S, Constantine, R, Tinker, A, Manthorpe, J, Biggs, S and Erens, B (2007) *UK study of the abuse and neglect of older people: Prevalence survey report.* Comic Relief and Department of Health.

Olsen, MR (1984) *Social work and mental health: A guide for the approved social worker.* London: Tavistock.

O'Rourke, M and Bird, L (2000) *Risk management in mental health.* London: Mental Health Foundation.

Parliamentary Health Service Ombudsman (2011) *Care and compassion? Report of the Health Service Ombudsman on ten investigations into NHS care of older people. Fourth report of the Health Service Commissioner for England Session 2010–2011.* London: The Stationery Office.

Parton, N (2006) *Safeguarding childhood: Early intervention and surveillance in a late modern society.* Basingstoke: Palgrave Macmillan.

Parton, N (1998) Risk, advanced liberalism and child welfare: The need to rediscover uncertainty and ambiguity. *British Journal of Social Work*, 28 (1), 5–27.

Patients' Association (2010) *Listen to patients, speaking up for change.* London: Patients' Association.

Payne, M (2005) *Modern social work theory.* Basingstoke: Palgrave.

Payne, M (2000) *Teamwork in multiprofessional care.* Basingstoke: Palgrave.

Penhale, B (1993) The abuse of elderly people: Considerations for practice. *British Journal of Social Work*, 23, 95–112.

Perkins, N, Penhale, B, Reid, D, Pinkney, L, Hussein, S and Manthorpe, J (2007) Partnership means protection? Perceptions of the effectiveness of multi-agency working and the regulatory framework within adult protection in England and Wales. *Journal of Adult Protection,* 9 (3), 9–23.

Pettinger, R (2000) *Mastering organisational behaviour.* Basingstoke: Palgrave Macmillan.

Pinder, M (2007) Were Ashley's parents right? *Community Care*, 15–21 February, 26–7.

Pratt, J, Gordon, P and Plamping, D (1999) *Working whole systems, putting theory into practice in organisations.* London: King's Fund.

Preston-Shoot, M and Wrigley, V (2002) Closing the circle: Social workers' responses to multi-agency procedures on older age abuse. *British Journal of Social Work*, 32, 299–320.

Pritchard, J (1999) Good practice: Victims' perspective. In Pritchard, J (ed.) *Elder abuse work best practice in Britain and Canada.* London: Jessica Kingsley.

Pyles, L (2006) Towards a post-Katrina framework: Social work as human rights and capabilities. *Comparative Social Welfare*, 22 (1), 79–88.

Quinney, A (2006) *Collaborative social work practice.* Exeter: Learning Matters.

Radford, L and Hester, M (2006) *Mothering through domestic violence.* London: Jessica Kingsley.

Rees, P and Manthorpe, J (2010) Managers' and staff experiences of adult protection allegations in mental health and learning disability residential services: A qualitative study. *British Journal of Social Work*, 40 (2), 513–29.

Rogers, C (1980) *A way of being.* New York: Houghton Mifflin.

Ryan, J with Thomas, F (1987) *The politics of mental handicap*. London: Free Press.

Samuel, M (2008) *No secrets* review: The key issues. *Community Care*, 20 February.

Scheepers, B (2010) Effective expert evidence to prove capacity: Legal and clinical perspectives. *10th Annual Brain Injury Legal Seminar*, 30 October. London: Brain Injury Social Work Group.

Schein, E (2004) *Organizational culture and leadership.* 3rd edition. San Francisco, CA: Jossey-Bass.

Schwer, B (2005) *The new Mental Capacity Act.* **www.careandhealthlaw.com.**

Scottish Executive (2007) The Adult Support and Protection (Scotland) Act 2007. **www.legislation.gov.uk**

Scottish Executive (2004) *Investigations into Scottish Borders Council and NHS Borders Services for people with learning disabilities: Joint statement from the Mental Welfare Commission and the Social Work Inspectorate.* **www.scotland.gov.uk**

Scottish Executive (2000) Adults with Incapacity (Scotland) Act. **www.scotland.gov.uk**

Scottish Social Services Council (2010) *Code of practice for social service workers.* **www.sssc.uk**

Scourfield, P (2010) Reflections on the serious case review of a female adult (JK), *Journal of Adult Protection*, 12 (4) 16–30.

Scragg, T (2010) Working with your manager. In Knott, C and Scragg, T (eds) *Reflective practice in social work*. 2nd edition. Exeter: Learning Matters.

Scragg T (2010) *Managing change in health and social care services.* Brighton: Pavilion Publishing.

Seddique, H (2010) *DPP release assisted suicide guidelines.* Available from: **www.guardian.co.uk/uk/2010/feb/25**

Shakespeare, T, Gillespie-Self, K and Davies, D (1997) *The sexual politics of disability.* Cassell: London.

Shaw, A, and Shaw, I (2001) Risk research in a risk society. *Research Policy and Planning*, 19 (1).

Smale, G (1998) *Managing change through innovation*. London: The Stationery Office.

Smith, K and Tilney, S (2007) *Vulnerable adult and child witnesses.* Oxford: Oxford University Press.

Smith, M (2005) *Surviving fears in health and social care: The terrors of night and the arrows of day.* London: Jessica Kingsley.

Social Care Institute for Excellence (2010) *Piloting the SCIE 'systems' model for case reviews: Learning from the North West of England*. London: Social Care Institute for Excellence. **www.scie.org.uk/publications**

Social Care TV (2009) *Safeguarding adults: Lessons from the murder of Steven Hoskin.* **www.scie.org.uk**

Stanko, E (2000) The day to count: A snapshot of the impact of domestic violence in the UK. *Criminal Justice*, 1, 2.

Stanley, R (1999) Learning disabilities: Supporting nurses in delivering primary care. *British Journal of Nursing*, 8 (13), 866–70.

Stevenson, O (1996) *Elder protection in the community: What can we learn from child protection?* London: Age Concern Institute of Gerontology, King's College London.

Sussex Multi Agency Policy and Procedures for Safeguarding Vulnerable Adults (2007) www.eastsussex.gov.uk

Teater, B (2010) *An introduction to applying social work theories and methods*. Maidenhead: Open University.

Thompson, N (2006) *Anti-discriminatory practice*. 4th edition. Basingstoke: Palgrave.

Thompson, N (2000) *Understanding social work: Preparing for practice*. Basingstoke: Palgrave.

Thompson, N (1999) *Promoting equality: Challenging discrimination and oppression*. Basingstoke: Palgrave Macmillan.

Titterton, M (2005) *Risk and risk taking in health and social welfare*. London: Jessica Kingsley.

Todd, J, Loewy, J, Kelly, G and Simpson, G (2004) Managing challenging behaviours: Getting interventions to work in non-specialist community setting. *Brain Impairment*, 5 (1), 42–52.

Walby, S and Allen, J (2004) *Domestic violence, sexual assault and stalking: Findings from the British Crime Survey*. Home Office Research Study. London: Home Office. **www.homeoffice.gov.uk**

Wallis, S (2007) Reflection and avoiding professional dangerousness. In Knott, C and Scragg, T (eds) *Reflective practice in social work*. Exeter: Learning Matters.

Walsh, C, Ploeg, J, Lohfeld, J, Horne, J, MacMillan and Lai, D (2007) Violence across the lifespan: Interconnections among forms of abuse as described by marginalized Canadian elders and their care-givers. *British Journal of Social Work*, 37, 491–514.

Warner, J (2006) Inquiry reports as active texts and their function in relation to professional practice in mental health. *Health, Risk and Society*, 8 (3), 223–37.

Watson, D (2003) Causes and manifestations of learning disabilities. In Gates, B (ed.) *Learning disability: Towards integration*. London: Churchill Livingstone, pp21–39.

Whittaker, A (1995) Partnership in practice: User participation in services for people with learning difficulties. In Philpot, T and Ward, L (eds) *Values and visions: Changing ideas in services for people with learning difficulties*. Oxford: Butterworth Heinemann, pp176–85.

Whittington, C (2003) A model of collaboration. In Weinstein, J, Whittington, C and Leiba, T (eds) *Collaboration in social work practice*. London: Jessica Kingsley.

Wilcox, P (2006) Communities, care and domestic violence. *Critical Social Policy*, 26 (4), 722–47.

Williams, P (2009) *Social work with people with learning difficulties*. 2nd edition. Exeter: Learning Matters.

Wolfensberger, W (1972) *The principle of normalisation in human management services*. Toronto: National Institute of Mental Retardation.

Yorkshire and the Humber Strategic Health Authority (YHSHA) (2010a) *Report of the independent inquiry into the Colin Norris incidents at Leeds Teaching Hospitals NHS Trust in 2002 based on evidence gathered up to December 2008, The independent inquiry team, Professor Pat Cantrill – Chair*. Leeds: YHSHA.

Yorkshire and the Humber Strategic Health Authority (YHSHA) (2010b) *The Airedale Inquiry: Report to the Yorkshire and the Humber Strategic Health Authority to be presented to the Strategic Health Authority Board on 8 June 2010*. Leeds: YHSHA.

Index

A

A vision for adult social care: Capable communities and active citizens 159
abnormal groupings 50
absolute rights 39
abuse
    assessment 14-16
    definitions 9-10
    emotive response to 82-4
    institutional 128
    reasons for 16-17
    zero tolerance 102, 162
    see also adult abuse; child abuse; domestic violence
abusers
    domestic violence 98-100
    financial abuse 28-9
    as vulnerable adults 16
abusing behaviours 16-17
Access to funds (Scotland) 70
accountability, risk associated with 172-3
Achieving best evidence in criminal proceedings 164
Action on Elder Abuse 22, 23
    financial abuse study 28-9
adult abuse
    assessing seriousness of 14-16
    case study 83-4
    categories 11-14
    inquiries 18
    key concepts 10-11
    legislation used to investigate 19-20
    prevalence survey 10, 11, 13
    societal recognition 17
    see also discriminatory abuse; emotional abuse; financial abuse; institutional abuse; neglect; physical abuse; sexual abuse
adult protection
    case conferences 31
    case study 23-4
    evolution of 17-19
    investigations good practice 112
    key stages in 29-30
    Scottish legal framework 70-7
    multi-agency working 163-4
    putting policy into practice 29-32
    using child protection experience 91-3
    see also safeguarding adults
Adult Protection Unit, Norfolk Police 165
Adult Safeguarding Boards 23, 31, 74, 182, 185
    conduct of SCRs 181
    partnership working 160
Adult Support and Protection (Scotland) Act 2007 21, 61, 67-70, 74-8
    definition of 'adult at risk' 74
    powers 75
    principles 74
    use of term 'harm' 74
adults
    empowerment of 10-11
    with incapacity 51, 70-4
    see also safeguarding adults; vulnerable adults
Adults Support and Protection: Ensuring rights and preventing harm 69
Adults with Incapacity (Scotland) Act 2000 21, 51, 70-4
    hierarchy of measures 70
    principles of Act 71
advance decisions 56-7
adversarial system 92
advice, constructive 136
advocacy 113, 116
advocacy skills 134-5
ageing, changing views of 86
ageism 115
Alzheimer's disease 125
anti-discriminatory practice 115
anti-oppressive practice 115
    empowerment through 117-19
    mental capacity and 62
Area Child Protection Committees (ACPCs) 88
assertiveness skills 134
assessment
    of abuse 14-16
    of mental health 60-1
    NHS and Community Care Act 1990 19
Assessment Order (Scotland) 75, 77
assumption of capacity 53
Auckland, Susan 87
audit of power 112-15
autistic spectrum disorder, communication impairment 124, 126, 132

B

Banking Code 29
banks and building societies 28
Banning Order (Scotland) 75, 77
'battered child' syndrome 86
Beech House inquiry (1993) 18
behavioural cues, as communication 132
behavioural model, partnership 157 (fig)
Belbin's typology, team workers 165-6
Bellwood, Simon 25-6
best interest 54-6

Bichard Inquiry 26
'Big Society' agenda 27
Bill of Rights 35
bipolar depressive illness, communication
    impairment 126
blame, risk associated with 172
blame avoidance 172
blame culture 172
Bournewood Gap 58
brain injury, communication impairment 124
British Crime Survey (2001) 98
British Sign Language 127, 132
business-like manner, working in 135

C

capacity
    acts in connection with care or treatment of
        someone who lacks 57
    Adults with Incapacity (Scotland) Act 2000 70-4
    establishing 72
    mental faculty required for 49
    not equated with wisdom 54
    presumption of 11
    restricting factors 49-50
    see also incapacity; mental capacity
capacity to consent 11, 51-2
Care Homes Regulation 2001 Reg. 37 25
Care Quality Commission (CQC) 24, 25, 161, 163
    new system of regulation 27-9
    concerns raised 27-8
Care Quality Commission (Registration)
    Regulations 2009 27
Care Standards Act 2000 24, 37
Carlisle, Kimberley 88
case recording 188
chairperson 166
'champions' of change 149
change 148-53
    different levels of 149-50
    importance of vision and values 148
    introducing in strong cultures 147
    leadership and management behaviour 151
    managing 149
    resistance to 149
    rhetoric and reality of 147
    styles of managing 151-2
    supporting staff through 152
    susceptibility to 142
Chapman, Jessica 26
child abuse
    case study 82-3
    definition of 86
    features and categories of 84-5
    perceived as a lower class problem 85
    see also child sexual abuse
child protection
    conferences 92
    evolution of 85-90
    legislative changes 91 (fig)
    procedures 87
    registers 87, 88

    see also safeguarding children
Child Review Committees 88
child sexual abuse 84
    Cleveland affair 88-9
child witnesses, achieving best evidence 164
childhood, construction of 86
children, consent to treatment 49
Children Act 1948 85, 86
Children Act 1975 86, 87, 92
Children Act 1989 89, 91, 92
Children Act 2004 18, 90
Children and Young Persons Act 1933 87
Children and Young Persons Act 1963 85
choice 63
civil rights 21
Cleveland affair 88-9
Climbié, Victoria 18, 89, 90
closed teams 165
co-evolution, partnership working 157-8
co-operation 157
co-ordination 157
Code of Ethics (BASW) 29
Codes of Conduct (GSCC) 29
cognitive behaviour therapy 126
cognitive impairment, and abuse 17
collaboration, managing change 152
collaborative culture 134-6
collaborative working 154-67
    across statutory organisations 163-5
    case studies 158, 165
    in context of adult safeguarding 159-60
    developing individual practice 165-6
    drivers for 161-2
    effective 156-8
    meaning of 155
    terminology 155-6
Colwell, Maria 86-7, 90
Commission for Racial Equality see Equality and
    Human Rights Commission
Commission for Social Care Inspection (CSCI) see
    Care Quality Commission
commitment, collaborative working 156
common sense 174
communication 121-37
    collaborative culture 134
    collaborative working 156
    early learning of 126
    impairment 124-8
    importance of 122-3
    improving user-focused 131
    managing change 151-2
    multi-modal 122, 134
    neurological basis 125
    organising the physical environment 133-6
    person-centred approach to 132-3
    poor health and 128-9
    see also user-focused communication
community profiles 117
company worker 166
competence, user-focused communication 132-3
competition, partnership working 157

completer-finisher (teamworker) 166
Comprehensive Area Assessment 161
compulsory removal from home 19-20
computer-based voice systems 132
confidence, collaborative working 156
conflict, collaborative working 156
consent, to treatment 49 see also capacity to consent
consultation, in decision-making 63
control
    in decision-making 63
    power and 96-7
control systems, organisational culture 145
Convention on Human Rights (UN 1948) 35
co-operation, partnership working 157
co-ordination, partnership working 157
Cornwall Partnership Trust 18, 144, 146, 150
correspondence, right to respect for 44-5
Court of Protection 29, 57, 58, 61
court process 92-3
criminal investigations 31
Criminal Records Bureau 26
cross-agency barriers 163-4
cruelty, freedom from 41-2
cultural diversity 109
cultural web 145-6
culture see collaborative culture; organisational cultures; professional culture

D

Data Protection Act 1998 25
debriefing, adult protection 31
decision making 169
    on behalf of individuals 56
    consultation 63
    enabling people in 53-4
    ethical dilemmas 174
    experience 62
    four-stage test of capacity 52
    knowledge and information 62
    provision of information 52
    resources 62-3
    shared responsibility 175
    stating value base behind 174
    support and encouragement 62
    support networks 63
    tick-box approach 168
    Titterton's model 175-6
defensive practice 174
Department of Health 161
dependency, assumption of link between capacity and 50
deprivation of liberty safeguard 59-60
deputies, appointed by Court of Protection 58
derogation, from HRA 39
detention
    of persons of unsound mind 42-3
    tension between police and mental health trusts 163
difference 108-20

anti-discriminatory and anti-oppressive practice 115-17
    case studies 109, 114, 118
    incapacity linked to 50
    meaning of 109
    PCS analysis 109-10
    power 111-15
    theories of empowerment 117-19
    vulnerability 110-11
direction, managing change 152
directions, in social work 21
disability
    abuse of women 96, 102
    assumption of link between capacity and 50
    investigation of abuse 19
Disability Discrimination Act 2005 21
Disability Rights Commission see Equality and Human Rights Commission
discrimination, prohibition of 45-6 see also anti-discriminatory practice
discriminatory abuse
    defined 13
    key principles combating 21
domestic violence 94-107
    abusers 98-100
    association with child abuse 82, 84
    case studies 99, 102-3
    defining 95-8
    gendered nature 100, 105
    links to safeguarding adults 105-6
    prevalence 99
    as a process 96
    research 96
    social work practice 106
    tensions in social work role 105
    understanding and responding to 100-3
    women's views about helpful responses 103-5
Domestic Violence, Crime and Victims Act 2004 22
Downs' Syndrome, communication impairment 124, 125
Duluth Domestic Abuse Intervention Project (DAIP) 96
duties, social work 20

E

education, managing change 151-2
elder abuse see Action on Elder Abuse
eligibility, service provision 171
emergency protection orders (EPOs) 91
emotional abuse
    of children 84
    defined 12
    serial 17
emotions, associated with change 152
employment checks 26-7
empowerment
    of adults 10-11
    perspective, domestic violence 102-3
    theory and method of intervention 117-19
encouragement, in decision-making 62

Enduring Power of Attorney 57
engagement, of people in decision-making 63-4
Equal Opportunities Commission *see* Equality and Human Rights Commission
Equality Act 2006 35
Equality and Human Rights Commission 35-6
Essential standards of quality and safety 159
ethical arguments, decision-making 174-5
ethical dilemmas 174
European Convention on Human Rights 35
European Court of Human Rights 35, 36
euthanasia 40-1
evaluation, adult protection 31
Every child matters 90
Everybody's business 164
evidence, gathering 93
experience, in decision-making 62
eye contact 126

F

family courts, failure to take account of domestic violence 99
family life, right to respect for 44-5
feedback, adult protection 31
financial abuse
    abusers 28-9
    Action on Elder Abuse study 28-9
    defined 12
    extent of 28
    possible legal remedies 29
    prevalence 13
    recommendations regarding 28
    serial 17
Financial Ombudsman Service 29
Fraud Act 2006 29
Freedom Bill 35
Freedom of Information Act 2000 25
front-line managers 151

G

gender, and domestic violence 100
Gillick v West Norfolk and Wisbech Area Health Authority 49
GPs, adult protection arrangements and 23
Grigg-Booth, Anne 183
group work, domestic violence 102
guardians *ad litem* 87, 92
Guardianship Order (Scotland) 71
guidance, in social work 21 *see also* multi-agency guidance
gut instinct 175

H

harm, use of term in Scotland 74 *see also* significant harm
Harold Shipman inquiry (2005) 18
health, and communication 128-9
Health and Social Care Act 2008 (Regulated Activities) Regulations 2010 27
Health Select Committee Inquiry into Elder Abuse (2004) 28

hearing impairment 127
Henry, Tyra 88
Herczegfalvy v Austria 36, 42
hindsight 169
hindsight fallacy 173
home
    compulsory removal from 19-20
    right to respect for 44-5
Homeshare 63
homophobia 111
Hoskin, Steven 23-4, 181
hospital care, poor quality of 186-7
housing, and abuse 13
HRA *see* Human Rights Act
human rights
    adult protection legislation 21
    case studies 37, 38, 42-3, 45
Human Rights Act 1998 34-47
    background to 35-6
    deprivation of liberty 58-9
    guiding principles 36-9
    least restrictive and intrusive principles 29
    proportionality of intervention 11, 39
    public authorities 36-9
    reflected in Scottish legislation 67
    reinterpreting the law 36
    rights enshrined within 40-6
    safeguarding adults 21
Huntley, Ian 26

I

impairment
    capacity to consent 51-2
    in communication *see* communication
    vulnerability linked to 122
incapacity
    adults with 51, 70-4
    four-stage test 52
    see also capacity
incremental change 150
Independence, wellbeing and choice 51
independent mental capacity advocates (IMCAs) 60, 92
Independent Safeguarding Authority 26-7
individualised budgets 28, 63
infant communication 125-6
infantilisation 50
information
    decision-making 62
    recording accurate handover of 132
    sources of 117
information deprivation 62
information sharing 69-70, 135-6
informed consent 49, 52, 56
inquiries *see* serious case reviews (SCRs)
institutional abuse 128
    case study 129-30
    causes 17
    defined 12-13
    whistleblowing failure 18
institutional racism 116-17

institutions 109
intellectual impairment 124-6
inter-agency co-operation 91
inter-agency consultation 31
internal management reviews (IMRs) 181
internet, sexual abuse on 84
intervention
    and assessment of abuse 32
    managing change 152
    proportionality 11, 39
Intervention Order (Scotland) 70
intimidated witnesses, achieving best evidence
    164

J

Jasmin Beckford Inquiry Report 87-8
Johnson v UK 43
joint interview training 164
joint police/social work ABE interviews 165
joint working, positive approaches to 164-5
JT v UK 36, 44

K

Kempe, Henry 86
knowledge
    in decision-making 62
    of legislation 119
knowledge of professional roles, collaborative
    working 156

L

Laming Inquiry (2003) 18
Lasting Powers of Attorney (LPAs) 29, 57
*Law Commission Review of Adult Social Care
    Law Consultation* (2010) 11, 19
Lawrence, Stephen 115-16
lead agency responsibilities, adult protection 30-1
leadership, and management behaviour 151
learned helplessness 130
learning difficulties
    assumption of sexuality 173-4
    communication impairment 124-8
    health problems 128-9
    institutional abuse (case study) 129-30
    risk perception/management 173-4
    sexual abuse of adults with 17
least restrictive intervention 56, 58
Leeds Teaching Hospitals NHS Trust (LTHT) 183
legal definitions 20-1
legislation
    adult protection 21-6
    child abuse 86-90
    compatibility with HRA 36
    directions and guidance 21
    knowledge of 119
    used to investigate adult abuse 19-20
    see also individual legislation; Scottish legislation
lexicon of terms 155
liberty
    deprivation of 43-4
    right to 42-4

life, right to 40-1
life stories 123
lifemapping 130
likes/dislikes profiles 130, 133
limited rights 39
local authorities
    central government constraints 20
    dominant role of social services 30
    involvement in MAPPAS 165
Local Authority Social Service Act 1970 21
local strategic partnerships 162 (fig)
long-term abuse 16
Longcare Inquiry Buckinghamshire County
    Council (1998) 18

M

Macpherson Report 116
Makaton 127, 132
management behaviour, and change 151
MARAC (multi-agency risk assessment) 186
medical care, incapacitated adults 51
medication, covert provision of 44
mental capacity
    and anti-oppressive practice 62
    assumption of link between dependency and 50
    case studies 53, 55, 58-9, 61
Mental Capacity Act 2005 46, 48-65, 91
    acts in connection with care or treatment of
        someone who lacks 57
    amended 43-4
    capacity to consent 11
    code of practice 55
    Court of Protection and deputies 58
    decision-making 56-7
    engaging with people who use services 63-4
    guiding principles 52-6
    human and civil rights 21
    least restrictive and intrusive principles 29
    mental capacity and anti-oppressive practice 62
    safeguarding adults 21
    self-neglect and 12
Mental Capacity Advocate 29
mental health, assessments 60-1
Mental Health Act 1983 36, 43, 44, 51, 58
Mental Health Act 2007 29, 36, 43, 56, 57
    section 136 163
Mental Welfare Commission for Scotland 67
mentoring 136
MIND 23
mistreatment 13-14
monitor-evaluator 166
Morris, Jenny 50
multi-agency adult protection committees
    (Scotland) 74
multi-agency guidance, adult protection 69-70
multi-agency protection, vulnerable adults 21-2,
    23-4, 68-70
multi-agency public protection arrangements
    (MAPPAs) 165
multi-agency teams 155
multi-agency working, adult protection 163-4

multidisciplinary teams 155
multi-modal communication 134
mutual respect, collaborative working 156

N

National Assistance Act 1948
    section 29 19
    section 47 19-20
National Confidential Enquiry into Patient
    Outcome and Death (NCEPOD) 187
National framework on Safeguarding Adults see
    Safeguarding Adults
National Minimum Standards 24
nearest relative 44
negative events 82
neglect
    of children 84
    defined 12
    perceived as a lower class problem 85
    prevalence 13
    reasons for 17
negotiation skills 135
neoliberalism 100
NHS, adult protection arrangements and 23
NHS and Community Care Act 1990 19
NHS Choices 117
No Secrets 9-10, 21-2, 51, 69, 92, 182
    expectation of agency collaboration 159
non-contact activity 12
Norfolk Police Adult Protection Unit 165
Norris, Colin 183
Northmore's checklist, partnership working 166

O

objectivity 178
Office for National Statistics 117
O'Neil, Dennis 86
open teams 165
opportunistic abuse 16
organisational cultures 141-53
    case study 144
    cultural web 145-6
    defined 142-3
    influence of 144-5
    inward-looking and abusive 147
    processes of change see change
    and socialisation 146-7
organisational structures 145
Our Health, our care, our say 51
Our safeguarding protocol: The Care Quality
    Commission's commitment to safeguarding
    163
over-proceduralisation 30

P

parents, right to overrule refusal to admission or
    treatment 49
participation
    collaborative working 156
    in decision-making 63
    managing change 152

partnership
    in decision-making 63
partnership working
    behavioural model 157-8
    checklist 166
    co-evolving 158
    elements of effective 156-7
    inhibiting factors 160
    see also local strategic partnerships
PASSING 148
pathologising 101
PAVA see Practitioners Alliance Against Abuse of
    Vulnerable Adults
peer advocacy 63
Performance Assessment Framework for Social
    Services 161
Performance Assessment Framework indicators
    (PAFs) 22
perpetrators see abusers
person-centred approach, to communication 132
personal, cultural and structural (PCS) analysis
    109-10
personalised safeguarding responses 30 (fig)
physical abuse
    of children 84
    defined 11-12
    prevalence 13
physical environment, to facilitate
    communication 133
'pic-syms' 132
picture boards, of staff 133-4
plant (teamworker) 166
police, tension between mental health trusts and
    163
power
    audit of 112-15
    collaborative working 156
    concept of 111-12
    and control 96-7
    structures, organisational culture 145
    see also empowerment
powers, social work 20
Powers of Attorney (Scotland) 71
Practitioners Alliance Against Abuse of
    Vulnerable Adults (PAVA) 31
precautionary principle 172, 174
pre-employment checks 26-7
Pretty, Dianne 40-1, 42
prevention, of abuse 22
private life, right to respect for 44-5
probability 170
professional culture, collaborative working 157
professionalism 135
proportionality, of intervention 11, 39
Protection from Harassment Act 1997 98
Protection of Freedoms Bill 26
Protection Order (Scotland) 75-6
    number of 76-7
psychiatric illness, and abuse 17
psychological abuse 12
psychotic illness, communication impairment 126

public authorities, applicability of HRA 36-9
Public Interest Disclosure Act 1998 25
punishment, freedom from cruel, inhuman or
    degrading 41
Purdy, Debbie 41

Q

qualified rights 39

R

R (Heather) v Leonard Cheshire Foundation 38
R (Johnson and others) v Havering Borough
    Council 37
R v DPP, ex parte Dianne Pretty and Secretary of
    State for the Home Department 40-1
Race Relations (Amendment) Act 2000 21, 115-16
refusal of treatment
    advance decisions 56-7
    parents' right to overrule 49
regulatory bodies, collaborative working 161
Rehabilitation of Offenders Act 1974 25
rehabilitation period 25
Removal Order (Scotland) 75, 77
resistance, to change 147, 148
resource investigator 166
resources
    adult protection 22
    decision-making 62-3
    rationing and preoccupation with risk 171
restraint 58-60
rights see human rights
risk 168-79
    acceptable and unacceptable 175
    decision making (case study) 176
    defensive practice 172, 174
    defining 169-70
    ensuring safe practice 177-8
    of interpersonal abuse 14
    perceptions of 48
    principles of good practice 174-6
    social construction of 171-4
    societal preoccupation with 172
    understanding concept of 169-70
    working with 174-8
risk assessment
    definition of 170
    increase in complex policies 172
    perception of 168
    stating value base behind 174
    tick-box approach 168
risk avoidance 169, 172
risk management
    activities of 170
    definition of 170
    perception of 168
    research 173-4
    stating value base behind 174
risk perception, research 173-4
risk society 172
rituals 145
routines 145

Rowan Ward (Manchester Mental Health and
    Social Care Trust) 147
rule of optimism 178

S

safeguarding adults
    collaborative working 159-60
    compared to safeguarding children 91-2
    domestic violence 105-6
    local strategic partnerships 162 (fig)
    right to life 40
    significant harm 11
    see also adult protection
Safeguarding Adults (ADSS 2005) 22, 51, 92, 161
Safeguarding adults: Report on the consultation
    on the review of No Secrets 159
safeguarding children
    compared to safeguarding adults 91-2
    see also child protection
schizophrenia, communication impairment 126
Scope 23
Scottish Borders Inquiry 67-8, 89
Scottish legislation 66-77
security of person 42
self-neglect 12
sensory impairment 126-7
separation, and abuse 13
serial abuse 17
serious case reviews (SCRs) 180-9
    limited understanding of 185
    number of agencies involved 186
    purpose of 182-3
    setting up 184-5
seriousness, assessment of 14-16 see also risk
service evaluation model 148
service provision, eligibility 171
sexual abuse
    adults with learning difficulties 17
    defined 12
    prevalence 13
    serial 17
    see also child sexual abuse
sexuality, learning disabled 173-4
shaper (teamworker) 166
Shaping Our Lives 107
Sheffield City Council inquiry (2004) 18
Sheriff Court 71
sign language 127, 131
significant harm 11, 14
situational abuse 17
situation incapacity 61-2
Social Care Institute for Excellence 117
social movement perspective, domestic violence
    101-2
social work
    areas of responsibility 20
    decision-making in 168-9
    directions and guidance 21
    domestic violence 105
Social Work Services Inspectorate 67
socialisation, culture and 146-7

society
cultural diversity 109
preoccupation with risk 172
solution-focused work 102
Solzhenitsyn's disease 42-3
staff
picture boards 133-4
resistance to change 147, 148
supporting through change 152
statutory framework, fragmented nature of 175
statutory organisations, collaborative working
across 163-5
stigma 50
stories, organisational culture 145
Strasbourg case law 36
structural perspective, domestic violence 101-2
Styles, Elin 186
suicide 40-1
supervision 136
support
collaborative working 157
in decision-making 62
support networks, decision-making 63
Sutton and Merton inquiry (2007) 18, 144, 146,
150
symbols, organisational culture 143

T
'tainting' evidence 93
targeting, resources 171
team workers, typology 165-6
teamworking 165-6
textual cues 133
Theft Act 1968 29
theft, fraud and deception 28-9
Titterton's model of decision making 175-6
torture, freedom from 41-2
transformational change 150-1
traumatic brain injury (TBI) 118-19
treatment
freedom from cruel, inhuman or degrading 41-2
unacceptable 17
see also consent to treatment; mistreatment;
refusal of treatment
trial, right to fair and public 44
trust, collaborative working 156
turn-taking, communicative 126

U
UK prevalence survey 10, 13-14
undue pressure 75
unlawful conduct 11
unsound mind 42-3
user-focused communication
developing competence 132-3
strategies for improving 131
user perspective, adult protection investigations
112

V
values, change process 148
Valuing people 148
verbal communication 122
verbal refusal of treatment 57
vetting and barring scheme 19, 23, 32
review of 26-7
victim blaming 100-1
vision, change process 148
visual impairment 126-7
visual symbols 133
voice, empowerment through 122
vulnerability
concept of 10
defining our understanding about 110-11
eligibility for service provision 171
legal protection, Scotland 70-4
linked to impairment 122
perceptions of 48
risk associated with 171
vulnerable adults 10
abusers as 16
definition of 172
multi-agency protection 21-2, 23-4, 68-70
protection see adult protection
vulnerable witnesses, achieving best evidence
164-5

W
Waldegrave, William 164
Wells, Holly 26
whistleblowing
fear of 25-6
organizational culture 147
policies 25
practitioner failure 18
Who decides? 51
Wisconsin Coalition Against Domestic Violence
106
wisdom, capacity not equated with 54
Women's Aid 102
Working together to safeguard children: A guide
to interagency working to safeguard and
promote the welfare of children 84-5

X
x-linked abnormalities, communication
impairment 124

Y
YL v Birmingham Council 38
Youth Justice and Criminal Evidence Act 1999
164

Z
zero tolerance 102